Editorial Manager	Judith Maxwell
Senior Editor	Lynne Williams
Editors	Bridget Daly
	Brenda Clarke
Series Designers	QED (Alastair Campbell and Edward Kinsey)
Designer	Kit Johnson
Series Consultant	Keith Lye
General Consultant	Theodore Rowland-Entwistle
Consultants	Michael Billington
	John Bishop
	Jenny McCleery
	Marshall Coombs
	James Monahan
	Betty Roe
Production	John Moulder
Picture Research	Jenny de Gex

©Macdonald Educational Ltd 1981
First published 1981
Macdonald Educational Ltd
Holywell House
Worship Street
London EC2A 2EN

2081/3200
ISBN 356 07008 5

Designed and created in
Great Britain

Printed and bound by
New Interlitho, Italy

WORLD OF KNOWLEDGE

The Arts and Entertainment

Ron Carter

Jean Cooke

Eric Inglefield

David Sharp

Keith Wicks

Macdonald

Contents

The Arts

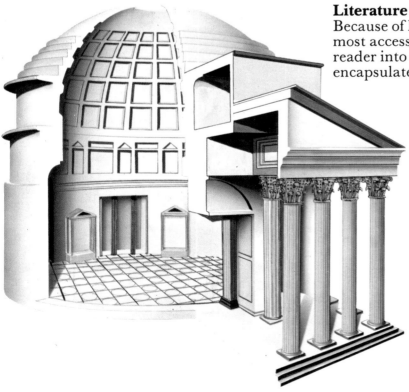

The Performing Arts

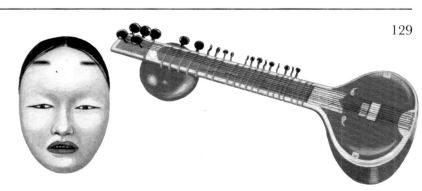

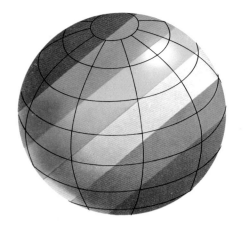

World of Knowledge

This book breaks new ground in the method it uses to present information to the reader. The unique page design combines narrative with an alphabetical reference section and it uses colourful photographs, diagrams and illustrations to provide an instant and detailed understanding of the book's theme. The main body of information is presented in a series of chapters that cover, in depth, the subject of this book. At the bottom of each page is a reference section which gives, in alphabetical order, concise articles which define, or enlarge on, the topics discussed in the chapter. Throughout the book, the use of SMALL CAPITALS in the text directs the reader to further information that is printed in the reference section. The same method is used to cross-reference entries within each reference section. Finally, there is a comprehensive index at the end of the book that will help the reader find information in the text, illustrations and reference sections. The quality of the text, and the originality of its presentation, ensure that this book can be read both for enjoyment and for the most up-to-date information on the subject.

WORLD OF KNOWLEDGE

The Arts

Eric Inglefield

Keith Wicks

Ron Carter

Introduction

Art has played an essential role in human society since prehistoric times. Much early art was linked with magic and religion and, even today, such sculptures as the haunting masks of West and Central Africa are made for use in religious ritual, although many pieces end up as *objets d'art* in western art galleries. Through a great variety of forms, which are described in this book, artists have enriched people's experience and appealed to their aesthetic senses, although their work is not always appreciated by their contemporaries. The fine arts, which appeal to us through sight, are covered in **The Arts.** They include painting, sculpture, photography, architecture, interior design and such creative arts as ceramics, metalwork and printing. There is also a section on literature, where the artist finds a means of self-expression through words.

Whether we regard them as a necessity or a luxury, the arts have to find sponsors. In the past, help for artists came from wealthy individuals, but governments and private companies are now making vital contributions.

Art in Society

Everything we know about mankind's past suggests that from the earliest times people have regarded art as an essential part of their lives. It might be thought that the beginning of civilization – literally, living in cities – would mark the beginning of art. Civilization developed around 10,000 years ago, but art was flourishing long before that. The paintings that adorn the walls of caves in France, Spain and elsewhere were made between 30,000 BC and 10,000 BC, and the skill of the STONE AGE artists who made them suggest an already long tradition of art.

A few Stone Age societies have survived into the present day, for example in the depths of the jungles of New Guinea. Although their ways of life are primitive, they have their own relatively sophisticated forms of art.

Throughout the ages art has been both an

Left: Leonardo da Vinci painted 2 versions of this picture, *The Virgin of the Rocks.* This one, now in the National Gallery in London, was commissioned for the church of S Francesco Grande in Milan. The other, earlier, version is now in the Louvre in Paris.

Below: *Blue Marilyn* is one of the works of the revolutionary American artist Andy Warhol. Many of Warhol's themes come from everyday life, and include such items as soup cans.

apparent necessity to humankind and a luxury. Through its art a society expresses something of its higher self, that subtle something which distinguishes the human race from other forms of animal life. Art probably dates from the time when humans learned to speak and therefore to exchange ideas as well as information.

Because it is a luxury, sophisticated art has usually depended on wealth. Economists tell us that wealth results from producing more than just enough for our needs. It was the PATRONAGE of royalty and wealthy noblemen which made possible the marvellous productions of the Renaissance artists, their paintings, sculptures and buildings. For example the banking family of MEDICI supported many artists including Fra ANGELICO *(see page 4)*, Paolo UCCELLO (1397–1475) and MICHELANGELO BUONARROTI *(see page 20)*, while several popes, notably JULIUS II, and monarchs such as FRANCIS I of France paid painters, sculptors and architects to create superb works of art.

Great composers too, largely depended on the help of rich patrons. For example, Joseph Haydn (1732–1809) spent most of his life in the service of the ESTERHÁZY family; Wolfgang Amadeus Mozart (1756–91) began his career at the court of the Archbishop of Salzburg. Richard Wagner (1813–85) was enabled to continue his work by the liberality of LUDWIG II of Bavaria.

Over much of the world today society tends to discourage the creation of large private fortunes. For this reason there are far fewer rich patrons to encourage today's artists. As a result a new patron has arisen: society itself, in the shape of national and local governments, often acting through special bodies such as Britain's ARTS COUNCIL. For it seems that art in all its forms is still an essential part of society, and society will always find ways and means of providing the money to fund it.

Reference

A **Arts Council of Great Britain** is the main government agency for helping the arts in Britain. It receives an annual government grant from which it gives subsidies to ballet companies, opera, orchestras, some theatre companies and a few writers and artists.

E **Esterházy** was the name of a noble Hungarian family whose members were distinguished both as

soldiers and patrons of the arts. Haydn's patron was Prince Miklós József (1714–1790); his grandson, Prince Miklós (1765–1833) made a large art collection.

F **Francis I** (1494–1547), ruled France from 1515 to 1547. He spent money lavishly on the arts, providing LEONARDO DA VINCI *(see page 18)* in his last years with a house and a pension.

J **Julius II** (1443–1513) (Giuliano della Rovere) was pope from 1503–13. He began the rebuilding of St

Peter's Basilica in Rome, and engaged many artists to work on it, notably MICHELANGELO *(see page 20)* and RAPHAEL *(see page 25)*.

L **Ludwig II** (1845–86) ruled over the south German state of Bavaria from 1864–86. He was a great admirer of Richard Wagner (1813–83), on whom he spent a great deal of money. He was declared insane, and is believed to have drowned himself.

M **Medici** is the name of a family which dominated

Florence in Italy for more than 300 years. The Medici made a fortune in trade and

Lorenzo dei Medici

by lending money, and many of them spent money freely on the arts. The outstanding patrons of the arts included Lorenzo the Magnificent (1449–1492), and Cosimo II (1590–1620).

P **Patronage** is support given to artists and others by wealthy people.

S **Stone Age** is the term used to describe any period in history when men used stone tools, not metal ones. Early men began using stone tools more than 2,500,000 years ago.

Art is constantly evolving, but pioneering artists sometimes displease their contemporaries. If we are offended by the apparent perversity of modern art, we must remember that Vincent van Gogh sold only one of his works in his lifetime.

Fine Art

Drawing: the basis of art

From prehistoric times the technique of drawing has been a popular pastime for both adults and children alike, and, in the hands of the world's greatest artists, has produced many beautiful works of art. Drawing is also an important preparatory stage in other forms of art, being used as the basis for various kinds of prints and for preliminary sketches and studies made before a painting is begun.

Any kind of material that will make a mark can be suitable for drawing, though pencils, chalk, charcoal and PASTEL are the most popular today, whilst BISTRE and SILVER-POINT were commonly used in the past. In the East, artists also mastered the art of sensitive drawing with brushes and ink. Drawings can be done on almost any surface. For example the black surface of scraperboard can be scratched away to reveal a drawing on the white board beneath.

Painting: the art of colour

In simple terms, painting is done by applying some kind of paint to a surface by means of a tool such as a brush. All paints contain a pigment, or colouring matter, mixed with a BINDER that permits it to be held and spread on a surface. The binder, also known as the vehicle or medium, consists of water for WATER-COLOUR paints, FRESCO, GOUACHE and ACRYLIC; oil, generally linseed oil, for oil paints, which can be thinned with turpentine; melted wax for ENCAUSTIC; and even eggs for TEMPERA, an early form of paint.

The most common surfaces for painting, apart from walls or ceilings covered with murals, are canvases stretched over frames of various sizes and supported on an easel. Wood panels and even glass, when properly prepared, are also suitable, whilst paper and board are generally used for water-based paints.

After thinking about the subject of a painting,

the artist may first make one or several rough sketches, followed by a CARTOON or a careful STUDY of details. For the picture's COMPOSITION, the various parts are arranged to achieve the desired effects and to produce a pleasing design, perhaps by following the traditional rule of proportion known as the GOLDEN SECTION. But because the composition is in two dimensions on a flat surface, the artist may give an impression of depth and space by the use of MODELLING, CHIAROSCURO, or techniques of ILLUSIONISM, such as PERSPECTIVE, FORESHORTENING and TROMPE L'OEIL.

When satisfied with the picture's composition, the artist may then make either a full-size CARTOON or a smaller SQUARED-UP DRAWING, from

Left: Albrecht Dürer: *Soldier on Horseback,* 1498. One of many accurately observed drawings that reveal Dürer's technical mastery of pen and water-colour.

Below: The basic equipment for painting includes tubes of different colours of paints (**5**); brushes of varying sizes and hardness, a palette on which to mix the paints, perhaps with a palette knife for applying paint thickly (**6**); white spirit for cleaning the brushes (**1**); turpentine for thinning the paint (**2**); and perhaps an easel to hold a large canvas (**4**). Charcoal is useful for preparing a preliminary sketch on paper (**3**).

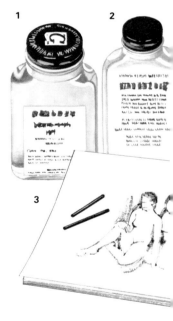

Reference

A

Abstract art is created when an artist 'abstracts' or leaves out, all the features of an object or scene which he considers unimportant, and in doing so captures what is for him the essence of its beauty or meaning. Abstract art can also be the result of building up lines or patches of colour into a composition of un-recognizable shapes which nevertheless appeals to the viewer through its beauty or emotional impact.

Acrylic is a quick drying form of emulsion paint. Because it can be thinned with water, it is useful for covering large areas with flat colour. It can also be applied as a thick IMPASTO.

Action painting is the pouring or splashing of paint on to a surface to create abstract compositions which express the subconscious feelings of the artist at the moment of working. The American artist Jackson Pollock (1912–56) was the best known exponent.

Alla prima painting is a method used by many artists today of completing an entire composition in one layer of thick paint.

Panel by Fra Angelico

Angelico, Fra Giovanni (1387 or 1400–55), a Dominican friar, is noted chiefly for the series of about 50 religious frescoes which he painted on the walls of the cells at the convent of St Marco, Florence, to help the friars in contemplation.

Angkor, capital of the Khmer empire (now Kampuchea), flourished AD 802–1413 as a centre of Indian-based culture. The vast stone temples of Angkor, with their galleries, staircases and towers, are decorated with thousands of finely-decorated carvings.

Anti-cerne is a white outline left between areas of colour in a painting. It was popular with FAUVE artists.

Aperture of a lens is a measure of its light-passing ability. The aperture, expressed as an 'f'-number, is equal to the FOCAL LENGTH of the LENS divided by its diameter.

Aquatint is a method of creating textured tones in printing by the INTAGLIO process. The metal plate is covered with a porous ground of resin or bitumen powder, which allows acid to penetrate and create a finely textured surface on which the composition can be transferred to the painting surface. Unless completing a whole picture in one session by the ALLA PRIMA method, an artist usually begins an oil painting by coating the surface with a GROUND of primer paint or GESSO. This is followed by an UNDERPAINTING, or LAY-IN, of the composition in monochrome (brown and white), or *grisaille* (grey and white), to work out the tone values achieved when building up the picture in COLOUR.

During the process of applying the colour, every artist adopts a characteristic style that reveals itself, for instance, in the BRUSHWORK. Other styles involve applying oil paints in thin layers, or employing the techniques of SCUMBLING or IMPASTO to create richly textured effects in FAT PAINT. STIPPLING with small dots produces the characteristic shimmering seen in the paintings of Neo-Impressionists, who invented the technique of DIVISIONISM. In addition, beautiful SFUMATO shading can be achieved through delicate brushwork, while sharply outlined shapes can be created by the ANTI-CERNE and SGRAFFITO methods. When completed, the whole painting

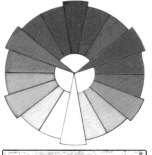

Top: The colour wheel shows the 3 primary colours (red, yellow and blue) with their complementary and intermediate colours.

Above: A detail of the brushwork in Seurat's *Bridge at Courbevoie* shows the small dots of paint used in the technique of Divisionism.

Right: Linocut printing: a shaped piece of lino is carefully lifted from the paper after printing a design cut into its surface.

can be sprayed with a FIXATIVE or brushed with a varnish to prevent flaking.

Printmaking: art in profusion
A large range of printing techniques, either with or without a press, is today being used to create beautiful works of art. These can be produced in the form of the single MONOPRINT or in editions of large numbers of identical copies. One basic method is ENGRAVING, which includes RELIEF engraving and the INTAGLIO process. The other is surface printing, of which LITHOGRAPHY and SILK-SCREEN PRINTING are the most important techniques. Each of these requires its own materials, tools and methods and produces characteristic effects.

The simplest form of relief engraving is the print taken from a design cut into a half-potato, a process also used for the LINOCUT, WOODCUT and WOOD ENGRAVING. Intaglio printing is done from designs cut into metal plates. The designs can be cut by sharp tools, as in line engraving, DRYPOINT and MEZZOTINT. They can also be produced by acid, as in AQUATINT, ETCHING and SOFT-GROUND

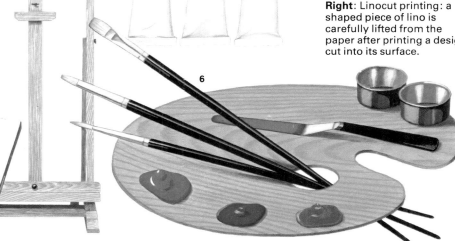

Art Nouveau menu by Mucha

the finished print. The Spanish artist GOYA used this process.
Armature is a framework of metal, normally lead, used to support the clay or wax when MODELLING a sculpture.
Art Nouveau was a style that appeared mainly in interior decoration, architecture and the applied arts between about 1890 and 1910. Two basic forms evolved: one with undulating lines often representing plants or human hair, as in the work of Alphonse Mucha (1860–1939) and Aubrey Beardsley (1872–98) and a more geometric style involving straight lines and rectangles, as practised by Gustave Klimt (1862–1918).
Ashcan School was a group of American painters of the late 1800s and early 1900s who realistically portrayed the seamier side of city life. George Bellows (1882–1925) was the most famous member of the group.
Autograph is a work of art done entirely by the person to whom is is attributed, without the aid of assistants.

B **Barbizon School** was a group of painters of the 1850s who gathered in the French village of Barbizon in the Forest of Fontainbleau to paint realistic scenes of country life. Jean François Millet (1814–75) was the best-known artist in the group.
Baroque was an elaborate, emotional style that dominated European art in the 1600s, particularly in Italy. Artists often chose dramatic religious subjects that had direct emotional appeal, and illustrated them in scenes packed with violent, swirling action. The leading exponents were RUBENS in painting and BERNINI in sculpture.

Benin 'bronzes' are brass heads of royal persons modelled on the works of the IFE metal masters, which Benin surpassed in the 1400s.
Bernini, Gianlorenzo (1598–1680), the leading figure of BAROQUE art in Italy, was both an architect and sculptor. His sculptures include early statues of classical subjects, such as *Apollo and Daphne*; portrait busts of which the impressive head of Louis XIV is the best known; religious works, which include his masterpiece, the dramatic *Ecstacy of St Teresa*; and late semi-

ETCHING. Textured effects can be created by HATCHING or STIPPLING.

Mosaic and stained glass

Mosaic is a form of art practised since ancient times. It is produced from small pieces of coloured stone or glass, called *tesserae*, which are cemented to a surface to form a picture or design. Stained glass consists of pieces of coloured glass held together by strips of lead called *cames*. It is used for window designs and is intended to be seen against the light. The colour can be produced by adding metal oxides to the glass when molten. Alternatively, a thin layer of coloured glass is fused over plain glass and a design is then ground into it. Acid can also be used to remove parts of the design. Details can be added in enamels, which are then fused to the glass by heating in a kiln.

Sculpture: art in three dimensions

The making of three-dimensional objects, known

Above: A majestic mosaic portrait of the Byzantine Empress Theodora in the church of S. Vitale, Ravenna, has real mother-of-pearl to represent jewellery in the design.

Below: Phillipe Asselin modelling a portrait head of Gabriel Loire in his studio in clay moulded on a frame. It will then be cast in a hard material such as bronze.

as sculpture, is one of the oldest arts. Three basic methods are involved: carving, modelling and construction. Carving requires sharp tools to cut a shape out of the material either as a free-standing object in the round or in RELIEF from wood, stone or other substances. In MODELLING, the sculpture is built up by hand from such plastic materials as clay or soft wax which is supported on an ARMATURE frame. Copies of sculptured models are often made by CASTING in metals, particularly BRONZE. For larger pieces the CIRE-PERDUE method is used. Using the construction process, sculptures can be pieced together from separate parts and fixed by such techniques as welding. Examples of this form of sculpture are the MOBILE and the sculptures of KINETIC ART and CONSTRUCTIVISM.

Photography

In the early 1800s, advances in chemistry made it possible to 'fix' in a permanent way the image which is formed when light reflected from an object passes through a LENS. Photography had arrived. But there was nothing new about the camera, which had been in use since the 1500s. The early camera, called the *camera obscura*, was used by artists as a drawing aid. Light from the artist's subject passed through the camera lens and formed an image on a screen. This image could then be traced or copied, enabling a realistic picture to be obtained quickly. Photography was introduced as a means of recording the camera's images automatically. The screen of the *camera obscura* was replaced by a plate coated with a light-sensitive chemical. All cameras work on the same basic principles. They consist of a light-proof box with a system for holding film flat, a lens to form an image and a mechanism for controlling the time the image falls on to light-sensitive film. When a photograph is taken, the SHUTTER opens and lets light pass through the lens forming a LATENT IMAGE on the film. During developing, DEVELOPER darkens the latent image where it is exposed, while a FIXER dissolves the unexposed areas leaving a negative image on the film. Reversal film used for transparencies produces a positive image.

At first, photography was a slow process, for the low sensitivity of the plates meant that an EXPOSURE of several hours was required to record an image. But better processes were soon intro-

---

architectural compositions using a mixture of colourful, rich materials, such as the *Chair of St Peter* in St Peter's, Rome.
Binder, also called the medium or vehicle, is the liquid constituent of paint which is added to the powdered pigment to bind it together.
Bistre, made from charred wood, is a brown pigment. It was often used for drawing by REMBRANDT.
Blaue Reiter, Der (The Blue Rider), was a group of artists working in Munich from 1911 until World War I and

who helped to create the German movement of EX-PRESSIONISM. The leading figures were Wassily Kandinsky (1866–1944), Franz Marc (1880–1916) and, later Paul Klee (1879–1940) See also DIE BRÜCKE.
Botticelli, Sandro (c. 1444–1510), an Italian Renaissance artist, is noted for the graceful, melancholy women who appear in his pictures, and for his clearly outlined painting style. Religious and mythological subjects were his special interest, the best known being *Primavera* and *The*

Birth of Venus.
Bronze, an alloy of copper and tin, with the addition of some lead has been used to make sculptures since ancient times. The sculpture is made either by CASTING the molten metal in a sand mould or by the CIRE-PERDUE method. The finished work is also known as a bronze.
Brücke, Die (The Bridge), was an influential group of German Expressionist artists formed in Dresden in 1905. A feeling of tension and foreboding pervades their work. The group helped to revive interest in the WOODCUT and

other printmaking.
Bruegel (or Breughel),

Brushwork on a Van Gogh painting

Pieter (c. 1525–69) was the first and greatest of several members of a Flemish family of artists, He is particularly noted for his satirical pictures of peasant life, and paintings on the months revealing his mastery of realistic landscape painting.
Brushwork is the pattern left in the paint by the artist's brush-strokes. It is as personal to him as his handwriting; compare, for example, the tiny dots of Seurat's DIVISIONISM with the frenzied slashes of VAN GOGH's last works.
Byzantine art was the art of

duced and, by the late 1830s, typical exposure times had been reduced to a few seconds.

Since the early days of photography, major improvements have been made in both cameras and photographic materials. Instead of using a separate photographic plate for each exposure, most modern cameras take a roll of film, on which several exposures can be made. Modern films give good definition, enabling high-qality images to be recorded in miniature. This has led to a general reduction in camera sizes. Improvements in film SPEED have made it possible to obtain satisfactory snapshots in quite dim light, and in bright light a very short exposure is often possible.

Art in ancient times

The first known forms of art date from over 30,000 years ago, when prehistoric artists drew simple outlines in wet clay on cave walls. From these beginnings evolved naturalistic paintings of deer, bison and horses, which early peoples

Above: One of 2 calotypes, showing W. H. Fox Talbot's Printing Establishment at Reading, England in 1844. It was the first of its kind and the print shows some of its activities – copying, engraving, portraits, printing positives and calotyping still-life.

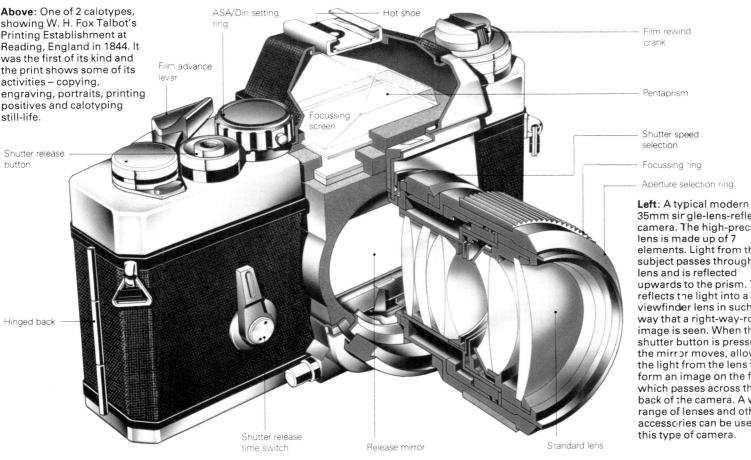

Left: A typical modern 35mm single-lens-reflex camera. The high-precision lens is made up of 7 elements. Light from the subject passes through the lens and is reflected upwards to the prism. This reflects the light into a viewfinder lens in such a way that a right-way-round image is seen. When the shutter button is pressed, the mirror moves, allowing the light from the lens to form an image on the film, which passes across the back of the camera. A wide range of lenses and other accessories can be used on this type of camera.

the East Roman, or Byzantine, Empire from the AD 400s to the 1400s (or to the 1700s in countries of the Eastern Orthodox Church). Christian themes were the main subjects of paintings (in the form of ICONS and manuscript miniatures) and of superb mosaics used for church decoration.

C **Calligraphy,** often quotations from the Koran or other sacred Islamic literature, became a leading art among the Arabs and Persians. Islam's many mosques and *madrasahs* (mos-

que colleges), illustrated books and paintings and used calligraphy as an art as Chinese painting did.
Calotype, (Talbotype), was a process patented in 1841 by Fox TALBOT for making paper photographic negatives. A print was made by shining light through a NEGATIVE on to another sheet of sensitive paper. Some of the paper negative's texture would appear on the print, obscuring finer details of the image.
Cameron, Julia Margaret (1815–79), was an English photographer noted especially for her outstanding

portraits. In her photographs of Tennyson, Browning, Darwin and other great men, Cameron exploited the soft, subtle images of the CALOTYPE process.
Canova, Antonio (1757–1822), was the most

Detail of Supper at Emmaus *by Caravaggio*

famous Italian sculptor in the Neoclassical style. As well as works on purely classical themes, he created a monument to Pope Clement XIV, several busts and statues of Napoleon, and his most famous work, *Pauline Bonaparte as Venus*.
Caravaggio, Michelangelo Merisi da (1573–1610), was a boisterous, somewhat quarrelsome Italian painter who, despite his great artistic gifts, was much criticized in his lifetime for portraying ordinary lower-class folk in his religious pictures. Apart from its realism, his work is

Above: A detail from the wall decorations painted in the tomb of Menna in about 1420 BC illustrates the conventionally flat, heavily outlined and colourful style of ancient Egyptian painting. The scene depicts the offerings supplied for the use of the dead in the next world.

Left: This detail from a colourful Indian painting, *Akbar crossing the Ganges*, is typical of the Mughal style of painting in the 1500s, in which Persian and Hindu artists worked together to depict court and historical events of the *Mughal* (Mongol Muslim) rulers of India.

believed would give them control over the animals' spirits and thus ensure successful hunting. The finest of these paintings were made around 12000 BC in deep caves at Altamira, Spain, and Lascaux, France. Early sculptures had an equally magical purpose. The so-called 'Venus' figures, found throughout Europe, were carved by prehistoric artists to ensure fertility, and were thus abstract in style, with an emphasis on sturdy hips.

When the world's first civilizations began in the Middle East around 5000 BC, painting and sculpture took on a decorative as well as a ritual function. Relief sculpture, often painted, was used to decorate Assyrian and Egyptian temples and palaces. Sculpture in the round portrayed great rulers in stiff, formal poses that conveyed their god-like majesty. The same stylization appears in Egyptian paintings of human figures (*see page 17*). Beautiful paintings of such figures in scenes from everyday life provided decorations inside tombs.

Eastern art

This section includes the art of that part of the world from Morocco eastwards, taking in all Asia except the Soviet Union. The main sources of inspiration for eastern art have been the Indian subcontinent, China, and the Arabian-based religion of Islam. The artistic traditions of several Afro-Asian countries have developed under these three dominating influences.

Hindu temple sculpture in India reached a high peak at KHAJURAHO by AD 1000. About 500 years earlier, INDIAN BUDDHIST ART reached near perfection in sculpture and painting. In contrast to its grace and serenity, JAIN ART was stiff and lifeless. A thousand years of Muslim rule (c. 700–1700) diminished the liveliness of Indian art. However, the MUGHAL DYNASTY (1526–1700s) did bring a resurgence of painting.

China's artists excelled in ceramics and pottery rather than sculpture. SILK SCROLL PAINTING began about AD 400, and 100 years later, HSIEH HO formulated 'six principles of painting' that have dominated Chinese painting since then. 'Mountain and water' landscapes characterized art of the SUNG DYNASTY (960–1279). Court painters of the MING DYNASTY (1368–1644) used rich colours and decoration, but court tradition stifled originality and painting declined.

---

also characterized by a dramatic use of CHIAROSCURO,
Cartoon is a full-size drawing done in preparation for a painting, or, in a modern sense, a comic or satirical drawing. *See also page 50.*
Casting is the method used to make a metal sculpture by pouring molten metal into a mould. The mould is made by covering the artist's clay or wax sculpture with plaster of Paris. When set hard and removed, the inside of the mould is an accurate replica in reverse of the original sculpture.
Celtic art comprises two

main periods: *La Tène* art of mainland Europe from the 400s to 100s BC, and the art

Cartoon by Raphael

of Celtic peoples in the British Isles from the 100s BC to the AD 1100s. Celtic art is characterized by the use of highly elaborate decoration in the form of spiral and curving strapwork, interlaced with animal shapes and stylized human figures. This was used to decorate pottery and gold objects, and, in the Christian period, stone crosses and religious manuscripts such as the Books of Kells and Durrow.
Cézanne, Paul (1839–1906), a French painter, was one of the most influential artists of the last 100 years. After a

period creating over-dramatic, violent and erotic scenes, he developed, via a period of IMPRESSIONISM, a more tranquil style, in which he used COLOUR and tone to reproduce the 3-dimensional shapes of solid objects in nature. His later subjects were therefore mostly landscapes and still-lifes.
Chiaroscuro is the artist's use of light and shadow in a painting. Its most dramatic effects can be seen in the work of CARAVAGGIO.
Cire-perdue, or lost wax, is a method of casting a hollow sculpture from molten

metal. A plaster of Paris mould taken from the artist's original clay sculpture is thinly lined inside with wax. The rest of the inside space is then filled with a core of plaster. The whole mould is then heated, and the molten wax runs out through pipes. The thin cavity left behind is filled with molten metal, thus forming an exact hollow replica of the original clay sculpture.
Classicism is the style of art and architecture created in ancient Greece and Rome. Generally considered to have set an unparalleled

Situated between the two 'super-cultures' of China and India – TIBET, Nepal, Burma, THAILAND, Kampuchea and INDONESIA borrowed heavily from them to create their own considerable artistic traditions. Buddhism and the great Hindu epic, RAMAYANA, have been especially influential in South-East Asian art. JAPAN adopted Chinese culture after AD 500, and Japanese artists cleverly adapted and developed Chinese forms into a uniquely Japanese art.

The early Muslims, zealous against idolatry, banned representations of human and animal figures. This encouraged Islamic artists to concentrate on architecture, tilework and CALLIGRAPHY. Muslim sculpture hardly exists, but book illustration is superb. Stricter application of religious principles virtually killed Arab painting in the 700s. East of Arabia the ban on image-making was less strict for secular art. The conquests of TIMUR THE LAME gave Islamic art a new lease of life. About 1600, travellers marvelling at the beauty of Persia's capital commented 'ISFAHAN is half the world'. But Islamic art was already in decline.

The art of Africa and the Americas
Some of the earliest remaining examples of African art come from the NOK CULTURE of 2,000 years ago. Sculpture reached its climax at IFE between the AD 1100s and 1300s and later at Benin, while the religious art of Africa has inspired such European artists as PICASSO and Amedeo Modigliani (1884–1920).

The pattern of art throughout ancient America was generally similar, suggesting a common origin. However, several settlements from Mexico to Peru developed distinctive styles of sculpture. Artists drew people and objects in symbolic outline, their drawings becoming almost a substitute for written languages. These early Americans also excelled in weaving techniques and designs. Colombian goldsmiths produced countless masterpieces over 1,000 years before the Spanish conquest, and the nimble fingers of MOCHICA craftsmen created lifelike artefacts.

The art of Greece and Rome
Soon after 3000 BC, Europe's first major civilization, the Minoan in Crete, emerged in the eastern Mediterranean. Its artists created painted pottery and wall paintings, first in a naturalistic, then in a more decorative style. The art of the Mycenean civilization which grew up around 2000 BC on mainland Greece and flowered in the 1500s BC was heavily influenced by the Minoans. The Myceneans excelled in the more decorative style of work in beaten gold, silver and bronze. After the overthrow of the Myceneans in the 1100s BC there was a 'dark age' of about 200 years where the only evidence of art was on vases decorated with simple linear designs. This abstract tendency formed the basis of the geometric style developed by Athenian artists after the 1100s BC and used, with scenes enacted by curious match-stick figures, to decorate pottery vases. The renaissance of Greek art occurred in the 800s and 700s BC with the development of a more settled society. The zigzags and geometric patterns became more elaborate and

Left: Japanese colour print artists flourished between 1740 and 1890. *Head of a Woman Reflected in a Mirror*, by Kigugawa (1787–1867) shows the elaborate hair styles of courtesans of the period. Despised by the ruling class, the colour print artists sold thousands of their prints for a few coins each.

Below: An altar carving in painted wood shows the peak of African sculpture reached by the Yoruba tribe of Nigeria. Yoruba sculpture emerged at the sacred city of Ife, and developed further at the royal court at Benin about 500 years ago.

---

standard of excellence, it was the object of detailed study and imitation, especially during the RENAISSANCE and the era of NEOCLASSICISM.
Collage is a form of art in which materials such as pieces of paper, cloth or wood are incorporated into the COMPOSITION.
Colour is used by artists in various ways to build up the COMPOSITION and create the effect or mood of their pictures. Each of the primary colours, or hues, of red, blue and yellow has a complementary colour formed by mixing the other 2 colours equally. Warm colours include red and yellow, which contrast with cool

Collage by Peter Blake

ones, such as blue and green. A tint is made by lightening a colour with white, whilst a shade results from adding black. A colour mixed with both black and white (that is, grey) produces a tone, which can vary in value depending on the amount of black or white in it.
Colour print artists of Japan (c. 1760–1890) shocked the Japanese ruling class with the topics of their unconventional art. Courtesans, geisha girls, ghosts, actors and monsters were their favourite subjects. They rejected the values of the old feudal overlords to please the rising merchant class centred on Osaka. Although colour printing originated in China and Korea, the Japanese, true to form, gave it an entirely new character. The colour print artists included Hishikawa Moronobu, Torii Kiyonobu, Susuki Harunobu, Kitigawa Utamaro, Toshusai Sharuku, Hiroshige Ando and Hokusai Katsushika.
Composition is the way an artist combines all the elements of a picture or sculpture to create a unified and satisfactory whole. In drawing and painting, it includes not only the organization of shapes on a flat surface in 2 dimensions, as in most ABSTRACT ART, but also the representation of solid, 3-dimensional objects or scenes by the skilful use of COLOUR, PERSPECTIVE and CHIAROSCURO.
Constable, John (1776–1836), was one of the greatest of British landscape painters. By working out of doors for his preparatory sketches, he was able to recreate, in naturalistic detail, a record of the Suffolk

As time passed, however, the human figure was portrayed with an increasingly lifelike appearance until, in the Golden Age or Classical period of the 400s and early 300s, an 'ideal' type of human beauty was created that has been admired ever since. Although most of their works, comprising paintings, statues and reliefs of gods, goddesses and athletes, are known only through later Roman copies, the names of the artists have not been lost. Among them were the painters Polygnotus, Apollodorus and Apelles, and the sculptors Polykleitos, Phidias, Scopas, Praxiteles and Lysippus.

During the next two centuries, the Hellenistic period, artists throughout the Greek world attempted to move away from this idealistic type of art and to give their work greater REALISM, a tendency that grew after the Romans conquered Greece in the 140s BC. The Romans employed artists, many of them Greek, to produce realistic portrait busts and relief carvings of their battles and victories on columns and triumphal arches. These, together with fine mosaics and wall paintings from the ruins of Pompeii, Herculaneum

Left: *Hermes Carrying the Infant Dionysos*, probably by Praxiteles, about 340 BC. The naturalistic style of Greek sculpture reached its peak in the physically perfect figures of gods and athletes created by sculptors of the Classical period (500–323 BC).

gradually figures of people and animals were introduced.

Right: Christian Celtic art at its most decorative. On a page from the Irish *Book of Kells*, dating from the late AD 700s, the figure of St Matthew appears enclosed in a typically intricate design incorporating animal forms and spirals.

and elsewhere, represent the great legacy of Roman art.

Medieval European art

Before the AD 300s Christianity was still outlawed and the first Christian art appeared in secret as wall paintings and carved stone coffins in the catacombs deep underground below the city of Rome. But from this timid beginning religious art came to dominate the entire medieval period. Throughout Europe the clergy decorated religious manuscripts with rich ILLUMINATION, and in south-eastern regions BYZANTINE artists produced ICONS and masterpieces of mosaic church decoration. In the far north-west CELTIC ART held sway.

With the building of the great Romanesque abbeys and Gothic cathedrals of western Europe, sculpture, wall frescoes, painted altarpieces and stained glass windows became important, not merely as decoration but also as a powerful means of providing pictorial instruction in the scriptures. More secular in tone was the art created in the INTERNATIONAL GOTHIC STYLE at

countryside in such paintings as the *Hay Wain*.

Constructivism is a modern method of creating abstract sculptures by building or constructing them from any suitable material, such as metal, wire, wood, or perspex. It began as a Russian art movement led by Vladimir Tatlin (1885–c.1953) and Antoine Pevsner (1886–1962) from 1913 to 1921.

Continuous representation is a method, often seen in medieval paintings, of recording successive scenes in a story on one canvas.

Conversation piece is a painting of a group of people informally portrayed in their usual surroundings at home.

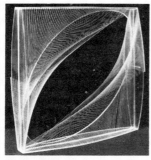
Contructivist sculpture, Naum Gabo

Cubism was a major European art movement from about 1907 to about 1914. Influenced by CEZANNE and African sculpture, Pablo PICASSO and Georges Braque (1882–1963) attempted to suggest the solidity of objects on a flat canvas by showing various viewpoints superimposed or next to each other. Misleading references were made by contemporary critics to the 'cubes' they saw in Braque's work, hence the name of the style. In this early phase, known as Analytical Cubism (1909–12), colour was of less

importance than form. But the paintings of Synthetic Cubism (1912–14) were characterized by the use of stronger colours, and of texture in the form of COLLAGE.

Dada was a form of anti-art created in Zurich from 1916 by European artists seeking refuge from World War I. Dismayed by the fighting, they deliberately set out to shock and outrage the complacent, neutral Swiss public. Apart from wild concerts, they created a form of art consisting of ready-made objects, such

as Marcel Duchamp's *Fountain* (a urinal) and his *Mona Lisa*, with added moustache and obscene new title. Dada lasted until 1922 and greatly influenced the artists of SURREALISM.

Daguerre, Louis Jacques Mandé (1789–1851), was a French stage designer and artist who invented a photographic process in the 1830s. His method, published in 1839, produced high-quality images on silver-coated copper plates. These photographs were called *daguerreotypes*.

David, Jacques Louis

Right: Michelangelo: *The Last Judgement*, detail, 1536–41. Covering the entire altar wall of the Sistine Chapel, in Rome, this immense fresco reveals the despondent mood and tension of Michelangelo's later work.

Below: Benvenuto Cellini: *Perseus with the Head of Medusa*, 1545–54. This famous bronze statue, cast by the *cire-perdue* process, takes its subject from classical mythology. Its emphasis on grace and its brilliantly executed detail mark this work as a masterpiece of late Renaissance sculpture.

the great courts of Europe from the end of the 1300s.

European art of the Middle Ages reflected the contemporary preoccupation with the transitoriness of human existence and the fear of damnation on the Day of Judgement, but with the Renaissance there emerged a more positive and self-confident view of the world.

The Renaissance

Though the reasons for the appearance of the Renaissance in Italy in the 1300s are complex, one essential factor stands out: whilst remaining faithful to their religion, Renaissance artists became interested in depicting this world rather than the next, and set out to explore and record its beauty. With classical art as their model, and with support from rich patrons, they were able to create the greatest flowering of art in European history. They portrayed the human figure, now nude as well as clothed, with a greater degree of realism than before and, alongside their portraits of contemporary celebrities, took their subjects from classical mythology as well as the Bible. In sculpture, DONATELLO and MICHELANGELO became unsurpassed masters, whilst a galaxy of great painters, in addition to Michelangelo, included Fra ANGELICO, BOTTICELLI, LEONARDO, RAPHAEL and TITIAN.

That northern European art retained its medieval character for much longer is evident in the work of such artists as Jan van Eyck (c. 1389–1441), Hieronymus Bosch (c. 1460–1516) and Mathis Grünewald (1480–1528) though the influence of Italy began to spread in the early 1500s through the work of Albrecht DÜRER, and Hans Holbein the Younger (1497–1543).

The Baroque and Rococo

The distortions evident in MANNERIST art of the

(1748–1825), was one of the leading French painters of

A daguerrotype

NEO-CLASSICISM. His *Oath of the Horatii* and *Sabine Women*, 2 of his major compositions on classical themes, were painted with the stark naturalism that characterized the neoclassical style. David later painted many imposing pictures of events in the life of Napoleon Bonaparte.

Depth of field in photography refers to a zone of sharpness. When a camera LENS is focused at any distance, objects at that distance will form a sharp image on the film, and, within certain limits, nearer and farther objects will appear acceptably sharp too. The zone between these limits is the depth of field. For a given lens, the depth of field increases when its opening, or APERTURE, is reduced in size. A small aperture is used when the photographer wants most objects to appear sharp.

Developer is a mixture of chemicals which changes the LATENT IMAGE on a negative to a visible one.

De Stijl (Style), or Neo-plasticism, was a movement in art and architecture that lasted for about 10 years from 1917. It was promoted by a Dutch design magazine of the same name, which set out to discover the essence of style and beauty in artistic creation. In painting, De Stijl is best seen in the abstract compositions of Piet Mondrian (1872–1944) consisting of rectangular areas of primary colours divided by thick black lines.

Divisionism, or pointillism, was a theory and technique of painting devised by the French artist Georges Seurat (1859–91) and the Neo-Impressionists. These artists applied colours in separate, small blobs, which then blend in the viewer's eye to produce much brighter effects.

Donatello, real name Donato di Niccolo Bardi, (c. 1386–1466) was the first great sculptor of the Italian Renaissance. His finest works, including his statue of David, the singing gallery for Florence cathedral, and the equestrian *Gattamelata* monument demonstrate his ability to create heroic, but lifelike human figures.

Drypoint is the simplest method of INTAGLIO engraving, and was often used by

late 1500s played an important part in the emergence of the BAROQUE style in Italy at the end of the century. Although continuing to use Biblical and classical mythological themes, Baroque artists, like the Mannerists before them, deliberately broke the Renaissance rules of restraint, balance and harmony. Their work has a highly emotional impact that directly involves the spectator in some vigorously dramatic incident, the excitement of which is effectively heightened by the compositional use of diagonal and swirling lines, as in Pieter Paul RUBENS' *The Lion Hunt*.

Around 1700, there was a reaction to the formal and grandiose splendour of Louis XIV's court at Versailles, in France. The lighter and more delicate ROCOCO style of interior decoration was created, starting in the palace itself. The new fashion soon spread to easel painting and was taken up by artists abroad. Many beautiful churches and royal buildings in southern Germany and Austria had astonishingly lavish Rococo decorations, among them Giambattista TIEPOLO's superb frescoes at Würzburg.

Classicism and Neoclassicism

During the 1600s several important artists, mostly French, refused to adopt the Baroque

Above: Pieter Paul Rubens: *Lion Hunt*, 1617–18 (detail) epitomises the Baroque style of the 1600s.

Below: Antonio Canova: *Pauline Bonaparte as Venus*, 1808. A coldly idealized, serene sculpture in the Neoclassical style.

style and persisted in following the example of their Renaissance predecessors, particularly RAPHAEL, by displaying emotional restraint and balanced, orderly composition. These artists, among them Nicolas Poussin (1594–1665), shared with their Baroque contemporaries an interest in mythological subjects, but rendered them in serene compositions devoid of Baroque theatricality. Their CLASSICISM led them to create a new art form: the ideal landscape.

By the 1750s growing hostility to the Baroque and Rococo styles and archaeological discoveries of ancient Greek and Roman ruins provided an opportunity for the creation of a new style that would, at least in theory, imitate ancient models at first hand. Typical of this Neoclassical style are Antonio CANOVA's smooth, highly finished sculptures and Jacques Louis DAVID's sharply outlined, heroic paintings on classical history and mythology.

Romanticism and Realism

The Neoclassicist's insistence on rules and the imitation of classical models was totally alien to the artistic, political and emotional freedom demanded by the followers of ROMANTICISM. This was a movement throughout the arts from the late 1700s to the mid 1800s. The world created by the Romantics revolved around a taste for the exotic, the mysterious and the sensational. In landscape painting some romantic painters were

---

REMBRANDT. The shaving, or *burr*, left on the metal plate during drawing with the sharp engraving tool, also holds some of the ink as well as the engraved groove, and gives the print greater richness in texture.
Dürer, Albrecht (1471–1528), was a German artist whose work helped to introduce the RENAISSANCE to northern Europe. His technical mastery is revealed in a wide range of drawings, a vast output of WOODCUTS and engravings, and a smaller number of oil and water-colour paintings.

E **Encaustic,** A mixture of pigment and melted wax, was used for painting in ancient times. LEONARDO DA VINCI tried to revive it, without success, for his mural of *The Battle of Anghiari* (now lost).
Engraving is a method of cutting a design into a metal, stone, wood, or other hard surface so that a paper print can be taken from it when the surface is inked. The 2 main techniques are RELIEF engraving and INTAGLIO.
Etching is a form of INTAGLIO engraving in which a design is scratched through a thin

acid-resistant film covering a metal plate. When dipped in

Engraved glass, c.1750

acid, the exposed metal is eaten away to form grooves exactly following the original design. These hold the ink when the plate is prepared for printing. REMBRANDT was a master of this technique, which began in about 1513.
Exposure in photography is the action of shining light onto light-sensitive material to produce a picture. The length of the exposure depends on the intensity of the light.
Expressionism is a method used by artists to communicate strong emotion by

means of exaggeration or distortion of line or colour. The Expressionist movement in modern art derived from the work of VAN GOGH and the FAUVES and became strongest in German art of the early 1900s. See also DER BLAUE REITER and DIE BRÜCKE.

F **Fat paint** is thick oil paint not thinned by turpentine. IMPASTO is created by using fat paint. Paint which has been thinned is called 'lean'. A traditional guide for beginners is to 'start thin and finish fat'.
Fauves were a loosely knit

Above: Claude Monet: *La Grenouillère*, 1869. French Impressionism can be said to have taken shape in the summer of that year, when Monet and Renoir devised the technique of small brush-strokes of colour to capture the fleeting effects of light on outdoor scenes. They painted almost identical pictures of this same spot on the Seine, a favourite place for day-trippers from Paris.

Below: Jan Davidsz de Heem: *Still-life with Ham, Lobster and Fruits.* The finely detailed realism of this painting is a characteristic feature of Dutch art in the 1600s, its greatest period.

oured objects cast shadows containing complementary colours offered them the chance to brighten their palettes. The result was the style of IMPRESSIONISM, in which artists captured the momentary play of light on objects in rapidly painted, and mostly outdoor, scenes. The Impressionists broke away from the tradition of painting historical events like DAVID, or idealized landscapes like Claude or Poussin (*see page 20*). They chose instead everyday landscapes and events from the area where they lived, around Paris and Normandy. The style took about 10 years to reach maturity and feature the characteristic short comma-like brushstrokes and the use of purple for shadows instead of black. But their experiments caused an outcry and they were excluded from the SALON.

After further experiments by the followers of NEO-IMPRESSIONISM, the late 1800s saw the emergence of POST-IMPRESSIONISM and the short-lived ART NOUVEAU style, together with the development of Symbolism and of more overt EXPRESSIONISM.

Art in the present century

The Impressionists' long, bitter struggle for the acceptance of their revolutionary form of painting opened the gates to a flood of exploratory styles in European art in the early part of the 1900s. ABSTRACT ART, in particular, has been a field of continuous experiment, although FIGURA-

attracted by the overpowering forces of nature, by its turmoil and atmospheric effects. The Romantics' unreal quality is excepted only in the naturalistic or realistic representation of human figures and objects. REALISM is thus not really an historical art style, although there was a vigorous attempt to create one in the mid-1800s, when Gustave Courbet (1819–77) extolled the realistic portrayal of ordinary working people in his violent rejection of both Neoclassicism and Romanticism.

Impressionism and Post-Impressionism

Experiments in photography and scientific studies of the colour composition of light had a major effect on the development of European painting in the late 1800s. Photography freed artists from the need to make exact copies of the world in their art, and the discovery that col-

group of French artists of the early 1900s, whose stridently coloured paintings prompted a critic in 1905 to refer to them as *fauves*, or wild beasts. Landscapes, still-life and everyday events were their subjects. The main figures in the group, were Henri Matisse (1869–1954), Maurice de Vlaminck (1876–1958), André Derain (1880–1954) and Raoul Dufy (1877–1953).

Figurative art represents recognizable objects, figures or scenes and is therefore distinct from ABSTRACT ART.

Filters are sometimes placed over a camera LENS to alter the quality of light falling on the film. A range of filters gives the experienced photographer more control over his pictures. In black-and-white photography, coloured filters are used to alter the TONE of selected parts of the picture. For example, a yellow filter will darken a blue sky, thus making any clouds more prominent. A colour filter will also lighten areas of the same colour. In portraiture, for example, freckles can be subdued by using an orange filter. Besides giving artistic con-

trol, filters have various technical applications.

Fixative is a thin varnish sprayed often over chalk or pastel drawings to prevent smudges and to stop flaking.

Fixer is a chemical solution which converts the unexposed surface area of film to a soluble form so that it can be washed away.

Focal length of a lens is the distance between it and the image it forms of a distant object. The focal length determines image size and the angle of view covered. A TELEPHOTO LENS has a long focal length, forms relatively

large images, and covers a narrow angle. A WIDE-ANGLE

Etruscan fresco, c. 520 BC

LENS has a shorter focal length and forms smaller images. The ZOOM LENS has variable focal length. *See also* DEPTH OF FIELD.

Foreshortening is an artist's method of representing an object in PERSPECTIVE.

Found object of any kind, whether a tree root or a stone, can be considered a work of art, according to the ideas of SURREALISM.

Fresco is a kind of wall painting completed section by section on damp plaster using water-based paint.

Futurism was an aggressively confident movement

TIVE ART has maintained its age-old fascination in the midst of this constant activity.

In 1905 the Parisian public was outraged by an exhibition of garishly bright paintings by a group of artists who were disparagingly referred to as 'wild beasts', or FAUVES, and the name stuck. Almost at once their experiments were superseded by the advent of CUBISM, devised by Pablo PICASSO and Georges Braque (1882–1963), which broke all the conventions governing the representation of solid objects on a flat canvas. A painting by Marcel Duchamp (1887–1968), *Nude descending a staircase* (1912) formed a link between Cubism and a new style concerned with expressing vigorous action and movement known as FUTURISM. Meanwhile Cubism was also influential in the appearance of abstract sculpture and the rise of CONSTRUCTIVISM. A preoccupation with

abstract pattern also characterized the work of Piet Mondrian (1872–1944), the leading painter of the DE STIJL (Style) movement of 1917.

During these early years of the century, EXPRESSIONISM as an art movement developed out of the work of VAN GOGH and other artists of the late 1800s and provided the impetus for the formation of the two German groups known as DIE BRÜCKE and DER BLAUE REITER. The interest of these painters in the emotional impact of their work was also shared by the artists of DADA and, later, SURREALISM, although in these there is a thinly disguised intention to shock, as in the provocative compositions of Salvador Dali (1904 –   ).

After World War II, POP, OP and KINETIC ART carried experimentation even further, whilst many other notable artists, such as Henry MOORE, have remained outside any particular grouping and have followed their own personal interests. Some of the more daringly original creations, particularly in sculpture and in the form of artistic 'happenings', have been received with predictable bewilderment, derision, or even anger by the general public, which has maintained its preference for the more readily 'understandable' kinds of representational art. New ideas and approaches are constantly appearing, and must continue to do so if art is to go on providing a dynamic outlet for expression.

Photography and art
Photography was invented so that permanent records of images formed by a lens could be made

Left: Henry Moore: *Three Sculptures: Vertebrae* 1968–9. Derived from smoothly rounded natural forms such as pebbles, Moore's sculpture is in total harmony with the materials he uses.

Left: Roy Lichtenstein: *Whaam!*, 1963. This lively example of Pop art exploits the garish colours and coarse printing technique of strip cartoons, from which it reproduces a single, action-packed frame.

---

in Italian art from about 1909 to 1915. Using an abstract style of composition derived partly from CUBISM, its artists extolled speed and the motor-car, modern warfare and patriotism, and danger and masculine courage. The leaders were Umberto Boccioni (1882–1916), Carlo Carrà (1881–1966) and Giacomo Balla (1871–1958).

G **Gainsborough, Thomas** (1727–88), was a British painter who became famous for his elegant portraits of fashionable

society, such as his renowned *Blue Boy* or *The*

Victorian genre painting, S.A. Forbes

Morning Walk, although he much preferred landscape painting.

Genre painting is a scene of everyday life, sometimes telling a story. Many fine examples were created by Dutch artists of the 1600s, such as Jan VERMEER and Pieter de Hooch (c. 1629–84) and by the French painter Jean Baptiste Chardin (1699–1779).

Gesso is an absorbent white GROUND of gypsum or chalk applied to a wood panel before painting with TEMPERA.

Giotto di Bondone (c.

1266–1337) was an influential Italian artist who moved away from the somewhat rigid, conventional style of late medieval painting and created dramatic religious frescoes peopled with lifelike human figures and town and landscapes that foreshadow Renaissance art.

Glaze is a transparent layer of oil paint which can be used to change the colour textures of another layer of paint beneath it. It is the opposite of the technique of SCUMBLING.

Gogh. See VAN GOGH.

Golden section is an imagi-

nary line drawn across a picture so that the ratio of the small part to the large part is as the large part is to the whole. The areas are in the proportion of 8 to 13. Since ancient times this proportion has been considered to give a picture harmonious balance.

Gouache is a form of watercolour paint to which white pigment has been added to make it thicker and opaque. It dries lighter than the wet colour.

Goya, Francisco de (1746–1828), a Spanish artist, showed his disgust at

Left: *Nude Descending a Staircase No. 2*, painted by Marcel Duchamp in 1912. The artist was inspired by photographs taken by the physiologist Etienne-Jules Marey (1830–1903). These showed the movements of animals and humans as series of superimposed images.

Right: *Portrait of Alice Liddell* by English amateur photographer Julia Margaret Cameron (1815–79). The distinctive soft tonal quality and the lack of fine detail are typical of the calotype process favoured by Cameron. The prints were made from paper negatives.

quickly. But now that the picture-making process had been automated, many artists felt that the camera had become a threat to their livelihoods.

Of all artists, those specializing in portraiture experienced most competition from the camera. Many were forced to give up painting and become photographers in order to survive, for there was an ever-increasing demand for quick, cheap portraits. Those who continued painting often resorted to photography in the course of their work. Instead of clients having to attend numerous sittings for a portrait, they could go to a single photographic session. The artist would then paint the portrait at his leisure, using the photographs for reference. Some artists adopted the technique of painting over a suitable photograph, thus greatly reducing the time taken to produce the portrait. However, competition from photography increased steadily with improvements to Talbot's negative-positive system. Unlike other processes, this enabled any number of prints to be made from one exposed plate.

From around the mid 1800s, with creative people like Tournachon and CAMERON, photography gradually emerged as a separate art form.

automatically. Notable among those who contributed to this new technology were Joseph Nicéphore NIEPCE, Louis DAGUERRE and William Fox TALBOT. Niépce was the first to find a way of fixing photographic images, so that they would not fade away on further exposure to light. The earliest surviving example of his work is a view from his house, taken in 1826. At first, photography was no more than an interesting novelty. Each exposure took several hours, and the picture showed little detail. But Daguerre perfected a much better system in the late 1830s. Exposure took minutes, rather than hours, and the photographs, called Daguerreotypes, were extremely clear and detailed.

Originally, the camera had been an aid to the artist, allowing him to trace or copy images

---

the political and social climate of his time in paintings

Goya, Los Caprichos

recording cruel events in the Napoleonic invasion of 1808, satirical portraits of royalty, and bitterly critical etchings in the *Caprichos* and *Disasters of War* series.

Grain, in most photographic images, is made up of tiny clumps of black, metallic silver particles. When a negative is greatly enlarged, its grain may become visible on the print. Fast (high-speed) films are generally more grainy than slow films. Where clarity is important, visible grain is undesirable, but it is often used to good effect in creating very

dramatic photographs.

Ground is the covering layer applied to a canvas, board or panel before beginning a painting. White oil primer paint is normally used on canvas and board, whilst GESSO is the traditional ground on panels.

H Hatching is a method of shading with parallel straight lines used in drawing and engraving. Denser shading is achieved by cross hatching, in which 2 sets of lines cross at an angle.

Hsieh Ho (c. AD 500) taught 6 principles of painting,

advising artists to: put life and vitality into their paintings; use firm brush-strokes; give each object its proper form and shape; use suitable colours; study space and arrangement; and imitate early masters.

I Icon is a small painting of Christ, the Virgin Mary or saints of the Christian Church on a wood or ivory panel. Icon painting was an important aspect of BYZANTINE ART and continued to flourish in the Eastern Orthodox Church.

Ife, the sacred city of the

Nigerian Yoruba tribe, was the site of superbly produced likenesses of royal heads, some in terracotta, some in brass, cast by the CIRE-PERDUE process around the 1200s.

Illumination is the art, perfected by medieval European monks, of decorating books and manuscripts with beautifully intricate lettering, figures, animals and scenes. The *Book of Kells* contains fine examples.

Illusionism is a skilful technique used by artists to deceive the eye into believing that flat surfaces are 3-

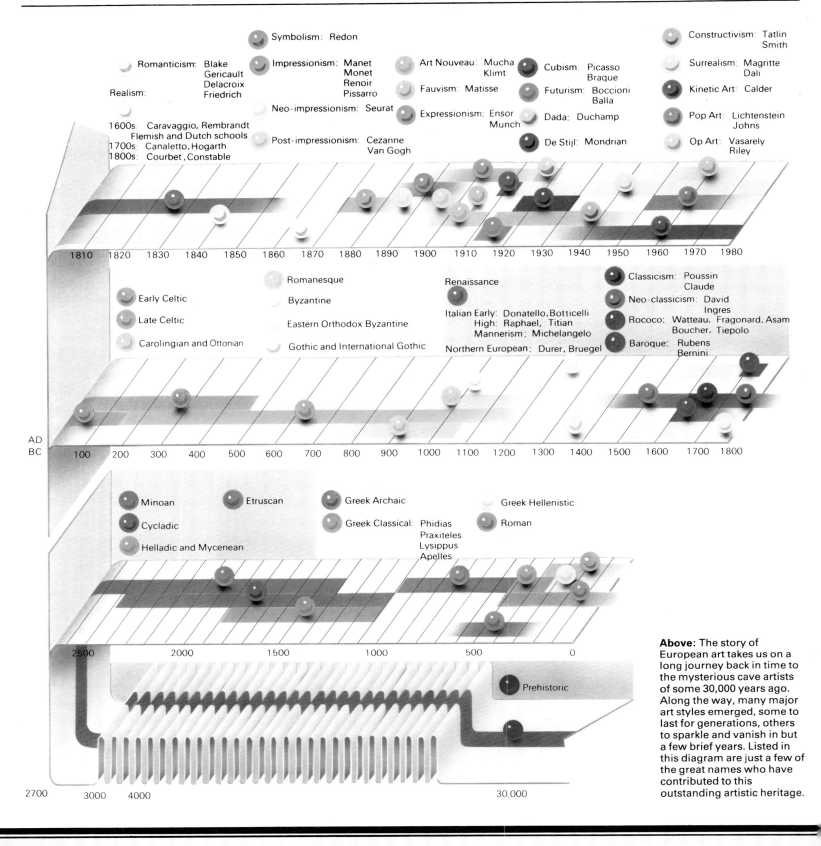

Symbolism: Redon

Romanticism: Blake
Gericault
Delacroix
Friedrich

Realism:

Impressionism: Manet
Monet
Renoir
Pissarro

Neo-impressionism: Seurat

1600s Caravaggio, Rembrandt
Flemish and Dutch schools
1700s Canaletto, Hogarth
1800s Courbet, Constable

Post-impressionism: Cezanne
Van Gogh

Art Nouveau: Mucha
Klimt

Fauvism: Matisse

Expressionism: Ensor
Munch

Cubism: Picasso
Braque

Futurism: Boccioni
Balla

Dada: Duchamp

De Stijl: Mondrian

Constructivism: Tatlin
Smith

Surrealism: Magritte
Dali

Kinetic Art: Calder

Pop Art: Lichtenstein
Johns

Op Art: Vasarely
Riley

1810 1820 1830 1840 1850 1860 1870 1880 1890 1900 1910 1920 1930 1940 1950 1960 1970 1980

Romanesque

Byzantine

Eastern Orthodox Byzantine

Gothic and International Gothic

Renaissance

Italian Early: Donatello, Botticelli
High: Raphael, Titian
Mannerism: Michelangelo

Northern European: Durer, Bruegel

Classicism: Poussin
Claude

Neo-classicism: David
Ingres

Rococo: Watteau, Fragonard, Asam
Boucher, Tiepolo

Baroque: Rubens
Bernini

Early Celtic

Late Celtic

Carolingian and Ottonian

AD
BC

100 200 300 400 500 600 700 800 900 1000 1100 1200 1300 1400 1500 1600 1700 1800

Minoan

Cycladic

Helladic and Mycenean

Etruscan

Greek Archaic

Greek Classical: Phidias
Praxiteles
Lysippus
Apelles

Greek Hellenistic

Roman

2500 2000 1500 1000 500 0

Prehistoric

Above: The story of European art takes us on a long journey back in time to the mysterious cave artists of some 30,000 years ago. Along the way, many major art styles emerged, some to last for generations, others to sparkle and vanish in but a few brief years. Listed in this diagram are just a few of the great names who have contributed to this outstanding artistic heritage.

2700
3000 4000
30,000

dimensional. PERSPECTIVE, FORESHORTENING and TROMPE-L'OEIL are the commonest forms.
Impasto is a thick application of paint to a surface.
Impressionism was a major art movement in France from the 1860s to the 1880s. Claude Monet (1840–1926) and Auguste RENOIR discovered a way of capturing a rapid, on-the-spot record of a scene by using small dabs of paint that merged together in the eye to give a dazzlingly colourful and naturalistic effect. Other artists who contri-

buted to the movement included Edouard Manet (1832–83) Camille Pissarro (1831–1903), Alfred Sisley (1839–99), Edgar Degas (1834–1917) and Paul CEZANNE.
Indian Buddhist art reached its peak about 1,500 years ago. Buddhist paintings, often of graceful, well-shaped women, reached superb standards at Ajanta (India) and Sigiriya (Sri Lanka). Buddhist sculpture attained excellence in the delicately carved Standing Buddha of Mathura.
Indonesia, although now a

Muslim country, developed its art under the conflicting

Indonesian batik work

influences of India, China, Polynesia and Melanesia, apart from Islam and the West. Indonesia excels in many minor arts, including textiles (especially batik), wood carving, metalwork-ing, mask making and pup-petry. Buddhist sculpture reached a high standard at Borobudur, a shrine in Java built in about AD 800.
Indus Valley was the site of one of the world's most ancient civilizations between about 2500 and 1500 BC.
Intaglio is the technique of cutting a shape or design into a surface, and is the

opposite of RELIEF. It is used in ENGRAVING and in making seals and industrial moulds.
International Gothic style developed in painting and sculpture in the courts of Europe in the late 1300s. Its main features were the choice of courtly and roman-tic subjects, the portrayal of elegant, graceful figures, and a greater attention to realism than before, although only in the fine details, such as the cos-tumes, flowers or animals in a scene. Leading artists in the style were the Limbourg brothers in France (early

Above: A 'Great Mother' figurine unearthed in Sardinia was carved in limestone thousands of years ago. In its stark simplicity it takes the widespread prehistoric theme of womanhood to its most abstract extreme.

Right: Mathis Grünewald: *The Mocking of Christ*, before 1503. In this earliest known work by Grünewald, a well-known religious episode is rendered with the emotional power typical of late medieval German art. The violence of the scene is reinforced by the distorted facial features of the scourgers and onlookers, which present a deliberate contrast with the resigned, suffering expression of Christ and the hesitant, uncertain gaze of Pontius Pilate. A further emotional emphasis is provided by the choice of bright colours – red and purple – for the scourgers' costumes, contrasting with the passively cool blue-grey of Christ's robe and the neutral-coloured tunic of Pilate.

The human figure

Throughout the ages the human figure has been a source of inspiration to artists in all parts of the world. The manner in which they have represented it, ranging from the realistic to the abstract, reflects not only their own individual styles and feelings about their subject but also the fashions and aesthetic outlook of their age.

The idea of creating beauty or a 'work of art' probably never entered the minds of those prehistoric artists who painted match-stick hunters on the walls of caves or those who carved contrasting plump fertility goddesses with well-developed breasts and hips. These were not portraits, but symbols or ritual objects. As such they were the earliest manifestations of ABSTRACT ART. A reduction of the idea of womanhood to its simplest form produced the stark 'Mother Goddess' figurine from ancient Sardinia which could understandably be mistaken for a piece of modern sculpture.

Artists living in the world's first civilizations – in Anatolia, Mesopotamia and Egypt – took the primitive, symbolic function of art a stage further with their portrayals of awesome kings and gods in reliefs, statues and paintings. Paintings from Egyptian tombs show that the art was very stylized with figures of a standard type, although at times there was an attempt to superimpose individual traits. It was not until the Classical period of Greek civilization that European artists began to create more naturalistic representations of athletes and gods. It was left to the Hellenistic Greeks and then the Romans, great admirers of Greek culture, to bring art down to earth with realistic portrait sculptures and paintings.

Outside Europe, the vigorous, sensual nature of Indian female figures had already become apparent in the lithe statuette of a dancing girl found in the INDUS VALLEY and cast in bronze over 4,000 years ago. Taken to the jungles of Kampuchea, this lively Indian art took on a new style in the galleries of ANGKOR. The difference between sophisticated Chinese and primitive Japanese tomb figures of 2,000 years ago is startling. Yet 1,000 years later sculptors of both countries produced LOHANS and other Buddhist figures of similar style.

The human figure in Islamic art is represented only in painting, where men appear stiffly formal and heavily clothed (except in some PERSIAN MINIATURES). In contrast, African tribal artists commonly produced nude carved figures with larger-than-life heads, breasts, abdomens and other bodily exaggerations. Ancient American human figures tended to be caricatures in the round, three-dimensional cartoons. Their con-

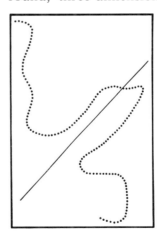

Left: Grünewald's painting is a masterpiece of unified, balanced composition, which brilliantly expresses the contrasting emotions of the action. The basic rectangle formed by the heads of the 4 principal figures is crossed from top left to bottom right by a snaking, tense diagonal formed by the wheeling scourgers, whilst a straighter, calmer line links the anxious figure of Pontius Pilate diagonally through his outstretched palm (notably not a fist) to the subdued Christ.

1400s) and Gentile da Fabriano (c. 1370–1427) in Italy.
Isfahan, the capital of Persia in the days of Shah Abbas (the 1600s), became a city of outstanding beauty, with splendidly decorated mosques and a central *maidan* (an open, rectangular area used in Isfahan for polo).

J **Jain art** includes impressive but stiff, otherwordly nude statues of saints of the Jain religion towering over 17 metres tall. Jain temples are often of finely carved marble. Colourful Jain paintings of human forms are charac-

Japanese Netsuke, 1700s

terized by a distinct style of eyes.
Japan has developed some unusual arts to a high degree, including: sword art; *netsuke* (miniature artefacts often of wood or ivory, used to fasten or hang objects from the dress); *inro* (small medicine boxes); sand gardens; and colour prints. Japan's outstanding artistic tradition derived from China, mainly through KOREA.
Jataka Tales were produced to teach unlearned people about Buddhism. They tell of the many lives of

the Buddha and were often illustrated in sculpture, as at Sanchi stupa, western India.

K **Key** is the degree of lightness or darkness of tone and colour in a painting. For example, paintings of Paul Gauguin (1848–1903) are high in key, whilst REMBRANDT's are low-keyed. The term is also used in photography, in which a high key is obtained by the use of soft lighting, which conveys a relaxed, light-hearted mood. Low key produces dramatic photographs consisting mostly of darker tones.

Khajuraho, in northern India, the capital of the Chandellas, a Rajput clan, became the centre of a large group of temples almost totally carved with beautiful sculptures of the human body, still to be seen.
Kinetic art comprises objects assembled so that they move or turn and, in doing so, form constantly changing colour patterns and shadow effects. the MOBILES of Alexander Calder (1898–1976) are examples.
Korea took its art forms and styles mainly from China and to a slight extent from

torted facial expressions and preposterous body proportions border upon the fantastic. Yet, amazingly, they convey the impression of being modelled on real people with individual personalities.

The advent of Christianity in Europe towards the end of the Roman era provided a wealth of new subject matter that found expression in BYZANTINE, CELTIC and medieval art. Amongst the multitude of apostles, saints and other biblical personalities, the central figure of Christ stood out, with large expressive eyes, long hair and dark beard, as in Mathis Grünewald's picture *The Mocking of Christ*. The medieval notion of the ugliness of sin is symbolized in this painting by the brutal faces of the floggers.

Renaissance artists held a less gloomy view of mankind and, with one eye on ancient Roman (and hence, Greek) art, created a whole gallery of paintings and sculptures extolling the beauty of the human form.

The MANNERISM in Michelangeló's *Last Judge-*

Right: Pablo Picasso: *Woman in a Fish Hat*, 1942. Although presenting one of the artist's favourite subjects, the female head, this is not a portrait in the sense that Rembrandt's is. Picasso's picture is a whimsical exercise in form and colour.

Left: Rembrandt van Rijn: *Portrait of Margareta Trip*, 1661. Rembrandt's ability to penetrate below surface appearances to reveal deeper, spiritual truths is well illustrated in this moving painting. Here he captures the universal human tragedy of a dignified 76-year-old woman, still insisting on lifelong high standards of grooming, although physically declining into sunken-faced and wrinkled old age.

ment is explicitly stated in the work of the Spanish painter El Greco (1541–1614) and the venetian Tintoretto (1518–94), whose elongated, distorted figures express deep inner tensions. More outwardly theatrical are the boldly vigorous men and plump nude women who people the Baroque art of RUBENS. A quieter dignity pervades the finely realistic portraits painted at this time by such masters as VELAZQUEZ, VERMEER, Frans Hals (1580–1666), Antony Van Dyck (1599–1641) and, above all, REMBRANDT, whose moving picture of Margareta Trip brilliantly captures the calm, gentle frailty of old age.

The tradition of naturalistic portraiture continued in the 1700s and 1800s, when royalty and fashionable society provided a steady living for many important artists, among them painters like Joshua Reynolds (1723–92), Thomas GAINS-BOROUGH, Francisco de GOYA, Auguste Dominique Ingres (1780–1867), and the sculptor Jean Antoine Houdon (1741–1828). The work of these artists of course reflected to some degree the major art styles current in their countries at the time; CANOVA's coldly classical *Pauline Bonaparte as Venus*, for example, represents Neoclassicism in sculpture. The same is true of the present century, in which the human form has been subjected to all the stylistic experiments of the

---

the Japanese and Mongols. However, its square-walled pagodas have a distinctive style.
Krishna, in Hindu theology, is the 8th reincarnation of the god Vishnu. He plays many divine roles, but is generally regarded as a friendly, merry god-hero, close to human beings.

L **Latent image** is the invisible image on film or paper after exposure and before development.
Lay-in. After drawing a picture on a canvas, artists who followed traditional painting

methods then 'laid in' the design in TONES of a single, dull colour, such as grey (known as *grisaille*) or brown. The final colour values could then be worked out and added.
Lens is a piece of glass or other transparent surface with both or one side curved for concentrating or dispersing light-rays.
Leonardo da Vinci (1452–1519), inventor, engineer, naturalist and artist, was one of the leading figures of the Italian Renaissance and perhaps its greatest creative genius. The

breadth of his interests is revealed in the sketches and copious notes taken in mir-

Drawing by Leonardo da Vinci

ror writing whilst his artistic achievements are represented by a small number of outstanding paintings, among them the 2 versions of *The Virgin of the Rocks*; the crumbling mural of *The Last Supper*; a fresco, now lost, of *The Battle of Anghiari*; and his most famous painting, the *Mona Lisa*.
Linocut is an engraving made by cutting a design into a piece of lino so that only the lines are left in RE-LIEF. When a print is taken from the inked design, only the lines léave an image.
Lithography is a method of

making prints without cutting into the printing surface. A design is drawn with greasy crayons or ink on to a metal plate (formerly limestone), which is then dampened. Greasy ink applied to the plate with a roller sticks only to the greasy design. The plate can then be used for printing. The technique was invented in Prague in 1798.
Lohans, priests or laymen on the threshold of attaining Buddhahood, became a favourite subject for Chinese sculptors and potters from the 700s to the 1200s.

period. PICASSO's *Woman in a Fish Hat* and sculptures by Henry MOORE demonstrate the extent of the exploration into non-naturalistic representation during these years, at a time when the art of photography has come into its own.

One advantage of photography over drawing or painting is its ability to produce a good likeness of the subject with little effort. This is particularly useful where portraits are concerned. For this reason, many artist started to make use of photography in the 1830s. Before that time, the extremely long exposures required made portrait photography difficult, for many sitters found it impossible to remain motionless, and a blurred picture resulted. To help the sitter remain still, a support was often provided for the head, and, for group photographs, it was common to pose each person in a position that could be held easily. As a result, many early photographs of people appear quite unnatural. One of the most accomplished portrait photographers was Julia Margaret CAMERON.

Right: Sensual sculpture of the female form was a leading aspect of Indian art for over 3,000 years. Sculpture of the human body reached its height in the temple complex at Khajuraho, northern India, which features this carving of a woman applying eye shadow about 1,000 years ago.

Below: A detail of one of the numerous movement studies by the English photographer Eadweard James Muybridge (1830–1904). In the complete study the action is captured at 12 stages and from 3 viewpoints. Having analysed movement in this way, Muybridge found that he could project each series of images to produce a moving picture. Hundreds of these studies appeared in *Animal Locomotion* (1887).

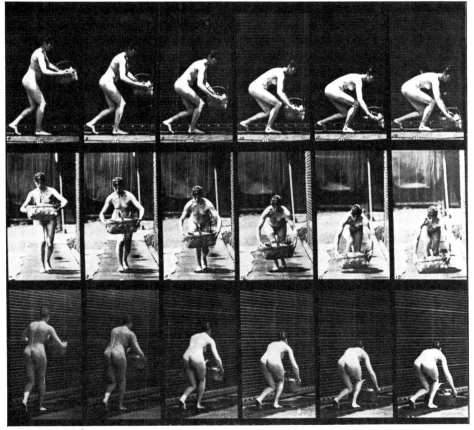

With modern equipment and materials, the problem of subject movement has been overcome. Portraits can be taken in a fraction of a second using daylight, continuous studio lighting or flash. And sharp, 'candid' pictures, showing people at work or play, can be taken without the subjects even being aware that a photographer is present.

Landscape

Views of the countryside, ships on the sea, and even city streets have enjoyed lasting popularity as subjects for art, and many of the world's finest artists are best known for their work in this field. But compared to pictures of the human figure, landscapes are a fairly recent form of art. The carved reliefs and tomb paintings of hunting scenes by the earliest artists did not make anything more than a passing reference to the countryside, and then only in the form of a solitary tree or bush, inserted without any concern for depth or space. Egyptian tomb paintings of the

---

Macrophotograph is an extreme close-up photograph, usually taken with a special lens or focusing facility on the camera. Like a PHOTOMICROGRAPH, a macrophotograph can be used for creative design work. The main difference between these 2 types of picture is one of scale. Macrophotography is generally used for image magnifications of up to 10 or 20 diameters. Higher magnifications are obtained by photomicrography, in which photographs are taken through a microscope.

Mahlstick has a padded knob at one end, and is used by an artist to support and steady the hand during painting.

Mannerism was a stylistic development in RENAISSANCE art and architecture in the later 1500s, in which the classical principles of harmony, balance and proportion epitomized by RAPHAEL, were deliberately flouted. Characteristic features were irregular and imbalanced composition; the distortion of human figures into elongated, muscular forms; the choice of harsh, bright col-

ours; and a general atmosphere of emotional tension. Apart from the later work of MICHELANGELO, the most important Mannerist art was created by Jacopo Tintoretto (1518–94), El Greco (1541–1614), Francesco Parmigianino (1503–40) and Jacopo Pontormo (1494–1556).

Masks, a feature of primitive societies the world over, have deep religious and magical significance. Masks gave their wearers new identities and inspired fear in others.

Master was a member of a medieval guild of artists who was permitted to set up in business after having a piece

Mezzotint by John Martin

of his work, his 'masterpiece' approved as competent by the guild. The term 'old master', meaning a painting by such a recognized artist, is a derivative.

Mexican codices are the picture books of ancient Mexico, made of bark, leaves or deerskin. They recorded happenings and ceremonies rather like modern strip cartoons.

Mezzotint is a technique of INTAGLIO printing invented in the 1600s. A copper plate is covered with dots using a tool with a serrated edge. A design is created by rubbing

1400s BC, depict charming hunting and fishing scenes in the Nile marshes, but again the emphasis is on the animals rather than the scenery. Among the earliest paintings that indicate an interest in landscape for its own sake were those done around 50 BC as fresco decorations in a house in Rome, which illustrate Odysseus's adventures in the land of the Lestrygonians.

Nature continued mainly as a backcloth in painting throughout the medieval period, although GIOTTO's *Flight into Egypt* marks a greater attention to modelling if not deep background perspective. Albrecht DÜRER's water-colour views of the Nuremberg countryside and the Alps, painted in the 1490s, however, went a long way towards establishing naturalistic landscape as a separate art form and paved the way for the superb series of pictures of the months painted by Pieter BRUEGEL in the mid 1500s, followed the next century by such masters of Dutch landscape as Jacob van Ruisdael (1628–82), Jan van Goyen (1596–1656) and Meindert Hobbema (1638–1709). This was also the age of the idealized classical landscape perfected in Rome by Nicolas Poussin (1594–1665) and Claude Lorraine (1600–82) incorporating classical buildings and figures distantly playing out an event from

Below: Claude Lorraine: *Landscape: Cephalus and Procris Reunited by Diana*, 1645. It is typical of the 'ideal landscape' of Classicism in the 1600s.

mythology. Claude's *Landscape: Cephalus and Procris Reunited by Diana* sums up this contrived, yet effective, form of art.

In the 1700s Francesco Guardi (1712–93) and Antonio Canale (Canaletto, 1697–1768), painted minutely observed views of Venice that have enjoyed lasting appeal, whilst John CONSTABLE and many others recorded the beauty of the English countryside. More imaginative and poetically atmospheric were J. M. W. TURNER's hazy, light-filled landscapes and sea pictures, which Constable described as 'airy visions, painted with tinted steam'. The ROMANTICISM evident in Turner's work was more overtly expressed, however, in the imaginary, theatrically lit scenes created by the German artist Caspar Friedrich (1774–1840).

In the first part of the 1800s Camille Corot (1796–1875) and the BARBIZON SCHOOL were the most important recorders of the French countryside before the Impressionists burst upon a shocked art world with their brightly coloured, blurry outdoor scenes. For one of the group, Paul CEZANNE, Impressionism was unsatisfactory as a means of exploring the solid forms in nature, and he broke away to create his own highly influential kind of landscape. At the same time Vincent VAN GOGH was producing increasingly tense,

---

some of the dots off. The resulting surface produces a wide range of tones.
Michaelangelo Buonarroti (1475–1564), a major figure of the Italian Renaissance, made an outstanding contribution to painting, sculpture, architecture and poetry. His carvings in marble are the consummation of Renaissance striving for perfection in the portrayal of the human figure. They include the heroic statues of *David* and *Moses*; the movingly dramatic and unfinished figures of slaves for the tomb of Pope Julius

II; and the 3 greatly differing PIETÀS. The Biblical scenes which he painted on the Sistine Chapel in Rome, and the awesome *Last Judgement* with which, some 25 years later, he covered the entire altar wall, testify to his creative genius and his technical mastery of FRESCO painting.
Ming dynasty of China (1368–1644), the only truly Chinese dynasty to rule after 1279, produced vast quantities of decorated 'blue and white' glazed porcelain for export. Although Ming court art declined, aristocrat-artists continued to paint.

Mobile is a form of hanging sculpture invented by the American artist Alexander Calder (1898-1976). It consists of bits of wood or metal connected by lengths of wire and delicately balanced. Any slight movement of air will cause it to girate. See also KINETIC ART.
Mochica (also called *Moche* or *Pre-Chimu*) civilization centred on northern Peru between c. 50BC and c. AD 750. Its artists produced large quantities of liquid-containing vessels often shaped in distorted human forms. Facial features, espe-

cially, were exaggerated much as they are in modern caricatures.

Mohica stirrup pot c. 400 AD

Modelling, in sculpture, is the technique of fashioning a 3-dimensional shape from a workable material, such as clay. In painting, modelling is the artist's method of making a 3-dimensional object look solid on a flat surface.
Monoprint, or monotype, is a single print taken from an inked design drawn in one or more colours on a glass or metal plate or engraving stone, or from an inked object placed on the plate.
Moore, Henry (1898–), a British sculptor, became a major figure in modern art. Concentrating on the tradi-

Far left: Giotto di Bondone: *The Flight into Egypt*, c. 1290. Giotto's frescoes on the lives of Christ and St Francis show a greater use of modelling in the figures and a more naturalistic rendering of landscape than in earlier European painting.

Left: Vincent van Gogh: *A Cornfield with Cypresses*, 1889. This landscape was one of many painted in a frenzy of activity when van Gogh was a patient at the hospital at St-Rémy. The visual reality of the scene is infected by the artist's mental state, so that everything in it – sky, trees, bushes and corn – writhe in a swirling turbulence.

Below: Paul Klee: *Ambassador of Autumn*, 1922. The seemingly primitive, even childlike, interpretation of nature in Klee's abstract water-colour nevertheless brilliantly evokes the atmosphere of early autumn. The eye is drawn to the browning leaves of the solitary, symbolic tree by the complementary blue tones of the mist-enshrouded fields.

expressionistic views of the French Midi, whilst Paul Gauguin (1848–1903) was recording on canvas the colourful, exotic world of the South Seas.

The coming of photography in the 1800s opened the eyes of the world, for no longer did people have to rely on verbal descriptions of far-away places, or on artists' impressions. At last, in photographs, they could see the truth for themselves. However, the photographer's technique, like the artist's, could greatly affect the impressions given by his pictures.

In the present century, landscape, like portraiture, has been an important element in the development of several major art styles. Garishly bright pictures of nature were painted by the FAUVES; nightmarish landscapes seemingly straight from the subconscious appear in starkly realistic detail in Surrealist art; and from German EXPRESSIONISM have come such abstract conceptions as Paul Klee's *Ambassador of Autumn*.

Non-European art has little landscape in the

tional technique of carving, he has created a characteristic style of monumental reclining figures and groups which are inspired by the smoothly rounded shapes of pebbles found in nature on the seashore.

Mughal dynasty of India (1526–1700s) reached the height of its artistic achievement in 1556–1658 under the emperors Akbar, Jahangir and Shah Jahan. Akbar developed the Mughal school of painting, setting Persian and Hindu artists to work together on Muslim themes.

Narrative painting depicts an incident in a story, either as one scene or as CONTINUOUS REPRESENTATION. It is assumed that the viewer will know or can guess the story and can therefore appreciate the significance of the action in the painting.

Nazarenes were a group of painters formed in Vienna in 1809 to recreate the style of religious art in the 1400s. They later worked in Rome. The British PRE-RAPHAELITE BROTHERHOOD were influenced by them.

Negative is a photographic image in which dark and light tones are reversed. During enlargement, light passing through the negative falls on to light-sensitive paper. Areas on which most light falls appear darkest when the paper is developed. Thus the original scene is reproduced correctly. Colour negatives show changes in colour as well as tone.

Neoclassicism was a revival of ancient classical art and architecture in Europe from the mid 1700s to the 1850s. It emerged partly as a reaction against ROCOCO frivolity and BAROQUE exag-

geration and partly as a result of the scholarly debates on art prompted by

Death of Marat *by David*

archaeological discoveries of Greek and Roman ruins at such places as Pompeii and Herculaneum. The leading figures of the movement included the painters Jacques Louis DAVID and Jean Auguste Ingres (1780–1867), the sculptor Antonio CANOVA, and the engraver Giovanni Battista PIRANESI.

Neo-Impressionism was a brief movement in painting in the 1880s. Following the interest of Impressionist artists in the colour values in light and shade, artists such as Georges Seurat (1859–91) and Paul Signac (1863–1935)

sense known to European artists. In Indian painting, landscape tends to be confined to mythical background scenes, whilst Tibetan religious landscapes take us into the world of fantasy. Landscape in Islamic art is even rarer than in Indian art.

Chinese 'mountain and water' artists of the late TANG and the Sung dynasties (c. 900–1279)

Below: Landscape took new form in the works of Japanese colour print artists, who developed Chinese 'mountain and water' painting into a uniquely Japanese form and style. This print, signed 'Hiroshige II – 1860', shows Mount Fuji seen from Nara.

illustrated Taoist-Buddhist themes in which saints, hermits, sages and immortals meditated in remote mountains separated by flowing streams. These delicate, hardly real landscapes contrast sharply with the more solid scenes of European painters. Under the brushes of Japanese artists, the Chinese landscape style became even less real. Inspired by SHINTO and the Japanese awe of natural forces, climatic tranquility gave way to storms, culminating in such works as *Mount Fuji seen below a wave at Kanagawa* by Hokusai Katsushika (1760–1849). In the hands of Hokusai, Hiroshige Ando (1797–1858) and other COLOUR PRINT ARTISTS (c. 1760–1890) the landscape took new, exciting forms, influencing Van Gogh and Gauguin, among others, in Europe. Manet and other French Impressionists also took inspiration from this 'new world' of art.

Everyday life and history
The ordinary activities of people going about

---

devised the theory of DIVISIONISM, in which, by a process of optical mixing, small, separate dots of primary colour seem to merge in the eye to create an effect of brightness.
Niépce, Joseph Nicéphore (1765–1833), was a French inventor who, in the early 1820s, discovered how to make photographic images permanent. The process is called fixing.
Nok culture of Nigeria produced maturely sculptured terracotta and polished stone heads in about 250 BC.

O p art, or optical art, is a form of ABSTRACT ART. which appeared in the 1950s and was devised to create beautiful and dazzling optical illusions in which the patterns of colour seem to move. The leading practitioners included Victor Vasarely (1908–) and the constructivist sculptor Günther Uecker (1930–).

P **Pastel** is a drawing medium consisting of powdered pigments mixed with gum or resin in the shape of sticks like thick crayons. Because the colour

tends to fall off or smudge, a FIXATIVE has to be used. One of the greatest artists in pastel was Edgar Degas (1834–1917).
Persian miniatures, which by the 1500s excelled in delicate representations of themes from Persian literature, owed their origin to the Timurid schools of painting encouraged by the patronage of the grandsons of TIMUR THE LAME in the 1500s.
Perspective is a technique used by artists to represent 3-dimensional objects receding into space so that they appear real on a flat surface,

Perspective

although Western perspective differs from that used by artists in the East. Aerial perspective also takes account of the increase in blue tones as distance increases. See also FORESHORTENING and MODELLING.
Photogram is a photograph made without a camera. The simplest form of photogram is made by placing various opaque objects on a sheet of photographic paper, which is then exposed to light. After processing, the paper shows the objects as white shapes against a dark background. More complex

their daily lives have provided a rich source of themes for artists since the world's first artists painted scenes on the walls of caves. But for thousands of years after the appearance of civilization, it was the world of kings and the gods that mainly concerned artists: art was exploited as a means of glorifying the king by recording his heroic battle victories and showing him in awesome communication with the gods. Not surprisingly, historians have been able to learn much about those ancient times from relief sculptures, statues, mosaics and paintings. The victories of the Roman emperor Trajan over the Dacians, for example, are set out in realistic detail in relief carvings on a commemorative column erected in Rome in about AD 113.

The activities of gods, kings and their courts were also emphasized in early non-European art. Many Indian paintings, for example, illustrate the life of KRISHNA. A popular theme is his romps with the *gopis*, or milkmaids. Tang artists painted plump Chinese court women busying themselves with silk weaving or other useful but ladylike occupations. Japanese painters recorded such events as the movements of European traders or the attacks of marauding RONIN. Toshusai Sharuku caricatured the lives of courtesans and actors in vast numbers of vivid prints. Indian

and Islamic paintings abound in 'historical' events. However, in many cases the court painters have either slanted historical fact to flatter their royal patrons or painted mythical rather than historical events.

African artists have shown little interest in everyday life. Ife and BENIN 'BRONZES' and Ashanti MASKS of Ghana portray mostly real persons but convey little about historical events. The gruesome rituals of the Aztec religion, however, are grimly recorded in the MEXICAN CODICES.

Everyday life was not seriously explored as a subject for European art until about the 1400s, when the miniatures of the Limbourg brothers in the *Très Riches Heures du Duc de Berri* and the drawings and engravings of the artist known as the Master of the Housebook marked the beginning of a long tradition of such GENRE art in northern Europe. The most notable artists to concern themselves with it in the 1600s and 1700s included Adriaen Brouwer (c. 1605–38) Pieter BRUEGEL, Pieter de Hooch (c. 1629–84) and Jan VERMEER in the Low Countries; Louis Le Nain (c.1593–1648) and Jean Baptiste Chardin (1699–1779) in France; Bartolomé Murillo (1617–82) in Spain; and in England William Hogarth (1697–1764) and Thomas Rowlandson (1756–1827).

Above: Trajan's Column, Rome, about AD 113. This detail of the superb reliefs carved on the column demonstrates the factual realism with which the emperor's successful Dacian campaigns were recorded.

Far above left: Chinese landscape painters specialized in 'mountain and water' scenes on Taoist-Buddhist themes. During the Mongol occupation of China (1279–1368), out-of-office noblemen occupied their time by developing landscape painting. During the Ming dynasty (1368–1644) they continued to produce paintings such as the one shown, despite the decline in the work of the professional painters, whose originality was stifled by the rigid etiquette of the Ming court.

Left: Pieter Bruegel: *Children's Games*, 1560. Lively, colourful Flemish scenes filled with ordinary folk doing everyday things were a recurring theme in Bruegel's work and earned this cultured artist the misleading nickname 'Peasant Bruegel'.

photographs can be made using semi-transparent and reflecting objects on the paper. Around 1920, photograms became popular with artists interested in producing instant abstract images from everday objects.
Photomicrograph is a photograph taken through a microscope. The high degree of enlargement in such pictures reveals shapes, patterns and textures not normally visible and often quite unlike those encountered in everyday life. These properties can be usefully explored and used

by the creative photographer. Compared with man-made objects, natural

Photogram of a leaf

subjects generally have a much more complex and delicate structure.
Picasso, Pablo (1881–1973), a Spanish artist, made an outstanding contribution to modern art through paintings, drawings, prints, sculpture and ceramics. His experiments in all these fields made him one of the most influential and controversial artists of his time. In the early 1900s, his explorations into the problem of representing 3-dimensional objects on a flat surface led to the appearance of CUBISM in painting. It was a totally

different style from his earlier naturalistic studies of poor folk (his 'blue' period) and his charming, rose-tinted scenes of the theatre and circus world (his 'rose' period). Subjects from classical mythology, acted out by monumental female figures, occupied him in the 1920s, followed by colourful bullfight scenes and the terrifying *Guernica*, Picasso's personal protest at the horror of the Spanish Civil War. Exiled in France, he continued until his death to experiment and left a vast amount of work.

Pietà is a form of sculpture portraying the Virgin Mary holding the dead Christ in her lap. It was first created by German sculptors of the 1300s, but the best-known examples are those by MICHELANGELO.
Piranesi, Giovanni Battista (1720–78), an Italian architect, became famous for the 135 ETCHINGS he made of ancient ruins and contemporary buildings in Rome, and for a series of imaginary scenes of prisons. His work greatly influenced the architects of NEOCLASSICISM.
Pisano, Nicolà (c. 1220–c.

Despite the great achievements of such artists, however, the academies of art established in several European countries from the 1600s regarded history and mythology, preferably ancient, as the most worthy and noble subjects for art. Most of the great European masters, among them RUBENS, TIEPOLO, GOYA and DAVID, contributed major works in this field, as did Winslow Homer (1836–1910) in the United States, with his factual, contemporary pictures of

Below: An Indian painting shows women in the holy city of Benares on the Ganges selling rice, vegetables and other foodstuffs. By the middle of the 1700s, Indian paintings often depicted such scenes from everyday life, but the style developed from earlier Mughal paintings concerned principally with life at court.

the American Civil War, but the fashion declined in the late 1800s as photography emerged.

The effectiveness of photography for recording historical events became apparent in the 1850s, when Roger Fenton (1819–69) took pictures of the Crimean War, and a few years later Mathew Brady (1823–96) photographed the American Civil War. Instead of the artist's portrayal of heroic deeds, the public now saw the terrible horrors of war.

Showing everyday life was a difficult task for the early photographers, for life usually involved movement, and movement could result in a blurred image, or even no image at all. Some early photographs of cities, for example, make them look like ghost towns, because an extremely long exposure was used. The camera, mounted on a rigid stand, would record buildings and other stationary objects, but most people and vehicles did not stay still long enough to be recorded on the film. So, as in portrait photography, shots of everyday life had to be carefully posed until the advent of snapshot photography gave greater freedom.

In the last 100 years everyday life and contemporary events have been variously interpreted in art according to current styles or the personal responses of individual artists free from the restrictions of academic convention. Impressionist art, PICASSO's 'blue' and 'rose' period works, the American ASHCAN SCHOOL, the art of FUTURISM, or the paintings of David Hockney (1937–) are thus diverse, but related, interpretations of contemporary life.

Objects and still-life

Paintings known as 'still-lifes', depicting simply an arrangement of various objects, were almost unknown in art history before the 1500s. Objects of all kinds had, of course, appeared as part of the composition in ancient and medieval art, and there was even a famous Greek mosaic of the 100s BC which represented nothing more than remnants of food scattered over the floor as if fallen from a banquet table. But it was in the 1500s that still-life as a separate art form fully emerged in highly detailed Spanish and Neapolitan paintings and was taken up by such artists as CARAVAGGIO, Francisco de Zurbarán (1598–1664) and that superb painter of musical instruments, Evaristo Baschenis (c.1617–77). It

---

84), and his son Giovanni (c. 1245–c. 1320), were important Italian sculptors who bridged the transition from Gothic to Renaissance art by using ancient Roman sculpture as a model.
Pop art developed in Britain and America in the 1950s and 60s, and consisted of paintings, sculptures and COLLAGES in which everyday objects were assembled together without any obvious link. Blown-up comic strips or photographs painted in garish colours were a typical form. The leading Pop artists were

Robert Rauschenberg (1925–), Jasper Johns (1930–) and Roy Lichtenstein (1923–).
Positive is a photographic image in which the light and dark areas correspond to those in the original scene. An enlargement is a positive print made by projecting a NEGATIVE on to light-sensitive paper.
Post-Impressionism is a general term applied to the reaction against IMPRESSIONISM and NEO-IMPRESSIONISM in the art of the late 1800s and early 1900s. Unlike the Impressionists, artists such

as CEZANNE, VAN GOGH, Paul Gauguin (1848–1903) and TOULOUSE-LAUTREC were concerned less with analyzing the colour effects of light than with the subject matter, composition and emotional expression of their work.
Pre-Raphaelite Brotherhood was a controversial group of very differing British painters of the mid 1800s who, dissatisfied with the low standard of contemporary art, set out to imitate Italian painting before the time of RAPHAEL. They concentrated on medieval, religious and mythological

subjects, which they presented in realistic detail and bright colours. The leading figures were William Hol-

Beata Beatrix *by Rossetti*

man Hunt (1827–1910), Dante Gabriel Rossetti (1828–82) and John Millais (1829–96).
Proof, in printmaking, is a first trial print made by the artist to see if any corrections need to be made.

R **Rajput painting** was patronized by the Rajputs (princes) of Rajputana, in north-west India. Rajput painters used Mughal techniques to portray Hindu themes. They developed *Raga-Ragini* pictures representing musical modes. Rajput sub-schools include

Right: George Stubbs: *Horse Frightened by a Lion*, 1770 (detail). A student of nature and anatomy, Stubbs became one of the finest of all animal painters. The experience of seeing a horse being eaten by a lion while travelling through North Africa remained in his mind all his life and provided the theme for many of his pictures.

Far left: A Crimean War photograph by Felice Beatto showing the 97th Light Infantry Division at camp before their attack on Sevastopol in 1855.

Right: Henri Matisse: *The Snail*, 1953. Throughout his life Matisse was the creator of brightly coloured pictures, first as one of the Fauves group at the beginning of the century, and in his final years as the inventor of abstract collage compositions of hand-coloured pieces of paper. In this large example, almost 3 metres square, the shape of the snail has become a barely discernible spiral.

was in the Protestant Low Countries, however, that still-life became most popular, following the decline of religious painting after the Reformation.

The objects in these early still-lifes often have a deeper significance than their surface appearance suggests. Objects such as skulls, hour-glasses, butterflies or flowers are often inserted as symbols of the vanity and brevity of human exisence. Other still-lifes were simply virtuoso pieces intended to display the artist's technical skill or, more particularly in the last 100 years, his interest in the formal problem of rendering objects in three dimensions, as in the work of CEZANNE or PICASSO.

Animals in art

Animals, both real and imaginary, have always been a favourite subject for artists. Paintings of bulls, bison and horses were among the first forms of art practised by prehistoric peoples, and Assyrian reliefs of lion hunts and Egyptian tomb paintings of birds, fishes and other animals stand out among the art forms of the early Middle Eastern civilizations. Imaginary creatures with part human, part animal features and representing gods of mythical beings appear prominently in the art of ancient Egypt, Greece and Rome, the sphinx and the centaur being two such composite

forms. Writhing animal shapes were a decorative feature of Celtic art. As late as 1500 monsters of all kinds, as well as real animals, filled the crowded panels of Hieronymus Bosch's (c.1450–1516) disturbingly imaginative TRIPTYCHS.

Throughout history the horse has been particularly popular in art, and the equestrian statue, portraying a mounted rider, became a test-piece for any aspiring sculptor. The most famous classical example was the Roman statue

Kangra and *Mewar*, which took KRISHNA as a favourite theme.
Ramayana, the greatest epic poem of Hinduism is basically the story of Rama, a semi-divine prince unjustly banished from his father's court, and of the fidelity of his wife, Sita. The epic combines myths, legends and historical facts. It is the fount of much of the visual art of India and THAILAND especially.
Raphael, or Raffaello Sanzio, (1483–1520) was, with LEONARDO DA VINCI and MICHELANGELO, one of the

Scene from the Ramayana

three greatest artists of the Italian RENAISSANCE. His finest completed paintings are the series of serene Madonnas, including the *Madonna del Granduca*, which he produced in Florence before 1508.
Realism, in the everyday sense, is the lifelike, naturalistic quality of objects or scenes in a work of art. However, the term also applies to the art movement of the mid 1800s led by the French painter Gustave Courbet. Socialist realism is the official style of art favoured by Communist regimes and used to promote their propaganda and glorify their achievements.
Relief, the opposite of IN-

TAGLIO, is the technique of carving or cutting into a material such as stone or wood so that an image or design stands out from the background. *High relief* involves deep cutting so that the image is almost detached, whilst *bas-relief* requires only shallow cutting. Apart from its application to sculpture, relief is a technique used to make LINOCUT and WOODCUT prints.
Rembrandt van Rijn (1606–69), the greatest Dutch painter, was primarily a master of portraiture, although he also concerned

himself with religious subjects. Among his group portraits of local celebrities is the so-called *Night Watch* and several family paintings. His single portraits include many charming studies of his wife Saskia in various guises, and a series of 60 moving and revealing self-portraits painted throughout his life.
Renaissance was the revival of Greek and, particularly, Roman learning and culture which began in Italy in the 1300s and lasted until the end of the 1500s. Artists studied and imitated the

Left: *Course de Chevaux à Epsom, le Derby en 1821* by Théodore Géricault. The 'flying-gallop' attitude of the horses seemed correct at the time. Later paintings of horses, after the advent of photography and photographic studies of movement sequences, show that the position of the legs was in fact incorrect if not impossible.

of Marcus Aurelius, which clearly inspired Donatello's superb *Gattamelata* monument in Padua, cast in the 1450s. Horses were also a favourite subject of the English painter George Stubbs, one of the most outstanding of all animal artists, as his *Horse Frightened by a Lion* demonstrates. The almost photographic naturalism of Stubbs' animals contrasts markedly with the wooden artificiality of the hobby-horses that wheel and kick in the three famous pictures of the battle of San Romano by the early Italian Renaissance painter Paolo Uccello (1397–1475).

An even greater visual contrast with Stubbs' realism is provided by the various kinds of stylistic treatment seen in modern art. In *The Snail*, by Henri Matisse (1869–1954) for example, the animal's form is reduced to a simple, abstract spiral composition.

Horses and horsemen also form a constant theme in Indian, Chinese and Islamic art. Animals and birds figure prominently in Indian Buddhist sculpture, particularly representations of the JATAKA TALES. A Chinese bronze ceremonial vessel of 3,000 years ago is owl-shaped, whilst a Chinese lacquer painting 2,300 years old shows a hunting scene reminiscent of prehistoric European cave art.

African masks are often made in the likeness of animal heads, and a well-known Benin artefact is a spotted leopard made of five elephant tusks. The sacred jaguar was a common theme of

Far left: India's Mughal rulers took Persian art themes into India after Emperor Babur conquered that country in 1526. This Persian-Mughal painting shows a delicate arrangement of birds illustrating a history of Babur in the late 1500s.

---

themes and style of classical art and took a fresh look at the rapidly expanding world around them, which they then recreated in naturalistic detail, following the ideas of 'humanism'. Human beings became the object of intense study and glorification, and harmony, balance and proportion became the guiding principles of artistic creation. The years before 1500 are generally termed the Early Renaissance; the years 1500–27, the High Renaissance; and the late 1500s, the period of MANNERISM.

Renoir, Pierre Auguste (1841–1919), A French painter, helped to create the new style of IMPRESSIONISM with Claude Monet (1840–1926) in 1869. He was less interested than other Impressionists in capturing the fleeting effects of light on outdoor scenes than in exploring the solidity of the human figure. This was a particular feature of the warm-coloured paintings of female nudes.

Rococo was a sumptuous style of interior decoration and painting popular in France, Austria and southern Germany in the first half of the 1700s. Its characteristic features include asymmtrical patterns incorporating 'S' and 'C' curves, garlands of flowers, and idealized rustic scenes. The style appeared in easel painting through the *Fêtes Galantes* of Antoine Watteau (1684–1721) and was consolidated by the gently erotic art of François Boucher (1703–70) and Jean Honoré Fragonard (1732–1806). In sculpture, leading exponents were Ignaz Günther (1725–75) in Bavaria, and Claude Michel Clodion (1738–1814) in France.

Rodin, The Kiss

Rodin, Auguste (1840–1917), the most important sculptor of the 1800s, created impressionistic bronze and marble sculptures that capture the feeling surrounding a figure rather than an exact likeness. Such works as the huge and somewhat theatrical statue of *Balzac* recall the monumental MANNERISM of Michelangelo's later sculptures; and like these, many of Rodin's figures incorporate highly finished portions which emerge from the untouched, rough block. Rodin also created an origi-

Far right: Jan van Eyck: *The Annunciation*, 1432–6. A favourite subject for European painters through the ages, the awesome Biblical event is here presented with an almost homely, quiet dignity in a northern Gothic setting.

sculptors from Mexico to Peru. North American Indians often carved animals and birds as tribal TOTEMS.

The photographer had an advantage over the artist when portraying animals in motion. In the late 1870s, the English photographer Eadweard Muybridge (1830–1904) perfected a method of taking several pictures in rapid succession. He used this technique in order to study the movements of people and animals. The pictures attracted great attention, as they provided man's first opportunity to study animal motion in detail. Although taken primarily to analyze movement, the photographs could also be used to synthesize it. With a special projector called a zoopraxiscope, Muybridge projected them on to a screen to produce a motion picture.

The modern nature photographer can take pictures of animals in the dark using infra-red radiation instead of light, and he can employ electronic devices to operate an unattended camera.

Religion and mythology

In the history of European art, religion and mythology have been by far the most important source of inspiration, providing a rich collection of themes for artists to exploit and interpret.

A belief in some unseen, supernatural force goes back to prehistoric times, when artist-priests known as shamans believed that by painting pictures while in a trance-like state, they could communicate with the spirits of the animals they depicted and in some way control or possess them. This being so, tribal hunters would then sally forth confident that by this magic they would be assured of a profitable expedition. Such shamanistic beliefs lie behind much of the art created by tribal communities as far apart as Africa, the Arctic and the Pacific islands.

It is a simple step from a belief in guardian spirits to the idea of supervisory gods as a means of explaining the universe. So, as the great civilizations of the Middle East emerged, a large number of deities appeared in art, some part human and part animal, some as imaginary animals, others simply as mere abstract symbols. In ancient Egypt, art was regarded as a means of continuing life after bodily death, so that, for example, colourful, lively tomb paintings of pleasant daily activities could be re-lived and

Above: Raphael: *Madonna del Granduca*, 1504–8. One of several paintings on the subject which Raphael completed while in Florence, this charming picture captures the serene beauty for which his work became universally admired.

---

nal form of sculpture: the fragment, such as a pair of hands.
Romanticism appeared in all the arts of western Europe in the late 1700s and lasted until the mid 1800s. Typical features were the theatrical and highly atmospheric subject matter drawn from medieval history and legend and incorporating such props as dark ruins and moonlight; the expression of revolutionary fervour in the struggle for liberty from tyranny and emotion exaggerated to the point of passion and an-

guish. Romanticism found expression in painting in the work of the French artists

Wreck of The Hope *by Friedrich*

Théodore Géricault (1791–1824) and Eugène Delacroix (1798–1863), and the German artist Caspar Friedrich (1774–1840).
Ronin were mercenary *samurai* (private soldiers) who became unemployed and destitute as feudalism declined in Japan and provided subject matter for writers and painters.
Rubens, Peter Paul (1577–1640), artist, scholar and international diplomat, was the most important and successful painter in the BAROQUE style. His vast output includes religious paint-

ings, mythological and allegorical scenes, landscapes and portraits, including many charming pictures of his young second wife, Hélène Fourment.

S **Salon** was an art exhibition begun by the French Academy in the 1600s, at first for members only and later for any artist. Controversy over the jury's choice of pictures reached a peak in the 1860s when the Impressionists were constantly refused acceptance, and the *Salon des Refusés* was instituted, followed by

the Impressionists' own independent exhibitions.
Scumbling is the technique of applying an opaque layer of paint over another of a different colour to achieve a broken textured effect.
Sfumato describes the gradual shading of tone or colour in a painting so that there is no abrupt dividing line.
Sgraffito, in early Italian panel paintings, was a technique of scratching a design through a surface layer of paint to reveal the gold GROUND beneath. The technique is also used in

enjoyed for eternity by the dead person's soul.

The Greeks, followed by the Romans, invented a whole hierarchy of gods headed by Zeus (Roman Jupiter), whose mythical lives provided themes not only for their own art, but also European art from the Renaissance until recent times. Praxiteles' statue of *Hermes*, is one of a vast number of Greek and Roman works of art inspired by the ancient myths.

Because Christianity was at first illegal in the Roman Empire, its artistic expression began unobtrusively in the form of painted or mosaic symbols such as fishes, or simple Gospel scenes carved on sarcophagi or painted on the walls of catacombs below Rome or of Christian community houses throughout the Empire. But after Christianity became the official state religion in about AD 380, its art came out into the open in a rich profusion of illuminated manuscripts, painted ICONS and sumptuous church decorations, such as those in Ravenna, Italy, that are masterpieces of BYZANTINE and medieval art. Also characteristic of this early period were numerous panel portraits of the Madonna painted against a gold background.

As Christianity spread northwards across Europe, Biblical themes fused with local styles to produce richly decorative CELTIC and Carolingian art and provided subjects for wall paintings, sculptures, stained glass and altarpieces for the great Romanesque and Gothic cathedrals. In late medieval times, Jan van Eyck (c.1390–1441), and Mathis Grünewald (the painter of the Isenheim altarpiece) were among the greatest religious artists of northern Europe.

In Italy, however, Giovanni Cimabue (c. 1240–1302) and GIOTTO had, by the 1200s, developed a more naturalistic, lifelike style for their paintings that foreshadowed the great religious art of the Renaissance. During this dazzling flowering of the arts some of the world's greatest Christian masterpieces were created by a long list of outstanding artists, as well as superb re-interpretations of ancient classical myths, which were almost absent from medieval art. Among the latter were Botticelli's graceful painting of *The Birth of Venus* and the triumphant bronze figure of *Perseus* by Benvenuto Cellini (1500–71).

In the 1600s and 1700s religion and mythology provided a vast range of subjects for major works

---

pottery and plaster decoration.

Shinto, Japan's age-old religion (practised along with Buddhism since the AD 500s), taught belief in the *kwami* (spirits) said to inhabit all aspects of being.

Shutter is the mechanism for allowing light to fall on the film for a controlled length of time.

Sikh art centres on the splendid golden Temple at Amritsar, northern India (AD 1500s).

Silk-screen printing, or serigraphy, is a method of making individual AUTOGRAPH prints. Ink is squeezed through a screen of material (originally silk), which has been partly masked by a design cut in a paper stencil

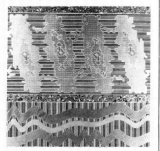

Silkscreen print by Paolozzi

or drawn on the screen in impervious lacquer, candle-wax, GOUACHE, or other media. The technique was developed by the Japanese in the 1600s.

Silk scroll painting often showed court scenes separated by CALLIGRAPHY that explained the scenes as the scrolls were unrolled.

Silver-point was a method of drawing popular in the 1600s and 1700s. The drawing was done on a thick, slightly tinted, white GROUND with a piece of silver (or gold or lead) wire fixed in wood like a pencil.

Soft-ground etching is a method of ENGRAVING. The metal plate is covered with an acid-resistant GROUND containing tallow. A sheet of paper is then placed over the plate and a design drawn on it in pencil. When the paper is removed, some of the 'soft ground' is taken with it. The etching acid is then able to bite through this area into the plate to give a soft, grainy effect.

Solarization is the production of a partially reversed image by exposing a negative to stray light during development. Reversal

occurs because light passing through the partially developed negative image causes a positive image to form.

Speed of photographic film is a measure of its sensitivity to light. The most sensitive film is described as fast, or high-speed. Less sensitive film is said to be slow, or low-speed. Fast film generally shows more GRAIN, and has less contrast than slow film.

Squared-up drawing is a means of accurately and quickly transferring a small drawing to a larger surface.

by RUBENS, TIEPOLO, Poussin and others, whilst the Christian faith was the driving force behind the Baroque sculptures of BERNINI, of which the dramatic *Ecstasy of Saint Teresa* is the best known. Mythological themes enjoyed a continuing vogue in the Neoclassical art of the 1800s, but by this time religion as a prime source of inspiration for art had begun to decline, although individual artists emerged from time to time, such as the English artists William Blake (1757–1827), the PRE-RAPHAELITE BROTHERHOOD, or Stanley Spencer (1891–1959), to express their own personal spiritual values.

Religion and mythology have together also provided the most powerful single influence on non-European art, and almost all Indian art is either Hindu, Jain, Buddhist, SIKH or Muslim. Religion has continued to predominate wherever art has spread from India, with the exception of Mughal painting and its successor schools, such as RAJPUT PAINTING.

Although Taoist-Buddhist influences pervaded most Chinese art intellectually, religion intruded less obviously into Chinese art except for specifically Buddhist themes. The thrusting

Right: Figures of *bodhisattvas* (saints who renounced Buddhahood in order to remain on earth and serve mankind) form a popular theme in Buddhist sculpture. This delicately-shaped Tibetan bronze of the 1500s of a female bodhisattva is set with semi-precious stones.

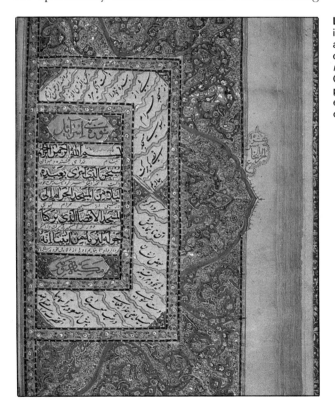

Left: Calligraphy developed into a leading art of Islam, and calligraphic tilework decorated mosques and *madrasahs* (colleges). Calligraphy also decorated paintings and books – especially the *Koran* and other religious works.

merchant class of Japan in the 1600s created a market for the highly secular, daring works of Japanese colour print artists from the mid 1700s. TIMURID court painting, like Persian, was often secular, but religion intertwined with sex was the inspiration for African tribal art. Much of the three-dimensional art of the Mexico-Peru region was also secular, showing abnormal medical conditions, battle scenes or sexual activities.

The vast literature of Hinduism and Buddhism has inspired much of the art of the whole region eastwards from China, Tibet and India. Sacred literature has also been the fount of Jain, Shinto, Taoist and Muslim inspired art in the way that Bible stories provided the subject matter of pre-Renaissance European art. Where sacred literature was taught by word of mouth rather than by books (among Oceanians and Australian Aboriginals, for example), it still provided the basis for visual art.

Ideas and emotions
Works of art are the creative expressions of human beings, and as such they reflect in various ways and on different levels, the ideas and feel-

The drawing is covered by a network of squares, the contents of each of which can be easily copied, enlarged, to corresponding squares covering the larger surface.
Stippling is the use of tiny dots to create the design in a drawing, painting or engraving.
Study in its strict sense, is a highly finished drawing or painting of a detail, such as a head or drapery fold, done in preparation for a work.
Sung dynasty (960–1279), which excelled in ceramics and landscape painting, fell to the YUAN DYNASTY.

Surrealism became a major European art movement after the decline of DADA in the early 1920s. Its artists portray a dreamlike world of fantasy, where everyday objects often appear in outlandish settings. Among the leading artists of Surrealism are Salvador Dali (1904–), René Magritte (1898–1967), Giorgio de Chirico (1888–1978), Max Ernst (1891–) and Joan Miró (1893–).

T **Talbot.** William Henry Fox (1800–77), an English inventor and amateur artist, invented the NEGATIVE-POSITIVE process of photography, and published details in 1839.

Tang sculpture 700s AD

Tang dynasty of China (618–907) was a brilliant period of culture generally, and of painting especially. Buddhist sculpture became more natural. Tang vitality imbued ceramics, textiles and metalwork.
Telephoto lens is used on a camera to increase image size. Photographs taken through a telephoto lens thus resemble images seen through a telescope. A telephoto lens has a relatively long FOCAL LENGTH, and its DEPTH OF FIELD is less than that of a standard lens with the same APERTURE.

Tempera is a kind of paint consisting of powdered pigment mixed with egg-yolk (or the white, or both), thinned with water. The colour dries much lighter than when wet. Tempera applied to a GESSO ground was the commonest technique of painting before the development of oil painting in the 1400s.
Thailand has developed a variety of arts inspired by Buddhism and by Indian influences. Thai classical dance-dramas are based on the *Ramakian* (the Thai version of the RAMAYANA).

ings of their creators. These may be immediately obvious in art that has a clear message, such as an agonizing Crucifixion or the socialist realist art encouraged by Communist governments for propaganda purposes. Often, however, the artist communicates with his viewers in a more subtle way, perhaps using symbolism or allegory. To some degree, of course, individual free expression has always been bound by outside factors such as the demands of patrons, the limitations of religion or politics or the imposition of 'rules' of art such as those put forward by the French SALON and other academic bodies in Europe, or HSIEH HO's 'six principles' in China.

Art has revealed attitudes to changing social, political and moral aspects of human life throughout history. In early civilizations art was geared to depicting the accepted social order of things, in which royal leaders were seen dispensing justice, winning battles, hunting animals or consorting with the gods. Although the artists presumably knew that they were creating something with aesthetic appeal, they had no notion of producing 'works of art' for their own sake. The expression of beauty as an end in itself was unheard of until the Greeks produced sculptures of gods and athletes whose major function was to arouse admiration for the sheer physical perfec-

tion of the human form.

Such an idea was of course alien to the Christian view of the world that dominated medieval European art. Christian concern for eternal salvation prevented any glorification of life in this world, in which humankind tended to steer a careless but disastrous course in the pursuit of frivolous pleasures.

Left: Victor Vasarely: *0519-Banya*, 1964. Vasarely's beautiful, ordered and inventive compositions in the field of Op art create dazzling illusions of movement in the viewer's eye.

Tibet, remote from the larger world, developed arts of its own, inspired by China and, to a lesser degree, India. Tibetan art, revolving around the Lamaist religion, includes brightly coloured scroll paintings (red and gold are favourite colours), bronzes, wood carvings, *mandalas* (colourful, geometrically composed pictures relating to the Tibetan concept of the universe), and illustrated manuscripts.
Tiepolo, Giambattista (1696–1770), the greatest Italian painter of the 1700s, became internationally fam-

ous in his lifetime for the sumptuous paintings in the ROCOCO style with which he decorated palaces in Italy, Germany and Spain.

Tibetan mandala

Timur the Lame (1336–1405), (better known as Tamberlaine) conqueror of central Asia, also encouraged the founding of a great culture that flourished under his successors, the *Timurids.* Their achievements in architecture and painting, especially, laid the basis for the exquisite mosques of Persia and the traditions of painting in Persia and Mughal India .
Timurid. See TIMUR THE LAME.
Tint. See COLOUR.
Titian (Tiziano Vecelli, c.1487–1576) was the greatest of all Venetian painters

and one of the leading figures of the Italian RENAISSANCE. His personal style developed from the highly finished paintings of his early years, through a period of MANNERISM in the 1540s, to the freer, impressionistic handling of his later works, done in rougher brushstrokes and finally with smudges made with his fingers.
Tone. See COLOUR.
Totems, like most forms of art – at least in the early stages – were produced for very practical purposes. A totem (often in the likeness

of an animal or bird) was the badge or emblem of a particular tribe.
Toulouse-Lautrec, Henri de (1864–1901), an aristocrat whose growth was stunted by a riding accident when a boy, became world famous for his boldly coloured posters and lithographs portraying people and scenes from the lively music-halls, dancehalls, brothels and circuses of Paris.
Triptych is a painting in three parts, often hinged together. A *diptych* has two panels. Both forms were commonly used for late

Right: Salvador Dali: *Outskirts of a Paranoiac-critical Town*, 1936. 'Paranoiac- critical activity', Dali's own definition of his art, perfectly summarizes the essence of Surrealism: the portrayal of the irrational, subconscious world that lies beneath our waking thoughts and often colours our behaviour.

Right: Pol Bury: *16 Balls, 16 Cubes in 7 Rows*, 1966. A representative of Kinetic art, Bury's construction achieves its aesthetic effect as the pieces move and jiggle when set in motion by a small motor.

Renaissance humanism swung the ideological balance towards a deeper appreciation of life in this world rather than the next, and art reflected this change of atmosphere, althougn retaining a strong Christian basis. In the 1600s the Catholic drive that resulted from the struggle with the Protestant Reformation found a powerful outlet in the theatrically emotional Baroque art of BERNINI and others, into which the spectator is intentionally drawn.

As the religious struggle subsided, an intellectual and aesthetic debate came to the fore in the mid 1700s, in which the 'noble simplicity and calm grandeur' of ancient classical art was put forward as a model for contemporary artists to emulate. The resulting adherence to 'rules' proposed by certain critics and the academies for this Neoclassical art, although accepted by such artists as DAVID and CANOVA, was anathema to the libertarians of ROMANTICISM in the early 1800s and then to the Impressionists. Thus, by the end of the century, artists had broken sufficiently free from the stultifying, conventional attitudes of the academies to produce the great flood of new styles and approaches that has revolutionalized the art of our time. Simply the creation of beautiful visual effects in the purpose behind both OP ART, represented here by *0519 – Banya*, by

medieval religious paintings.

Trompe l'oeil, a French phrase meaning 'deceive the eye', is the highly skilled technique used by painters to make the viewer believe that a painted object is real and not part of the artistic composition.

Turner, Joseph Mallord William (1775–1851), a major figure in British landscape painting, was the subject of much controversy in his day on account of his stylistic originality. An accomplished draughtsman and water-colourist, he produced thousands of landscapes and topographical and architectural pictures. He turned to oil painting in about 1796, and from the

Turner, The Golden Bough

1820s began to produce the light-filled, misty landscapes for which he is especially remembered.

U **Underpainting** is a monochrome layer of paint, or LAY-IN, in which the artist works out the design and tone values, usually in *grisaille* (grey), before completing the finished composition in colour.

V **Van Gogh,** Vincent (1853–90), a Dutch painter, became one of the most popular of all artists, yet sold only one painting during his lifetime. His constant tragic loneliness, eventually led to mental imbalance and final suicide. After a period in which he created gloomy, dark-coloured pictures of poor country folk, he moved to southern France, where he lightened his palette and painted the brightly coloured landscapes, interiors and portraits for which he is best remembered. Violent, swirling brush-strokes and intensely foreboding skies mark his final characteristic style and reveal the anguish of his last days.

Velázquez, Diego de (1599–1660), one of Spain's greatest painters, was a master of sensitive, naturalistic portraiture, as in his famous *Drunkards* and the large number of revealing pictures of Philip IV and his court, among them the superb *Maids of Honour* (*Las Meninas*). His other work includes records of historical events, such as *The Surrender of Breda*.

Vermeer, Jan (1632–75), a Dutch painter, left fewer than 40 pictures, but is regarded as one of the world's greatest painters of

Victor Vasarély (1908–) and KINETIC ART, of which *16 Balls, 16 Cubes, in 7 Rows* by Pol Bury (1922–) is an example. A deeper intellectual and emotional response, however, is demanded by SURREALISM, seen at its most provocative in such works as Salvador Dali's *Outskirts of a Paranoiac-critical Town*.

Many Surrealist paintings depict strange, illogical scenes, acceptable in dreams, but never encountered in everyday life, in which highly realistic objects are shown in totally unexpected surroundings. The need for a high degree of realism in the images makes this type of work ideally suitable for photography, for it is easy to cut out an image from a photograph and stick it on to a new background. In this way, a ship can be made to sail up a city street, or a traffic policeman can be placed in the middle of a field. This technique of re-arranging photographic images by cutting out and sticking is called *photomontage*. It also enables parts of different photographs to be combined to produce fantasy objects, such as a flying pig or a man with three heads. Further fantasy effects can be obtained by varying the scale of the individual images during enlargement. Children can thus become much larger than adults, and harmless insects can be made to appear like menacing beasts.

Above: *The Happy Elephants*, a striking example of photomontage by John Heartfield. This satirical picture was used on the front cover of *Picture Post* magazine following the 1938 Munich Agreement.

Left: Masks, a prominent feature of primitive art the world over, have deep religious and social significance. They provide the wearers with new identities suitable to the assumption of new roles. This wood and fibre helmet mask is from Sierra Leone.

Besides arousing the viewer's curiosity, photomontage can be used to provoke much stronger emotional responses on issues of political or social importance. Outstanding in this field was John Heartfield (1891–1968), whose carefully contrived montages of the 1930s forcefully condemned the rising terror in Nazi Germany. However, the absolute realism of straightforward photography can be even more effective in arousing emotional responses. Hence the success of appeals for famine relief that use photographs of sick, starving children.

The freedom that today's artists feel to express their ideas and emotions about any subject they choose has created an atmosphere in which art can explore new directions with renewed vigour.

---

domestic scenes. These usually contain only one or 2 figures performing some simple task in a gently lit, simply furnished interior.

W **Water-colour,** a popular painting medium, consists of colour pigments mixed with gum arabic or some other water-soluble BINDER. To apply the colour to the picture surface – usually paper – it is softened with a wet brush. Among the world's finest water-colourists were Albrecht DÜRER, J. M. W. TURNER and Paul CÉZANNE.

Wide-angle lens is used on a camera when the standard lens cannot cover the subject to be photographed. This situation often arises in small rooms, where the photographer is unable to move far enough away from the subject to get it all in. The wide-angle lens has a relatively short FOCAL LENGTH, and a greater DEPTH OF FIELD than a standard lens of the same APERTURE, so that the close and distant parts of a scene can appear equally sharp.

Woodcut is a form of ENGRAVING by the RELIEF method.

The design is cut into a wood block along the grain. Softwood, such as pine, is used for the block. The technique dates from the

Woodcut by Edward Munch

700s in Chinese art, and from the late 1300s in Europe, where Albrecht DÜRER was one of its greatest practitioners. Superb woodcuts were also made by many Japanese COLOUR PRINT ARTISTS of the 1700s and 1800s.

Wood engraving is a method of RELIEF printing. It resembles WOODCUT, except that the design is cut into the block across the grain.

Y **Yuan dynasty** (1279–1368) was that of the Mongol conquerors of China. Pushed out of office,

many Chinese noblemen occupied their enforced leisure by developing new art styles that combined painting and CALLIGRAPHY with literary themes. Many painted on paper or bamboo in place of the traditional silk.

Z **Zoom lens** has variable FOCAL LENGTH, and enables the photographer to alter the camera's angle of view. In general, the zoom lens is used to replace a range of fixed-focal-length lenses.

Buildings, whatever their function, can be works of art. But the architect is not only an artist. He must also have the skills of the engineer, the town planner and the businessman.

Architecture

The large cities of today are made up of a conglomeration of buildings of all shapes, sizes and styles. All of them have been created over the centuries by people who are not only skilled in the technical business of putting buildings up but have also been trained to design them to fulfil their intended function and to look pleasing in their surroundings. This is what we call architecture, and the architects who practise it help to determine the kind of environment in which we live. Over the ages they have exploited all kinds of materials and methods for buildings that range from the simplest of shelters to the complex structures of today.

Materials and methods: simple shelters

In prehistoric times, when people lived by hunting wild animals, there was no need for architects; families found shelter from the weather in rock caves or beneath cliffs. But many centuries later, when they began to grow crops,

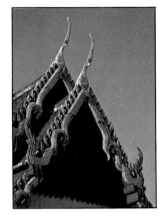

Above: A temple in Bangkok, Thailand, demonstrates the functional and decorative use of wood in Oriental roof structures.

they had to stay in one place until the seed ripened, so they built simple shelters from whatever materials lay to hand: leafy branches, rushes from the river banks, or the skins of wild animals tied over a twig frame. In this way a rudimentary form of architecture began: people had started to think about constructing, not merely finding, a place in which to live. Even today, there are communities of people in remote areas of the world who still build and live in such simple dwellings.

The flexibility of wood

Because trees grew over most of the areas where the first peoples lived, it was not long before suitably cut, sturdy branches came to be used for the construction of large buildings. The strength and durability of wood were particularly useful in the basic framework and roof structure, and these qualities were fully exploited both by the early Greeks and by Chinese and Japanese crafts

Below: Traditional forms of shelter around the world are constructed from materials that are readily available, in styles that are adapted to environment and climate.

Right: (1) a round house made from tree branches in northern Kenya; (2) a buffalo hide tent, or *tipi*, of the North American Indians; (3) a thatched, round house of mud and clay of southern Africa and (4) a bamboo house, raised on stilts, of Borneo.

Reference

A **Acropolis** is the citadel built on the highest point of ancient Greek cities to contain the main temples and other buildings. The best-known is at Athens.
Agora was an open-air space used for meetings, markets or entertainments in ancient Greece – the equivalent of the Roman FORUM.
Amphitheatre is a circular or oval arena surrounded by tiers of seats, such as the Roman Colosseum.

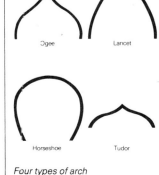

Ogee   Lancet

Horseshoe   Tudor

Four types of arch

Arcade is a series of arches supported on columns or piers and either attached to a wall or free-standing. It is often used to form a covered walk around a courtyard.
Arch is a structure devised to bridge an opening too large for only one stone or brick and supported only at the sides.
Art Nouveau was a style of decoration in the visual arts between about 1890 and 1910. Two basic forms evolved: the use in France and Belgium of sensuously undulating lines, and a more geometric approach (in

Austria) using straight lines and sharp angles influenced by architects such as Charles Rennie Mackintosh. In Spain, Antoni GAUDÍ created his own highly original form. The style was known as *Liberty* in Italy and *Jugendstil* in Germany.

B **Baroque** was a highly decorative and theatrical style that dominated European art and architecture, it developed out of Renaissance MANNERISM, and became popular in Roman Catholic areas of Europe, where magnificent churches

were erected to promote the faith in the struggle against the Protestant Reformation. Elsewhere a more restrained form of Baroque, known as Baroque Classicism, was prevalent. The best-known Baroque architect is Gianlorenzo BERNINI.
Basilica, a rectangular building used for public meetings in Roman times, was adopted for use in worship by the early Christians. The design incorporated a high central nave with one or more aisles on either side, and lit by CLERESTORY windows above the aisle roofs.

men, who developed strong, timber-framed buildings and gateways with complex pitched ROOF systems and ornamental, bracketed eaves.

Pitched timber roofs also evolved in the rainier parts of Europe, reaching a peak of technical perfection during the Middle Ages in the elaborate hammerbeam form seen at Westminster Hall, London. Much simpler was the cruck construction of Saxon houses, in which curved upright timbers met at the top to form the main framing for both walls and roof, with an in-filling of wattle and daub. The next development was the timber-framed, or half-timbered, house, with its eventual brick in-filling.

Whole buildings in wood were also built, such as the tall stave churches of Scandinavia, the first onion-domed churches of Russia and, much later, the clap-boarded buildings of colonial North America. In more recent times, wood has played an important decorative role in architecture, though it has also been exploited for beautiful structural uses by the Finnish architect Alvar Aalto (1899–).

The massive strength of stone

Much heavier and stronger than wood, stone demanded different building techniques, yet the ancient Egyptians showed that, with thousands of workers to haul the huge blocks up specially built ramps, even the great PYRAMIDS could be constructed. In the Far East, too, stone was impressively mastered in the construction of such massive temples as Angkor Wat, in present-day Kampuchea, or Borobudur, in Indonesia, whilst some of the early Buddhist and Hindu temples of India including the magnificent CHAITYAS at Karli, Ajanta and Ellora, were hewn out of the living rock. Everywhere the stone was marvellously carved into a profuse display of rich ornamentation.

In Europe, the beautifully proportioned stone temples of ancient Greece influenced the whole course of later architecture throughout the continent, and Rome contributed such engineering marvels as the aqueduct (an artificial channel for conveying water) as well as fine buildings. In medieval times, stone was fashioned into soaring VAULTS, flying BUTTRESSES and delicate forms of window TRACERY as well as walls for the great Christian cathedrals. It was a heritage of craftsmanship that was to continue in European architecture for many centuries.

Across the Atlantic, the Incas of South America took masonry to such a peak of skill that, like the Greeks, they could fit huge stone blocks so tightly together that they needed no mortar. Farther north, the Aztecs of Mexico filled their capital, Tenochtitlan, with magnificent stone buildings that amazed their Spanish conqueror, Hernan Cortes, when he first saw them in 1519.

Apart from its structural qualities, stone can indeed produce effects of great beauty. Granite, sandstone and limestone are only three kinds of stone that offer differing colours and textures that can be exploited for decorative purposes. Marble, too, has a particular richness of colour suitable for the creation of sumptuous interiors as a layer rather like tiling called 'cladding'.

Below: The Pantheon, Rome, is a masterpiece of Roman architecture, completed in its present form in the AD 120s. Its structure consists of a massive, circular, domed temple, lit only by an 8-metre opening at the top, and joined to a huge portico supported on Corinthian columns.

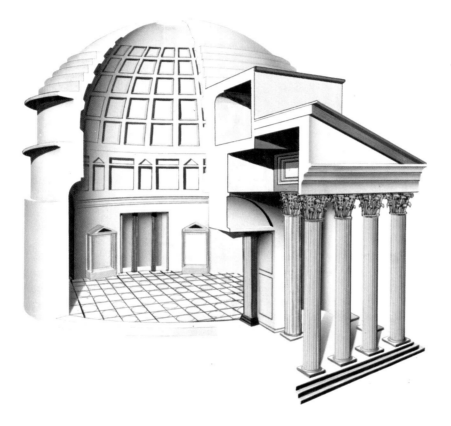

Bauhaus was an influential school of art and design in Germany organized by the architect Walter GROPIUS in 1919 and later headed by Mies van der ROHE. It gave its students an awareness of good craftsmanship and the close relationship between the design of a building and its function. The school was closed by the Nazis in 1933.

Bernini, Gianlorenzo (1598–1680) was the most important Italian architect working in the BAROQUE style. he spent virtually all his working life in Rome, where he designed the imposing COLONNADE facing St Peter's, such buildings as the Palazzo Odescalchi, and the oval church of St Andrea al Quirinale.

Box-frame, or cross-wall, construction is a kind of building technique employing small, box-like cells so that the weight is carried on the cross walls.

Bramante, Donato (1444–1514) was one of the greatest of Italian Renaissance architects. His finest works are in Rome: the circular Tempietto in Roman style in the cloister of St Peter in Montorio; the Palazzo Caprini, later the house of the artist Raphael; and his square, Greek-cross plan for the new church of St Peter.

Flying buttress, Chartres Cathedral

Brunelleschi, Filippo (1377–1446) was the first great Italian architect to study ancient architecture in his search for solutions to practical building problems. Balance, proportion, and a feeling of lightness and spaciousness are features of his work. His best buildings are in Florence.

Brutalism, a recent style of architecture, has large surfaces and beams of rough, exposed concrete.

Buttress is a masonry support built against a wall, often to carry some of the outward thrust of a roof or vault. A flying buttress, a feature of Gothic cathedrals, leans against the wall, like an arch, at the top of a separate pier.

Byzantine architecture evolved after AD 330 in the East Roman Empire, which had its capital at Constantinople (now Istanbul), and continued in Russia until the 1700s. Early Byzantine architects first adapted the Roman BASILICA as a church, and then created a form of centrally domed church based on the Greek-cross

brickwork were the rule. In 'English bond' the brickwork is laid in alternate courses of bricks laid lengthwise (known as stretchers) and crosswise (headers) while in 'Flemish bond' stretchers alternate with headers in the same course.

Structures in concrete and iron

The development of a form of concrete by the Romans before the 100s BC made it possible to design buildings that incorporated vast, round-shaped features such as arches, vaults and domes, and consequently differed from the rectilinear, TRABEATED architecture of ancient Greece. The Romans thus had the means to erect such impressively spacious buildings as the Baths of Caracalla or the Pantheon, with its huge concrete dome 43 metres in diameter.

The next major development in concrete, how-

Left: The stone façade and towers of the great Romanesque cathedral at Santiago de Compostela in Spain were remodelled between 1650 and 1750 in the elaborate Spanish form of Baroque decoration known as the *Churrigueresque* style.

Bricks and mortar

In the dry, desert areas of the world where stone was not plentiful, people in ancient times discovered how to make bricks from sun-dried mud, called *adobe*, or from baked clay. Small and light enough to be carried in the hand, bricks could be laid in rows and bonded together with mortar to build not only straight walls but also rounded ARCHES and curved VAULTS much more easily than with stone. The ancient Babylonians and Assyrians found that bricks glazed on one side, or covered with a separate lining of thin stone slabs, would last much longer. It was the start of a tradition that continued in this area into the Islamic era; from the AD 700s onwards decorative plasterwork and then coloured tiles were used over bricks to create dazzlingly ornate interiors in palaces and mosques.

Courses (continuous layers) of larger, flatter bricks were used by Roman builders in walls of rough stone to give greater strength, and in many of their buildings the Romans showed their skill with brick structures, particularly in the use of brick ribs with light concrete to span huge openings with vaults and domes.

In early Christian times, builders employed brick PENDENTIVES and SQUINCHES to support the domes of Byzantine churches, on the outside of which they laid bricks in various ways to form patterns with stones of a different colour.

In northern Europe, where brick is a traditional building material, less ornate forms of

Above: The Eiffel Tower, constructed for the 1889 Paris Exhibition, is the best-known example of the use of iron for architectural structures in the 1800s.

Right: The Engineering Building at Leicester University, in Britain, was completed in 1963. It displays an arrestingly original concept based on functional requirements and realized in red brick, tile and glass.

---

plan and richly decorated inside with marble cladding and mosaic (and later painted) scenes. Many churches had beautiful exterior brickwork. Apart from St Sophia, in Istanbul, the finest Byzantine churches are in Greece and at Ravenna, in Italy.

Cantilever is a projecting part of a building, such as a balcony, canopy, or beam, which has no visible means of support. It is in fact supported in the middle or along half its length and weighted at one

end to carry a proportionate load on the other.

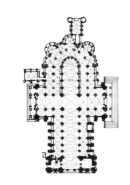

Cathedral plan

Cathedral is the main church in the diocese, or district, of a Christian bishop. The greatest period of cathedral building lasted from the 1000s to the 1400s and spanned the ROMAN-ESQUE and GOTHIC styles. Cathedrals are generally based on the plan of a cross, with the top of the cross facing east.

Chaitya is an Indian Buddhist assembly hall containing a reliquary and broadly similar in plan to a Roman BASILICA.

Chicago School was a loose group of American

architects who adopted the new steel FRAMED BUILDING method of construction for tall offices and commercial buildings in Chicago after the city centre was destroyed by fire in 1871.

Classicism (or Classical style) is the style of ancient Greek and Roman architecture. Because of its adherence to well-defined principles of proportion and balance, it came to be regarded as a standard of excellence to be emulated by later European architects. Several classical revivals occurred, the most impor-

tant being the RENAISSANCE and the period of Neoclassicism in the late 1700s and early 1800s.

Clerestory is the upper part of the wall of a building above an adjoining roof, as in a BASILICA.

Colonnade is a series of columns, often bearing arches.

Crypt is a chamber beneath the main floor of a Christian church. It was used to house the relics of saints.

Curtain wall is the outer defensive wall of a castle. It is also, in modern architecture, a non-load-bearing wall

Above: The church of Notre Dame du Haut, built in 1950–4 at Ronchamp in France, is an amazingly imaginative concrete structure designed by Le Corbusier. Admirably appropriate to its setting, the building seems to spring from the surrounding meadow like a gigantic mushroom.

ever, did not occur until the early 1900s, when reinforced concrete (followed, after 1928, by pre-stressed concrete) was devised by inserting steel rods into concrete beams to strengthen them against tensile, or stretching, stresses. This gave considerable freedom to architects such as Eero Saarinen (1910–61), LE CORBUSIER and Pier Luigi NERVI to design buildings with exciting shapes that made full use of CANTILEVERS.

The use of metal in architecture goes back to the lead-covered iron cramps with which the Greeks secured large stone blocks in place of mortar. Much later, horizontal iron tie-beams were used to strengthen the walls of medieval cathedrals, and supporting iron chains were placed around the domes of St Peter's in Rome (1590) and St Paul's in London (1710) to prevent their collapse. Iron in the form of structural members was used from the 1700s and appeared in such obvious examples as the Eiffel Tower in Paris (1889). The principle of the metal FRAMED BUILDING was developed in Chicago in the 1880s and has provided a major method of construction which is still in use.

Recent materials and methods

The increasing use of pre-fabricated construction units and synthetic materials has considerably influenced the course of architecture in recent years. Buildings can now be constructed of mass-produced factory units, such as pre-cast concrete sections, and this has greatly reduced the time needed for construction on site. Synthetic materials, at first used for such decorative purposes as plastic panelling, have also been exploited for their structural properties in such buildings as the globular 'radomes' housing electronic equipment in North America. Among the most exciting architectural achievements of recent years have been the immense SPACE-FRAME domes and suspended, tent-like roofs designed for major sports arenas.

Periods and styles in architecture

With the growth of settled communities thousands of years ago, people began to build permanent homes for themselves, palaces for their rulers and temples for their gods. In Mesopotamia from about 3500 BC, these temples took the form of vast brick-built stepped pyramids called *ziggurats*. In the Nile Valley of Egypt, the people's preoccupation with life after death led to the construction of enormous tomb complexes and funerary temples, sometimes cut out of solid rock. The Pyramids which they built to house the mummified bodies of their pharaohs were listed among the SEVEN WONDERS OF THE WORLD. Their post and lintel method of building, seen for instance in the great HYPOSTYLE temple at Karnak, involved the use of massive carved columns which were a development in stone of the papyrus reed bundles used in traditional mud houses.

Early architecture around the world

Great buildings were also constructed all over the world wherever civilizations evolved. During the 100s BC the advent of Buddhism in India prompted the appearance of great rock-cut temples, and the building of monasteries, and mounds for relics of the Buddha known as *stupas*. The fine carving on these buildings was surpassed only by that on Hindu temples built from the AD 600s, with their massively thick walls and characteristic *sikharas* or tower-like structures.

Around the same time, the Chinese and Japan-

---

added to the outside of a FRAMED BUILDING as weather protection, often in glass.

D **Dome** is an evenly curved roof with a circular base, which is placed on a building like an inverted cup. Sometimes it is supported on a circular wall called a drum and carries a decorative LANTERN on top. The problem of supporting a round dome on a square tower is solved by the use of PENDENTIVES or SQUINCHES.

E **Elizabethan** style of English architecture

spans the reign of Queen Elizabeth I (1558–1603). It represents a mixture of Italian Renaissance decoration with the native Perpendicular Gothic style.
Entablature, in ancient Greek and Roman architecture, is the entire structure of one of the ORDERS of architecture above the column. It comprises the architrave, FRIEZE and cornice.
Entasis is a slight bulge given to a column because a normal straight-sided column forms an optical illusion and seems thinner at the middle.

F **Formwork,** or shuttering, is a temporary timber mould to hold wet concrete while it sets in the shape required.

Framed building

Forum, the ancient Roman equivalent to the Greek AGORA, was an open space surrounded by public buildings and used as a market and meeting place.
Framed building has an interior framework of steel or concrete beams that carries the main loads. CURTAIN WALLS added to the outside of the building keep out the weather.
Frieze is part of an ENTABLATURE below the cornice on a classical building. The term is also loosely applied to the decorative top part of an interior wall.

G **Gable** is the triangular upper part of a wall supporting the end of a pitched roof. Sometimes the gable has a shaped, decorative top, as on traditional Dutch houses.
Gallery is an upper floor open on one side to the outside or to the main interior area of a building. A long gallery, a long interior passage, is a feature of English mansions in the ELIZABETHAN style.
Gargoyle is a projecting stone water-spout designed to throw rainwater from the roof away from the walls of a

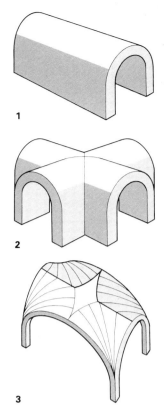

Above: The main forms of vault used in the building of European cathedrals developed from medieval times to about the 1500s from the tunnel, or barrel, vault (**1**) via the groin vault (**2**) to the rib and fan vault (**3**).

Above right: Henry VII's Chapel in Westminster Abbey, London, was built between 1503 and 1519. It contains the most dazzlingly ornate form of fan vaulting in English Perpendicular (late Gothic) architecture.

Right: The bedroom of Sultan Murat III in the Topkapi Sarayi Palace, Istanbul, Turkey. The palace, built in the 1500s, is luxuriously decorated in typical Ottoman style with ornate tiles that create an atmosphere of coolness and opulence.

ese established a form of architecture based on wood, as in the SHINDEN-ZUKURI style, and created richly ornamented curving roofs for their temples, PAGODAS, palaces and gateways. Sumptuous decoration, in the form of tiles and plasterwork, was also a feature of Islamic palaces and MOSQUES built from the 700s, the mosques in particular having magnificent domes and towering, slender MINARETS. Religious buildings in Central America during this period took the form of flat-topped, stepped pyramids.

The glory of Greece and Rome

The ancient civilizations of Crete and Mycenae, which thrived in the eastern Mediterranean before 1200 BC, created forms and styles of building that played an important part in the evolution of later Greek architecture. The *megaron*, a rectangular chamber with entrance PORTICO, was, for example, the basis for the style of colonnaded temple that reached its peak of technical perfection and beauty in the 400s BC in such buildings as the Parthenon, splendidly sited atop the ACROPOLIS in Athens.

The Greek trabeated method of building involved the use of an ENTABLATURE supported

medieval cathedral. They were often carved in grotesque animal or human forms.

Gargoyle, Essex, England

Gaudí, Antoni (1852–1926), a Spanish architect, created a highly individualistic form of ART NOUVEAU, using undulating surfaces, fantastic excrescences and inlaid bits of broken crockery. His masterpieces include the unfinished cathedral of the Sagrada Familia and two apartment blocks, the Casa Battló and the Casa Milá, all in Barcelona.

Gothic style dominated the architecture of north-western Europe from the mid-1100s for about 250 years. Its main features are seen in cathedrals of the period:

pointed arches, increasingly elaborate ribbed VAULTS and window TRACERY, flying BUTTRESSES, and large windows of beautiful stained glass that fill the interior with coloured light.

Gropius, Walter (1883–1969), one of the leading architects of the present century, was head of the influential BAUHAUS school of design from 1919 to 1928. A firm believer in the essentially functional basis of architecture, he created houses and factories that were models of the INTERNATIONAL MODERN style.

H Hip is the edge along which 2 sloping roof surfaces meet. In a hipped roof the gable ends slope inwards to form 2 further roof surfaces.

Hypocaust was the underground furnace and system of air ducts used to heat ancient Roman buildings.

Hypostyle, in ancient Egyptian architecture, was a large building with a flat roof supported on a large number of closely spaced columns.

I Iconostasis is a screen separating the chancel from the nave in BYZANTINE

churches. It was often covered with panel paintings of Christ or saints, known as icons.

International Modern style was created in North America before World War I and later in Europe by such architects as Walter GROPIUS and Frank Lloyd WRIGHT. Its buildings have asymmetrical cubical or rectangular shapes, large horizontal windows and little or no decoration apart from the use of white rendering.

L Lantern is a small turret with windows on all

on columns, a system that developed through three major styles, or ORDERS, known as the Doric, Ionic and Corinthian. The Romans adopted the Greek style of architecture but added variations of their own to the Greek Orders and made their own architectural innovations. Out of their discovery of concrete and great engineering skills came a characteristic style of architecture that made greater use of curving forms – arches, vaults and domes, and even the basic structural plan of such buildings as the oval Colosseum and the circular Pantheon, in Rome.

Above: The Villa Rotunda, near Vicenza, Italy, was designed in the Renaissance classical style by Andrea Palladio in about 1550. It is one of the most beautifully symmetrical and elegant houses in the world.

Right: The World Trade Centre in New York, taken with a fish-eye lens, designed by the Japanese architect Minoru Yamasaki and others, was opened in 1977. It consists of twin towers rising to 110 storeys.

European styles since Roman times

After the collapse of the Roman Empire in the AD 400s, the early Christian Church adapted the rectangular Roman BASILICA for purposes of worship, whilst the more compact, domed Greek-cross plan, seen to perfection in St. Sophia, Istanbul, became widespread in the BYZANTINE architecture of eastern Europe. From the Roman basilica, too, came the basic plan for the great medieval cathedrals built in western Europe in the ROMANESQUE and GOTHIC styles.

In the 1400s Italian architects of the RENAISSANCE, such as BRUNELLESCHI, BRAMANTE and PALLADIO, tried to recreate ancient Greek and Roman, or CLASSICAL styles of architecture, based on the principles of symmetry, balance and pleasing mathematical proportions, and employing the ancient ORDERS of design. Individual treatment of these principles by MICHELANGELO, Giulio Romano (c.1492–1546) and others led to

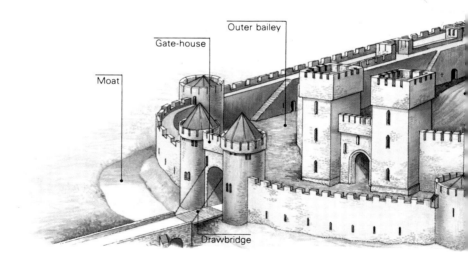

Inner bailey

Outer bailey

Gate-house

Moat

Drawbridge

sides on top of a roof or dome. It is often used to let light through to the interior below.

Le Corbusier (Charles Edouard Jeanneret, 1887–1965) was an influential Swiss architect and town-planner known particularly for his mastery of concrete. His work ranges from the cleanly rectangular Unite d'Habitation apartment block scheme in Marseilles to more aggressively expressive designs, such as the little mushroom-shaped chapel at Ronchamp, France. The city of Chandigarh,

India, represents his work in the field of international town-planning.

Mannerist style, or Mannerism, was a late Renaissance development in Italian architecture. Designers went on using the classical elements of the RENAISSANCE style but combined them in unusual ways, thus disregarding classical principles of balance and proportion. The tendency was first seen in the work of MICHELANGELO BUONARROTI.

Mausoleum is an impressive tomb, so named after

the magnificent memorial built for Mausolus, the Persian ruler of Caria, at Halicarnassus in Greece in about 350 BC. This was regarded

Mausoleum, Ravenna c. 440 AD

as one of the SEVEN WONDERS OF THE WORLD.

Michelangelo Buonarroti (1475–1564), one of the leading artists of the Italian Renaissance, also created important architectural works. Never bound by slavish adherence to detailed drawings, or even to architectural 'rules', he was wont to modify his designs during building. His individualistic approach, which gave rise to the MANNERIST STYLE, can be seen in his designs for the sacristy in the church of St Lorenzo and for the reading room of the

Laurentian Library, both in Florence, and in the reworked facades for the Palazzo Farnese and Palazzo del Senatore, in Rome. His most important commission was the completion of St Peter's Rome, though his designs were much altered after his death.

Minaret is a tall, slender tower forming part of a MOSQUE complex and used for calling muslims to prayer.

Mosque is an Islamic building for prayer. The congregational, or Friday, mosque used for communal worship

the MANNERIST style of the late 1500s, whilst in northern Europe Italian Renaissance details were grafted on to local styles, as in English ELIZABETHAN architecture.

Out of Mannerism came the grandiose BAROQUE style of Catholic Europe, exemplified by BERNINI. Elsewhere during the 1600s a more classical style, called PALLADIANISM, was preferred – or a mixture of the two, known as Baroque Classicism, seen in the work of Christopher WREN. A short-lived flight of elegant fantasy known as the ROCOCO style created sumptuous interiors in the early 1700s, but it was replaced in mid-century by the more sober designs of NEOCLASSICISM, typified by the severe, Roman-style Pantheon in Paris. Many of these styles were taken to colonies overseas by European settlers.

The 1800s saw a revival of a wide range of historical styles of architecture, followed by the attempt, at the turn of the century, to create a totally new style in ART NOUVEAU. Much greater in influence, however, have been the teachings of the BAUHAUS design school and the architecture of the INTERNATIONAL MODERN style.

Buildings of all kinds

The complex way of life that has evolved with the growth of civilization has brought with it a wide range of activities that require special buildings –

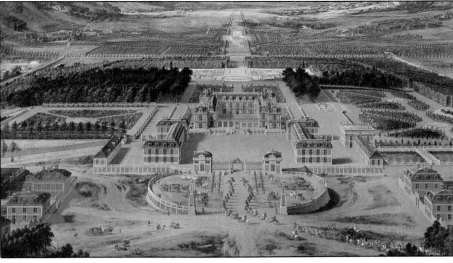

Above: The Palace of Versailles, France, depicted in a painting of 1668 by Pierre Patel before the additions by Louis Le Vau and Jules Hardouin Mansart transformed it from a hunting lodge to the grandest palace in Europe.

Below: The early form of European stone castle evolved from the simple motte (moat) and bailey (fortifying wall) system. The main building was the keep.

homes in which to live, churches or mosques in which to pray, schools where children can be taught, and stadiums where people can watch or take part in sport or athletics, to mention just a few.

Castles, palaces and houses

Built essentially for purposes of defence in times of war, castles can be looked upon as merely functional products of military engineering, yet these rugged and romantically beautiful structures do have an important place in the history of architecture. In Europe the first ones were simple wooden towers, but they were soon replaced by high, stone-built keeps or donjons, built upon earth mounds called mottes and surrounded by walled enclosures known as baileys. As time passed, these simple medieval fortresses became more complex in design to meet the challenge of changing methods of warfare. Eventually whole towns, known as bastide towns, came to be fortified with huge defensive walls and towers, such as those at Carcassone in France.

From the late 1500s the Japanese evolved their own form of castle, rectangular in plan and standing on a sloping stone base often inside a moat. The upper storeys consisted of a series of shuttered wooden galleries, each with its own tiled, up-turned roof.

Unlike castles, houses around the world have largely depended for their design on the kinds of building materials available, the climate they have to withstand, and the degree of aesthetic

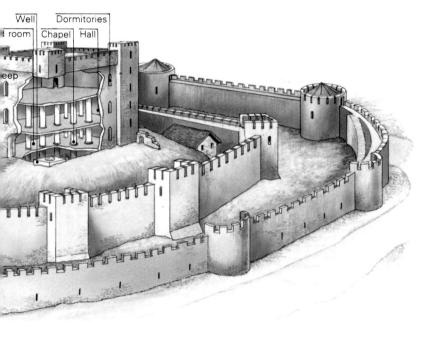

Well | Dormitories
room | Chapel | Hall
Keep

on the Muslim sabbath, generally has a large arcaded space in front.

N **Nervi,** Pier Luigi (1891–1979) was an excitingly inventive Italian architect and engineer. His genius in covering huge buildings with concrete vaults or domes is seen, for example, in his aircraft hangars, exhibition halls, and the delightful Palazzetto dello Sport in Rome.

O **Orders,** in western architecture, are the various designs of columns and

their appropriate ENTABLATURE created by ancient Greek and Roman architects and adopted by later imitators. The main Orders

Orders of Architecture

were Doric (in Greek and Roman forms), Tuscan, Ionic, Corinthian, and Composite.

P **Pagoda** is a timber, or brick and timber, tower in a Chinese Buddhist temple precinct. Generally polygonal in plan, it has from 3 to 15 storeys, each with an encircling, widely projecting and ornate roof.
Palladianism, a style derived from the work of the Italian Renaissance architect Andrea PALLADIO, became popular first in England through the designs of Inigo

Jones (1573–1652) and then spread to Germany, Russia and the United States in the 1700s.
Palladio, Andrea (1508–80), the most influential of all Italian Renaissance architects, created a style of building characterized by its symmetry and proportion, though displaying an occasional hint of MANNERISM.
Pediment is a low, triangular gable on a classical temple or above a PORTICO.
Pendentive is a curved, triangular area of masonry in the space between the base of a dome and the

corner formed by 2 supporting walls underneath it.
Pilaster is a shallow, rectangular column attached to and only slightly projecting from a wall. Not load-bearing in function, it is purely decorative and, in classical buildings, conforms to one of the ORDERS of architecture.
Pilotis are pillars like stilts supporting a building above the ground so that there is a space beneath.
Plateresque style is a highly ornamental form of decoration applied to Spanish buildings of the 1500s.

Right: The pilgrimage church built by Dominikus Zimmermann at Wies, in southern Germany, between 1745 and 1754 is a masterpiece of sumptuous Rococo decoration.

beautiful villas designed by Andrea PALLADIO, after whom a whole style was named. Yet perhaps the most grandiose and imposing of European palaces was that built during the 1600s at Versailles for the 'Sun King' Louis XIV and emulated throughout the continent. Its oriental counterparts at this time were the palaces of Shah Jahan in Delhi and Agra, India, and the Imperial Summer Palace near Peking, China.

In modern times, Frank Lloyd WRIGHT is but one of the many designers who has created beautiful homes for individual clients, but the need to house the mass-populations of today's cities has called for more large-scale architectural solutions. Architects such as LE CORBUSIER and Mies van der ROHE have contributed huge apartment blocks in their characteristic styles, but from Japan have come some of the most exciting schemes in urban planning, such as Kiyonori Kikutake's vision of extending the city of Tokyo into the sea on a series of artificial islands.

Buildings for worship
One of the major concerns of builders and architects throughout the ages has been the construction of special buildings for the followers of the world's great religions. Built in stone in order to last, many are still standing and provide a faithful record of the architectural styles favoured by each generation. The simple lines of Greek and Roman temples were followed by increasingly decorated Christian cathedrals, churches and monasteries, whilst in the East appeared Shinto, Buddhist, Hindu and Jain temples and shrines, and later the lavishly decorated mosques of Islam. The examples are too numerous to list, but the little mushroom-shaped concrete church at Ronchamp, in France, designed by Le Corbusier in the 1950s, serves to represent the many fine contributions made by today's architects to the long tradition of religious building around the world.

Buildings for the community
In the first great civilizations of thousands of years ago, the administration of trade, justice and other important civic activities was in the hands of court officials in the palaces of all-powerful rulers. It was only with the development of more democratic forms of government in

appeal considered appropriate. Yet the remains of houses in the Roman city of Pompeii, destroyed by the volcano Vesuvius in AD 79, show that even in such early times homes could be specially designed that had high standards of comfort and were pleasant to live in. In Rome itself many people lived in overcrowded apartment houses, or *insulae*, much as do millions in the world today, and in medieval times the housing of ordinary folk was not far from squalid.

In contrast, ruling families world-wide could afford to employ the finest craftsmen they could find to build luxurious palaces, among which the Moorish palace of the Alhambra at Granada in Spain must rank as one of the most magnificent. Renaissance Italy could also boast many superb palaces and, somewhat smaller in scale, the

---

Portico is a porch with columns supporting a PEDIMENT and roof.
Projection, in architecture, is a geometrical drawing to show a building in three dimensions. The vertical sides of the building remain vertical in the drawing, but horizontal lines are drawn at an angle.
Proscenium was the acting area in front of the permanent rear scenery in an ancient Greek theatre. Today it refers to the stage area in front of the curtain and includes the arch facing the audience.

Pylon was a large, flat-topped rectangular building

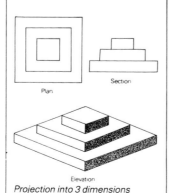

Projection into 3 dimensions

with sloping sides that stood on either side of an ancient Egyptian gateway.
Pyramid is a large building with a square base and sloping triangular sides that meet at a point at the top. The Pyramids of ancient Egypt were built between 2700 and 2000 BC as tombs for royalty. The flat-topped pyramids constructed centuries later in Central America supported temples for religious rituals.

R **Renaissance,** meaning rebirth, was a period covering broadly the 1400s

and 1500s, in which classical (mainly Roman) art and architecture was studied and imitated to create a style that was characterized by symmetry, harmony and proportion. The Renaissance began in Italy and spread to other European countries, where its details were combined with local styles.
Rococo was a lavish, elegant and dainty style of interior decoration that became popular in France, Austria and southern Germany in the early 1700s. Its characteristic features included elaborate stucco-

work, asymmetrical decoration incorporating delicately coloured patterns based on 'S' and 'C' curves with garlands and flowers, flying Cupids and country scenes.
Rohe, Mies van der (1886–1969) followed Walter GROPIUS as director of the BAUHAUS design school. He created a distinctive style of plain FRAMED BUILDING that was devoid of surface ornament except in the colour and texture of the materials used (glass, bronze, marble, etc). His finest work included buildings at the Illinois Institute of Technology, apart-

Left: The Pompidou Centre, designed by Renzo Piano and Richard Rogers, was opened in Paris in 1977. A bold concept combining engineering with architecture, the structure is based on a steel framework with the main service ducts (and even escalators) on the outside.

Below: The Johnson Wax factory at Racine, Wisconsin, in the United States, is a fine modern design by Frank Lloyd Wright. A major feature of the low Administration building (1936–9) is the glass top-lighting supported by slender mushroom columns in concrete. The elegant Research Tower (1946–9) has external curtain walls forming bands of red brick and glass.

ancient Greece that separate buildings for such functions began to emerge. Thus the Roman senate house had a long line of successors in the magnificent Renaissance town halls of Italy, the grandiose city halls of industrial Britain, the imposing Capitol building in the United States, the huge Law Courts of Brussels, and the futuristic Congress building in Brasilia, to name but a few – all of them reflect changing styles and tastes in architecture through the centuries.

The same is true for schools, universities and libraries. Apart from those linked to the world's major religions, separate institutions were gradually founded all over the world, following local styles of architecture and, more recently, international methods of building. The engineering laboratories at Leicester University, in Britain, provide an example.

The growth of trade and of manufacturing industry in many countries has brought a need for factory and office buildings which are appropriate to their functions. Unlike the appallingly grimy mills of the 1800s, the well-designed buildings of many modern industrial concerns, such as those planned by Frank Lloyd Wright for the Johnson Wax factory at Racine, Wisconsin, in the 1930s, are models of good architecture. The Van Nelle tobacco factory at Rotterdam was influential in promoting the INTERNATIONAL MODERN style during the same period.

ments, Chicago, and the Seagram building, New York.

Romanesque style was current in western European architecture from about the early 900s to the mid-1100s. It evolved during the construction of great abbeys, cathedrals and pilgrimage churches, which were designed on the Roman BASILICA plan and had massively thick walls, sturdy columns, rounded arches and vaults, and small windows.

Roof, a weather protection covering a building, varies in design according to climate.

In hot, dry countries the flat roof is common, but where rainfall is heavy, pitched, or

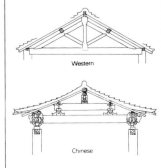

Pitched roofs

sloping roofs of various designs are necessary. Different traditional systems of structural support for pitched roofs evolved in western and oriental architecture. In western roofs the weight thrust is both downwards and outwards; in oriental roofs it is only downwards and requires no BUTTRESS. *See also* HIP.

Rose window, or wheel window, is a large, round window with ribs or TRACERY that often contain beautiful stained glass, as in GOTHIC cathedrals.

S Seven Wonders of the World were chosen by the Greek poet Antipater of Sidon in the 1st century BC. In addition to the statue of Zeus at Olympia and the Colossus (a statue of a sungod) at Rhodes, they included 5 great architectural works of the ancient world: the PYRAMIDS of Egypt; the hanging gardens of Babylon; the temple of Diana at Ephesus; the MAUSOLEUM at Halicarnassus; and the lighthouse at Alexandria.

Shinden-zukuri was a form of Japanese architecture favoured by the nobility during the Heian period (AD 794–1185). It consisted of a group of rectangular buildings set in an elaborate garden landscape and often linked by covered passages.

Space-frame is an exceptionally strong three-dimensional framework used to cover large areas. An example is the huge domed roof of a factory built at Baton Rouge, Louisiana, in 1958 and designed by Buckminster Fuller. It has a diameter of 117·4 metres.

Squinch is an arch, or series of arches, one above the

Single-roomed shops opening on to the street were already known in ancient cities, but by the late 1800s they had evolved into large, multi-storeyed department stores based on the metal-framed method of building developed by the CHICAGO SCHOOL of architects. From these, the next step was the soaring skyscraper block that gives the New York skyline its unique character. Modern techniques and materials have also gone into the design of much-needed hospitals around the world and in the planning of whole new urban schemes, among which must be mentioned Le Corbusier's work at Chandigarh, India, and Kenzo TANGE's exciting development plan for Tokyo.

Travel and transport buildings

As travel becomes easier in the rapidly shrinking world of today, architects have had to design buildings to service the needs of travellers and machines alike. Successors to the old coaching-inns of yesterday are the modern motorway service areas, whilst the iron-vaulted railway stations of the last century are now being replaced with such superb examples of modern design as the cantilevered Stazione Termini, in Rome. Even more spectacular than Pier Luigi Nervi's concrete aircraft hangars of the 1930s are the passenger terminals designed in recent years for many of the world's major airports. Among the most beautiful must be Eero Saarinen's

Above: The Trans-World Airlines terminal at Kennedy airport, New York, designed by Eero Saarinen and completed in 1962.
Below: The Paris *Opéra* (1862–75) was designed by Charles Garnier with the Baroque-style grandeur favoured in the 1800s.

Trans-World Airlines terminal at Kennedy airport, New York, designed to look like a bird in flight.

Buildings for leisure

Buildings where people can watch or take part in sporting activities or other kinds of entertainment were an important aspect of architecture as long ago as ancient Greece and Rome. The semicircular, open-air Greek theatres and the circular or oval arenas of ancient Rome, such as the immense Colosseum, were two characteristic forms. Today, architects have been able to take advantage of modern materials and building techniques to create beautiful, well-equipped theatres and adventurously original structures for huge sports stadiums that give greater protection from the weather. Nervi's Palazzetto dello Sport, in Rome, is one such building.

Despite its worldwide importance, the radio and television industry has required less originality in the design of its buildings, which, for the most part, remain essentially functional. Nevertheless, some attempt has been made to give aesthetic appeal to the communications towers that soar above the skyline of many of today's major cities.

---

other and increasing in radius, and built diagonally across a top interior corner of a square tower. Its purpose is to transform the square shape of the tower to an octagon suitable for carrying the base of a DOME. *See also* PENDENTIVE.

Tange, Kenzo (1913–), the most important Japanese architect and town-planner of the present century, created many outstandingly original works. They include the exciting suspended roof of the National Gymnasium designed for the 1964 Olympics; the remarkable Yamanashi broadcasting centre at Kofu; and imaginative town-planning schemes for Skopje, Yugoslavia, and Tokyo, the latter a scheme for expanding the city into the sea on piles.

Trabeated construction is a simple building method in which upright posts or columns are used to support horizontal lintels, or beams. Good examples can be seen in Egyptian and Greek architecture.

Tracery is the pattern of shapes formed by the stonework mullions holding the glass in Gothic cathedral windows. From the earliest simple plate tracery evolved the increasingly elaborate form known as bar tracery.

Vault is an arched ceiling or roof constructed in various designs.

Wren, Christopher (1632–1723), England's greatest architect, designed many fine buildings in the BAROQUE Classical style, He is best remembered for his Sheldonian Theatre, Oxford; St Paul's Cathedral and the 51 churches he designed for London after the Great Fire of 1666; Greenwich Hospital; and Kensington and Hampton Court palaces.

St Paul's Cathedral, London

Wright, Frank Lloyd (1869–1959), the most original of all American architects, is best known for creating a distinctive style of low, rambling house based on strong horizontal lines and consisting of rooms and terraces that interlock with each other and with the surrounding gardens. He also designed fine commercial buildings.

Interior design is a form of art which we encounter in everyday life. Interior designers are concerned not only with creating a beautiful environment, but also a comfortable one.

Interior Design

The interior design of a building, even more than the exterior design, has to be closely related to the purpose for which it is intended. Often, however, an interior is a compromise between being functional and fitting in with a pleasing exterior. In the Middle Ages interiors had to fit in with a fortress-like exterior, as most dwellings were built with defence in mind. Furnishings in this case evolved as a means of reducing the austere nature of the accommodation. But from the early 1700s the influence of the architect began to be felt inside as well as out.

Style and purpose

An outstanding example of the way in which purpose has influenced the style of the interior, and from that the design of the exterior, is the

Above: In contrast to the elaborate decoration of an Adam room, a traditional Japanese room is extremely bare, simple and cool – something which suits the Japanese way of life.

Left: The saloon at Saltram House in Devon was designed by Robert Adam in 1768. He planned every detail – even the Axminster carpet was specially woven.

Christian church of western Europe from the Middle Ages onwards. The shape is determined by the need for a long nave for processions, with attention focused on the altar at the eastern end, and in the larger churches a chancel for the clergy's own worship, and often various side chapels for quiet individual prayer.

Traditional Japanese domestic interiors, which seem positively bare to Western eyes, are again the result of the way of life. Living in a country much of which has mild winters and very hot summers, the Japanese plan their houses for warm-weather living, simple and uncluttered. Sliding paper screens serve as doors. By contrast the domestic interiors of northern Europe tend to be more heavily furnished, with thick curtains and carpets designed for a cool climate.

Reference

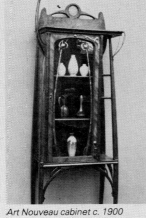

Art Nouveau cabinet c. 1900

A **Adam,** Robert (1728–92), a Scot, was the most well-known of 4 brothers who set up as architects in London in 1758. Although he designed many houses he was noted for his interiors, and for the style named after him.

Antimacassar was a covering for chair-backs to protect them against macassar oil, used as a hair dressing in early VICTORIAN times.

Arras, a town in northern France, was a leading centre of TAPESTRY-making in the 1500s – so much so that its name came to stand for tapestry.

Art Deco was a decorative style of the 1920s and 1930s. It was an abbreviation of the French phrase *art décoratif*. It emphasized streamlined and geometrical shapes, and was adapted to mechanical production methods.

Art Nouveau, literally 'new art', was a style that flourished from about 1890 to 1910. (*See also page 5*).

Arts and Crafts Movement was active in England during the late 1800s. It opposed the new machine-based ideas of the industrial age, and placed most emphasis on crafts executed by hand. WILLIAM MORRIS was one of the prime movers in the movement, and it was greatly influenced by the writings of JOHN RUSKIN. It died out just before World War I (1914–18).

Axminster is a small town in south-western England, famous for its carpet factory (1755–1835). The factory produced a particular weave in which the pile tufts are knotted singly to the back-ing. A new factory was opened at Axminster in 1937.

B **Bakelite** was the first man-made resin plastic. It was invented in 1909 by a Belgian-born American chemist, Leo H. Baekeland (1863–1944). Bakelite is a trade name.

Behrens, Peter (1868–1940) was a German painter who became an architect and designer. He specialized in industrial design of all kinds, and believed that machine-made articles should have their own style, not that of hand-made things.

While the Middle East preserved the ancient Greek and Roman ideas of comfort in interior design, Europe during the Dark Ages which followed the fall of the Roman Empire paid little attention to interior design. Defence was of paramount importance, and people lived largely inside their defences, rather than in rooms designed for a purpose. The Renaissance, that rebirth of the arts which began in the late 1400s, saw a change in attitudes. This change was made possible by the better law and order kept by strong governments. Architects began to pay a great deal of attention to proportion. They sought to relate spatial ideas to those of music: because notes that produced harmonies had certain proportions to one another, they felt that similar proportions would produce a visual 'harmony' in the size and shape of rooms.

Wall coverings

We know very little about the houses of ordinary people in ancient times because they were built of materials that have perished, such as timber and mud bricks. The few remains that have survived from Egypt and the ancient Middle East suggest that poorer people whitewashed their walls, but richer people used colour washes. The more durable ruins of stone-built palaces show that kings, at any rate, had their walls more elabo-

Right: A William Morris room in a house in Hammersmith Terrace, London. The chair covers, curtains and wallpaper were all designed by Morris; the tiles in the fireplace are Delft.

Below: The Romans decorated the walls of their larger houses with wall paintings. These are in the House of the Vettii in Pompeii, built by 2 rich merchants, Aulus Vettius Restitutus and Aulus Vettius Conviva.

rately decorated, usually with painted figures or scenes. This use of painting developed most strongly in Greece and Rome. The well-preserved ruins of Pompeii, near Naples, buried by ash from the volcano Vesuvius in AD 79, have many examples of fine wall paintings.

The Romans also began the use of MOSAIC panels on walls, and this practice spread to the Eastern Roman Empire (Byzantium) and to the world of the Arabs who conquered Byzantium. A form of mosaic wall decoration had been used by the ancient Sumerians some 2500 years earlier, but the practice seems to have died out. Today simple mosaic patterns are often used in public parts of large buildings, particularly in hallways and on staircases.

The cold and draughty stone buildings of northern Europe were frequently fitted out with PANELLING to take away some of the chill of the stone and help keep down the draughts. This panelling, known also as wainscoting, developed during the late Middle Ages, and was a feature of Gothic architecture. One of the most popular patterns was LINENFOLD.

Leather or fabric wall hangings were used even earlier, and contact with Arab culture during the crusades led to the introduction of woven TAPESTRY to Europe, often called ARRAS. Tapestries remained popular up until the end of the 1700s, when they gave place to WALLPAPER, which was cheaper and allowed for decorations to be changed easily. It was laid on smooth PLASTER surfaces, the art of plastering having been practised for at least 4,000 years. Wallpaper has

---

Biedermeier style lasted from the late 1820s to about 1860 in German-speaking countries. The name came from 'Gottlieb Biedermeier', a fictional character in the journal *Fliegende Blaetter* who was supposed to typify so-called 'middle-class vulgarity'. It combined features from many earlier styles, and tended to be solidly elaborate.
Boulle, André-Charles (1642–1732), a French cabinet-maker, used a style of INLAY with metal and tortoiseshell, which later became known as buhlwork.

C Chippendale, Thomas (1718–79), was an Eng-

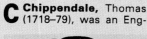

A Chippendale chair

lish cabinet-maker and furniture designer. Although furniture was made in his large workshops, Chippendale himself did not make it. He is best known for his book *The Gentleman and Cabinet Maker's Director* (1754), then the largest book of patterns of its kind. Most of the designs are in the ROCOCO style.
Cressent, Charles (1685–1768) was official cabinet-maker to Philippe d'Orléans, regent of France. He was one of the originators of the REGENCE style, and a skilled maker of ORMOLU mounts.

D Deutscher Werkbund was an association of German industrial designers. It was founded in 1907 by Peter BEHRENS and others, and included businessmen and manufacturers. Its aim was to improve the standard of industrial design, particularly manufactured objects.

E Empire style derives its name from the period in French history when the Emperor Napoleon I ruled the country. As well as elements of Greek and Roman styles it included Egyptian ideas.

F Federal style is the name given to the American version of the ADAM style in England, and was based on the designs of George HEPPLEWHITE and Thomas SHERATON It was a style of the 1700s.

G Goddard was the name of a family of cabinet-makers at Newport, Rhode Island. John Goddard (1723–85) invented the block-front style of making furniture in which such things as drawer-fronts curve in at the centre and out at the ends.

remained the most popular form of wall decoration in Western civilization. It achieved recognition as an art form through the work of William MORRIS, whose papers in rich, dark colours have recently become fashionable again. Modern processes have improved the texture of wallpapers, notably in the use of PVC (poly-vinyl-chloride), a plastics product which gives a durable, washable finish.

Floor coverings

The art of floor covering probably began when Stone Age people spread animal skins on the floor of a cave, and the practice of using pelts for rugs has still not died out. By the late Stone Age people were weaving rush mats to put on their floors.

For at least 3,000 years, however, the most popular form of floor covering has been rugs and carpets. These durable fabrics are made by a variety of techniques. Some are woven like tapestry, or by knotting threads of wool through a coarse canvas. The most commonly-used method is the woven pile, which leaves tufts sticking up at right angles to the fabric. In this it imitates a sheep's fleece, which was probably one of the earliest pelts used as a rug. The oldest known knotted-pile rug was found in Siberia, and was made about 400 BC. However, Assyrian carvings

Below: Persian carpets laid side by side cover the floor of the El Aksa Mosque in Jerusalem.

Right: A carpet made from synethic materials covers this modern European living-room.

show that rugs were being made before 1000 BC.

Carpet-making developed in Persia, where the principal centres of manufacture were Herat, Isfahan, Kashan and Tabriz. From there it spread to Turkey and the lands ruled by Islam. The earliest European carpets were made in Spain under Moorish influence. Factories were set up in England and France during the 1500s. Among the most famous names in carpet making are AXMINSTER and WILTON. These factories founded in the 1700s gave their names to styles of weave. Carpets were made exclusively on hand looms until 1841, when the first machine looms were brought into use in the United States. The practice of using wall-to-wall carpeting which grew after World War II (1939–1945) led to an enormous growth in the carpet industry. And whereas older carpets had woollen pile, many man-made fibres are used today.

Hard surfaces are needed for floors which have to resist a great deal of wear or damp. Stone slabs have been used for thousands of years, and the use of mosaic on floors is even older than its use on walls. Decorative tiles were also popular, and many fine examples from medieval times survive in old churches. The first modern smooth-surfaced floor covering was LINOLEUM, invented about 1860. It has now been largely supplanted by VINYL floorings.

Early furniture

Since most furniture throughout the ages has been made of wood, a perishable substance, little has survived from ancient times. Treasures found in the dry tombs of Egypt, paintings and written accounts show that the peoples of Egypt, Greece and Rome had a variety of tables, chairs and couches, which they decorated with carvings. There were also simple cupboards and boxes.

Medieval Europe also had very simple furniture, much of it made from oak – then a plentiful wood. At first the construction was comparatively crude: the timbers were fastened together with wooden dowels, or even with hand-made nails. Some crude MORTICE AND TENON JOINTS were used. Jointed furniture in the modern sense came into use at the end of the Middle Ages, and from this practice came such terms as the JOINT STOOL.

A great deal of early furniture was plain or painted. Some was enriched by carving, and turning was a popular method of shaping legs. INLAY and, in particular, MARQUETRY came into

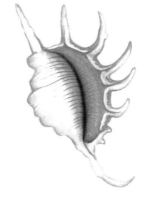

Above: A shell (in French *coquille*) the shape of which inspired the style of decoration known as rococo. The term rococo is believed to have originated in a combination of *rocaille* (rockwork) and *coquille*.

Below: Chairs through the ages: **1**, Greek; **2**, a box-type carved oak chair of the 1300s; **3**, a carved and turned walnut chair of the late 1600s with cane back and seat; **4**, an oval backed chair of the late 1700s, gilt with silk upholstery; **5**, a mid-Victorian mahogany chair with buttoned upholstery; **6**, a chair made in the 1900s from laminated plywood.

use in Italy in the 1400s, and gradually spread to other countries. In France it was carried out especially by André-Charles BOULLE, famous for his VENEER work. LACQUER also became a popular method of decoration in the early 1600s.

Furniture in the 1700s

The 1700s was perhaps the greatest period in the history of furniture-making. Its influence lasted until about 1825. The great source of ideas was France, where Charles CRESSENT, cabinet-maker to Philippe d'Orléans, regent of France, established a style known today as REGENCE. He made great use of bright-coloured woods and ORMOLU mounts, and it was during his time that the term commode first came into general use in France for a chest of drawers.

The *régence* style soon gave way to ROCOCO, and that was followed in the mid-1700s by a revival of the classical styles of Greece and Rome, which became known as NEO-CLASSICAL (*see page 21*). It coincided with the reign of Louis XVI, and is often referred to as *Louis Seize*. The rococo and *Louis Seize* styles were widely copied in England and North America. The chief English exponent of rococo was Thomas CHIPPENDALE, a designer who did not apparently make any furniture himself. Chippendale was also greatly influenced by Chinese styles, but his more extravagant ideas were not followed in American Chippendale.

The neo-classical style in England was

M Marquetry is a pattern made from VENEERS of wood, ivory, metal, mother-of-pearl and other materials. It is used as an INLAY on furniture. Craftsmen have employed it since the days of ancient Egypt, and it was revived in Italy in the 1400s.
Morris, William (1834–96) was an English poet and artist. In 1861 he founded a business (nominally an artists' co-operative) to revolutionize design, particularly of fabrics, carpets, TAPESTRY and WALLPAPER. He was the main driving force behind the ARTS AND CRAFTS

MOVEMENT. He changed people's ideas of interior

Marquetry on walnut desk, 1600s

decoration and was the greatest single influence on the art of his time.
Mortice and tenon joint is where the end of a piece of wood (tenon) is shaped to fit into a corresponding hole (mortice) in a framework.
Mosaic is the art of making patterns from small pieces of different coloured stone, glass or other materials, which are called *tesserae*. It was particularly used on floors in ancient Greece and Rome, and as a wall decoration by the Romans and in the Byzantine (Eastern Roman) Empire. It was also

used by Indians in Central America.

O Ormolu is the name given to gilded bronze mounts and other ornaments applied to furniture made in France during the 1700s.

P Panelling is a form of decoration or structure in which a flat rectangular surface (the panel) is sunk inside a raised framework. Thin panels of wood held in this way do not warp; they make for lighter construction than more solid timbering.

Panelling is used in furniture making and as a wall covering.
Papier-mâché is a hard substance made by pulping paper and mixing it with a material such as clay or sand to give it body. It is then pressed into a mould and allowed to dry. (It can also be made by LAMINATING sheets of paper). Once it is LACQUERED to keep it dry it is very strong. A range of items including furniture and imitations of plaster ornaments for decorating interiors used to be made from it.

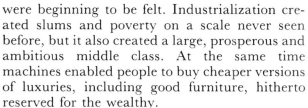

were beginning to be felt. Industrialization created slums and poverty on a scale never seen before, but it also created a large, prosperous and ambitious middle class. At the same time machines enabled people to buy cheaper versions of luxuries, including good furniture, hitherto reserved for the wealthy.

Led by the BIEDERMEIER style of the German-speaking countries of Europe, furniture in what we now think of as the VICTORIAN AGE ran riot, without having the delicate lines that prevailed in the 1700s. Furniture was heavy and bulbous, with solid, overstuffed upholstery and a tendency to excessive drapes and curtains. There were frills everywhere, notably on the ANTIMACASSARS which were found on every chair back. A new material, PAPIER-MACHE, was introduced at this time, and was often finished by JAPANNING.

A reaction against this over-exuberance led to John RUSKIN and William Morris, forming the ARTS AND CRAFTS MOVEMENT. Its keynote was a return to simpler hand craftsmanship instead of a total reliance on machine-made goods.

pioneered by Robert ADAM. and he may have evolved it independently of the French. Primarily an architect, Adam designed 'complete' houses for his wealthy clients, down to the decoration of walls and ceilings and the furniture. His ideas were popularised by the cabinet-makers George HEPPLEWHITE and Thomas SHERATON, who were copied in North America.

Above: The furniture produced by the Shakers – members of the United Society of Believers – is light and elegant.

Below: In contrast to the simplicity of a Shaker room, a typical Victorian sitting-room was over-furnished and upholstered.

Furniture in the 1800s

Furniture in the 1800s is of two basic kinds. First came the elegant pieces, strongly influenced by the tradition of the previous century, known in France as EMPIRE and in England as REGENCY. both Empire and Regency had their extravagant moments, perhaps best seen in the Royal Pavilion at Brighton England, designed for the Prince Regent (later George IV) in 1815–1821. Again, the style was followed in the United States, but there it became a distinctive form known as the FEDERAL style, among whose principal exponents were Duncan PHYFE and the later members of the GODDARD family. A completely independent style of furniture was that made by the SHAKERS, strong, simple and light.

The Regency period came to an end in 1830, just as the full effects of the Industrial Revolution

Modern furniture

Furniture design in the 1900s began with a hangover from the previous century, the style known as ART NOUVEAU. The Arts and Crafts Movement also persisted, and it was taken up in

Above: Indian furniture makers borrowed ideas from the many Europeans who invaded their land. This armchair with incised veneer of ivory, made in Vizagapatnam, north-east Madras, in the first half of the 1700s, is in the Dutch burgomaster style.

Germany by the DEUTSCHER WERKBUND. Its supporters, particularly the designer Peter BEHRENS, differed from the Arts and Crafts Movement in thinking that machine made things could also look good, and founded industrial design.

The 1900s have been a time of great social change, brought about partly by two devastating world wars, and partly by the rapid advance of science and technology. This led to changes in patterns of people's ways of life, and the introduction of new materials. These included the early plastics, particularly BAKELITE, tubular steel, and the use of LAMINATED materials. One of the earliest applications of these materials was in ART DECO, in the 1920s and 1930s.

A new angle on interior design was provided by the architect LE CORBUSIER (*see page 38*), who described houses as 'machines for living'. The Dane Kaare KLINT followed this idea through by working out standard sizes for furniture to give the maximum ease of use. Greater comfort in upholstery came with the introduction of foam rubber and plastics.

Oriental furniture

Of the Oriental countries probably India has laid the least emphasis on furniture. However, the rich carving and inlay found on some pieces had a strong inflence on Western design. The Chinese made much more use of furniture, and the use by both the Chinese and the Japanese of lacquer was also much imitated in the West. Both China and Japan lay much emphasis on simplicity of line coupled, for religious or ritual purposes, with richness of decoration and embellishment.

Early visitors to the Orient found that the cabinet-making was of relatively poor quality compared with that of Europe. For many years Western-made pieces were shipped out to China or Japan to be lacquered, until European makers themselves mastered the art of lacquer. One item of furniture much in use in the Orient was imported to Europe, and that was the SCREEN, which in the West was mainly a fixed feature in church interiors. The East also provided one important material, bamboo, which is widely used in China and Japan.

Right: The streamlined style of Art Deco is shown clearly in these examples. Art Deco had its vogue during the 1920s and 1930s.

1806) was an English furniture designer. Although trained as a cabinet-maker, he does not seem to have made furniture himself. He is best remembered for his books of patterns, especially *The Cabinet-Maker's and Upholsterer's Drawing Book* (1791–94). His designs were light and delicate, and he advocated the use of satinwood.

T **Tapestry** is a decorative fabric made by WEAVING (*see page 56*). It has plain warp (lengthways) threads, and through these a picture

is built up by using different coloured weft (widthways) threads. It differs from EMBROIDERY (*see page 51*), which is made by stitching on to an already woven fabric.

V **Veneer** is a thin sheet of decorative material glued on to a solid base. Most veneers are of wood, but metal, ivory, and in these days plastics are also used. Veneers can be used for purely ornamental purposes, as in MARQUETRY or INLAY, but they are also used to conceal inferior wood with an outer layer of an expen-

sive one. Early veneers were cut in sheets across the grain of wood, but modern ones are mostly made by peeling a sheet off a rotating log, as for making plywood.

Victorian Age corresponds with the long reign of England's Queen Victoria (1837–1901). It was a time of industrial development.

Vinyl is a form of plastics, which can be made rigid or flexible, transparent or in solid colours. Vinyls are a petroleum by-product.

W **Wallpaper** came into use in Europe at the

Chinese wallpaper, 1700s

end of the 1600s, though it had been known for at least 150 years before. For about 250 years it has been sold in rolls 10·05 metres long and 530 mm wide. Design was strongly influenced by William MORRIS in the 1800s, and by improved printing techniques in the 1900s.

Wilton is a small English town in Wiltshire where carpets have been made since the 1690s. Wilton carpets are woven on a loom which can use up to 6 different colours

The decorative arts are concerned with the production of beautiful objects, many of which are displayed in museums. But most of these objects originally had a practical application.

Decorative Arts

The term 'decorative arts' is now widely used by museums to describe those arts which have a practical application. In this way it includes all the crafts, from cabinet-making to macramé, whose end product is a useful object showing fine workmanship and a pleasing appearance. In this context it is worth remembering that one person's idea of beauty is not necessarily everyone's. People also have different ideas of what is a decorative art. Furniture making, for example, can be considered so, though in this volume we have grouped it as an important element of interior design. And there is of necessity a certain overlap with fine art.

Art in fabric

Fabric making is one of the oldest crafts. It began sometime in the Stone Age, at least 11,000 years ago. Primitive sewing, in which leather thongs were used to lace together animal skins, is older still. The first fabrics were undoubtedly very plain, but archaeological remains show that at an early stage people started WEAVING patterns into their cloth. The discovery of plant and insect dyes led weavers to make coloured patterns – though we know very little about coloured fabrics in ancient times apart from the way in which they are pictured in Egyptian wall paintings. EMBROIDERY seems to have come into existence almost as soon as there was woven material to embroider on.

KNITTING is a more recent invention, first worked by Arabs some 2,500 years ago. KNITTING pins as used today came into use in medieval times, and the first knitting machine was made in England in 1589. LACE making is even more modern, the earliest known lace being produced in Venice in the 1500s.

The most 'artistic' form of weaving is undoubtedly tapestry, whose practical application as a wall hanging is described on page 44. Tapestries are woven by hand on huge looms, the weaver copying a full-sized painting on paper or linen known as a CARTOON. The weaving is done from the back of the fabric, and the weaver has to walk round to the other side or use a mirror to see the finished pattern. Tapestry-making is very much a living art following a revival in the 1920s. Embroidery, however, once a flourishing industry and a craft practised by the aristocracy as well as by peasants is now largely an amateur occupation or one for the independent artist-craftsman who has exploited the use of machine embroidery. Many fine artists concentrate on the design of woven or printed fabrics.

Above: A detail of the phoenix robe which belonged to the Empress Dowager Tz'u Hsi of China – a fine example of Chinese silk embroidery of the 1800s. The phoenix (Feng Huang) was one of the 4 symbolic creatures which guarded the Celestial Empire of China.

Left: Some idea of the way in which tapestry is woven can be gained from this small, simple loom. The weaver has drawn the design on to the warp threads.

Reference

A **Alloy** is a mixture of metals, or of a metal with some other substance such as carbon (used with iron to make steel). Most alloys are harder than the metals of which they are composed, but melt more easily.

B **Beardsley,** Aubrey (1872–98) was an English book illustrator in the tradition of ART NOUVEAU (see page 43). His sinuous, grotesque figures were condemned by many people as 'decadent'.

Biscuit is pottery or PORCELAIN which has undergone FIRING but not GLAZING. Some biscuit porcelain is made to imitate marble; the English Parian ware, made in Staffordshire, is an example.

Bone china is a form of PORCELAIN which contains up to 40% bone ash. It came into use in England in the early 1800s and is now the standard form of English porcelain.

Böttger, Johann (1682–1719) was a German alchemist employed by Augustus the Strong, King of Poland and Elector of Saxony. He was engaged to

Derby bone china tea set c. 1790

try to turn lead into gold, but instead found out the Chinese secret of making PORCELAIN. As a result Augustus set up a factory at Meissen, near Dresden, and so gained gold in a way that he had not expected.

C **Cane** is a rod of coloured glass, used for making, among other things, MILLEFIORI paperweights.

Carat is a term used in defining the amount of gold in an ALLOY, 1 carat equalling 0·04 of the total weight. The number of carats given are those of the gold in the

Left: Blue and white painting applied under the glaze was at its finest during the period of the Chinese Ming Dynasty (1368–1644).

Ceramics

Pottery as a craft is almost as old as weaving, and so skilled were prehistoric potters that their various designs and styles can be used by archaeologists for dating prehistoric finds. Early pots, like early bricks, were baked hard by the heat of the sun, but for the past 6000 years or more pottery has undergone FIRING in a kiln. All pottery is made from clay of one kind or another, and from the Greek name for potter's clay, *keramos*, comes the word ceramics, used to describe all kinds of pottery.

There are three basic kinds of ceramics, made from clays which fire at different temperatures. EARTHENWARE, the crudest form of ceramics, and also the oldest is fired at the lowest temperatures. STONEWARE is much harder, and is fired at higher temperatures until VITRIFICATION takes place, giving it a smooth surface. PORCELAIN is the finest kind of ceramics, and unlike the other two is generally translucent. Like stoneware, it was invented by the Chinese, who guarded the secret jealously. Porcelain was imported from China into Europe from the 1500s onwards, as soon as a regular sea trade between West and East was established. It was known as China ware, a term

which was later abbreviated to 'china'.

European potters made strenuous efforts to imitate Chinese porcelain, but at first they could not match the PASTE of the Chinese ware. French and English potters evolved their own SOFT-PASTE ware, made in such factories as SEVRES and CHELSEA. The secret was finally discovered by Johann BÖTTGER, at Meissen near Dresden in Germany in 1709. This was a true HARD-PASTE porcelain. The products of the Meissen factory were widely sought all over Europe, particularly the delicate figures modelled by Johann KAENDLER.

With the production of BONE CHINA in England in the early 1800s porcelain became available to people other than the very wealthy. Poorer users still had to be content with the existing large range of pottery wares. In the 1600s and 1700s much of this was decorated by glazing it with a white glaze containing tin to make it opaque. That from Italy and Spain was known as MAIOLICA, and that from France as FAIENCE. DELFT WARE was made in many countries. Faïence, delft and maiolica were eventually driven off the market by the invention of creamware, or Queen ware, a fine pottery produced by Josiah WEDGWOOD. It was copied by pottery

Below: Imari ware was the name given to porcelain exported to Europe from Arita, in the Japanese province of Hizan, during the early 1700s. The 'brocaded Imari' in blue, red and gold was particularly popular and was widely imitated by European factories.

---

alloy: for example, 18 carat gold contains 18 parts of gold to 6 of some other metal. Carat is also a measure of weight used for precious stones: 1 carat=200 milligrammes.
Cartoon is a full-sized preliminary drawing, often in full colour, for a painting or a tapestry. The word comes from the Italian *cartone*, a big sheet of cardboard or paper. The modern meaning, a humourous or satirical drawing, dates from 1841, when the British magazine *Punch* made fun of cartoons for murals in the new

Houses of Parliament under the heading 'Punch's cartoons'.
Cellini, Benvenuto (1500–71) was an Italian sculptor and goldsmith of considerable skill. He is best known for his *Autobiography*, in which he describes his adventures and his love-life in greatly exaggerated terms.
Chasing is a method of decorating metal, particularly gold and silver, by hammering it to raise a pattern. The term is also used for the removal of rough parts from castings.

Damascened iron plaque Italian c. 1550

Chelsea was one of the best-known English SOFT-PASTE porcelain factories. It was founded near London about 1745 and closed in 1784. Its products were marked first with a triangle, then successively with an embossed anchor, a red anchor and a gold anchor.
Cutting, in glass-making, is a means of incising decoration with a revolving metal disc, using sand or emery powder and water as a cutting agent.

D **Damascening** is the process of decorating

works throughout Europe and North America.

Glazed pottery and porcelain had to be fired twice. The first stage, known as BISCUIT, is fired at a high temperature, and the glaze is then fused to the ceramic at a lower temperature. Much early delft ware was decorated by painting on designs by hand over the glaze before firing. A great deal of pottery and porcelain was, and is, decorated at the biscuit stage and then covered with a translucent glaze. Some over-glaze decoration required a third firing to set it, possibly with the addition of a further clear glaze. Hand-painting requires great skill and a good deal of time, and high-quality work was (and is) necessarily expensive. Cheaper wares were often very crudely decorated.

Cheaper decorated ceramics became possible with the invention of TRANSFER PRINTING in the mid-1700s. Blue-and-white printed ware was a very popular product of the English ceramics factories of the 1700s. The best-known is the WILLOW PATTERN, in continuous use from about 1780 to the present-day. English potteries did a roaring trade to North America in the late 1700s and early 1800s with 'American views' – plates and other wares transfer-printed with pictures of American scenes copied from engravings of the

Right: A group, *Leda and the Swan*, made at the Chelsea factory near London about 1765. This is an example of the finest English soft-paste porcelain of the 1700s.

Left: A Meissen figure of a shepherdess with a birdcage. It was made about 1750 by the factory's chief modeller, J. Kaendler.

time. Oriental designs were widely copied, particularly the IMARI and KAKIEMON patterns of Japan.

Glass

Glass vessels have been made for at least 3,500 years, and glass beads are known to have existed in Egypt, for perhaps 1,000 years before that. Glass is sometimes formed naturally by the action of lightning on sand, which may have given early people their first ideas on this useful and beautiful substance.

Glass is made by melting sand in a furnace, using a FLUX to help it melt more readily and at lower temperatures. Other minerals are added in small quantities to give the glass special qualities. For example, arsenic, nickel or manganese make glass absolutely colourless. The addition of lead makes glass shine brilliantly, and all fine modern cut glass is produced in this way. So is the so-called 'paste', a fine glass used for making imitation gemstones since the 1700s.

The two basic techniques of glass-making are blowing and moulding. In moulding (the older technique) the molten METAL was poured into or over a mould. In blowing, invented about 30 BC,

---

iron or steel with a design in gold and silver. A pattern is cut in the iron and gold and silver wire is hammered into the grooves so formed. The name comes from the city of Damascus, where the technique originated.

Delft ware is a kind of pottery coated with an opaque white tin glaze. It was made in many countries but took its name from the town of Delft in the Netherlands which was an important centre for its manufacture in the 1600s and 1700s.

Doré, Gustave (1832–83) was a French artist who

made his name as a book illustrator. He used wood engravings, heavily detailed and dramatic. His sculptures and his large religious paintings are not so well known or highly thought of.

E **Earthenware** is pottery made with clay that is fired at comparatively low temperatures – about 800° C–1200° C. It is slightly porous. Flower-pots provide a good example of earthenware.

Electroplating is the process of coating a base metal, generally copper or one of

its ALLOYS, with a thin layer of silver or gold. The article to be plated is put into a solution of the metal to be deposited, and an electric current is passed through the solution to the article. This causes metal from the solution to be deposited on the article. The process came into use in England about 1840.

Embossing is a process for making a relief design in gold, silver, copper or other metal by hammering it from the reverse side.

Embroidery is the art of making designs on fabric

with needle and thread. Many techniques and

Engraving, Hogarth 1733

stitches are used. Some forms of embroidery involve cutting the base fabric (cutwork) or removing some of its threads (drawn threadwork. Silk, cotton, wool, man-made fibre or metallic threads may be used.

Engraving is the process of cutting a design composed of fine lines into metal or glass. The term engravings is used for prints made by cutting a design or picture on a plate of metal or very hard wood. In commercial printing the term is used for a printing plate made by a photographic process.

Above: A Roman glass ewer. The hexagonal lower part shows the influence of metalworking on the design. The greenish colour is probably caused by burial in the soil.

Below: Venetian glass was the envy of other European countries in Renaissance times. On the left is a wine glass of the 1500s, its deep bell bowl set on a squat foot. On the right is a *tazza*, a wine cup with a broad bowl set on a centre stem and foot.

a long metal tube is dipped into the metal to pick up a blob of it. The operator blows gently into the tube to produce a hollow bulb. While the glass stays red-hot he can shape it with various tools, reheating it from time to time and possibly blowing into it again. When the object is shaped it is broken off the end of the blowpipe and allowed to cool completely. The two techniques can be combined by blowing the glass into an iron mould.

The decorating of glass can be carried out in many ways. For example, CANES of coloured glass can be twisted together while semi-molten, or blended into clear glass to form a pattern. MILLEFIORE paperweights are made in this way. A thin layer of coloured glass can be applied to the outside of a vase or other article. When part of the coloured glass is removed the clear glass underneath shows through. Stained glass for windows is made in this way.

Once the article is formed it can be decorated by CUTTING, ENGRAVING, ETCHING or SAND-BLASTING. It can also be enamelled – that is, painted with colours containing a glassy substance which, when fired at a relatively low temperature, fuses to the article. One of the finest artists at this kind of work was Johann SCHAPER.

The Romans made very fine glass, some superb examples of which have survived despite their fragility. The next great name in glassmaking is that of the city of Venice, which had a well-organized craft of glass-blowers by the

Below: Glassblowing in medieval times. Similar techniques are still used for hand-made glass.

Right: This elaborate gold and silver salt-cellar was made about 1540 by the Italian goldsmith Benvenuto Cellini for Francis I of France. It shows allegorically the production of salt from the sea (represented by Neptune).

Far right: A splendid display of Georgian silver set out as it was meant to be seen, on a table. It is in the dining-room of Ickworth, a great house in Suffolk, England, built in the 1790s.

1200s. They made very thin, beautiful glassware, known as *Cristallo*. It was greatly sought-after, and to keep their trade secrets glass-makers were threatened with capture and death if they left the city. However, some did get away, and as a result a busy glass industry was set up in Bohemia (modern Czechoslovakia).

England became a leading glass-making country in the 1500s, and rose to pre-eminence after the invention of LEAD CRYSTAL there in 1674. This glass was much heavier and more brilliant than Venetian glass, and lent itself to cutting as the main means of decoration. The American glass industry began with the opening of a factory in New Jersey in 1739. The great American contribution to glass technique was PRESSED GLASS, which brought beautifully patterned glass within the reach of all purses. Some patterns are so sharp that they resemble cut glass. Modern glass-making in all countries either follows traditional patterns, or else adapts existing techniques to current styles.

Gold and silver

Gold was one of the earliest metals known to man, because it is often found as nuggets or lumps of metal. It is soft and easy to work and it resists chemical action so that it retains its lustre. For thousands of years it has been a symbol of wealth and a main ingredient of jewellery. Silver, though it turns black in the presence of oxygen, has been almost as highly valued for nearly as long. Platinum a white, metal-like silver with the

untarnishability of gold, was discovered only in 1557.

Because gold is a very soft metal and silver a relatively soft one, they are generally used as ALLOYS with some harder but less valuable metal, such as copper. The pureness of gold is measured in CARATS. Silver alloys are described in terms of fineness – the number of parts of silver in 1000 parts of the alloy. The English standard of sterling silver, which contains 92·5 per cent silver, is said to have a fineness of 925.

Goldsmiths and silversmiths have been highly respected craftsmen from very early times, often organized into guilds, or craft unions. For the past 500 years or so such craftsmen in the West have tended to mark their products. Guilds or even governments have frequently insisted on other marks as a standard of metal purity, the most outstanding example being the HALLMARKING of PLATE in England. Outstanding craftsmen in gold and silver include the French Huguenot (Protestant) refugees Paul de LAMERIE and Paul REVERE, the Italian Benvenuto CELLINI, and the Englishman PAUL STORR.

Techniques used in gold and silver work include CHASING, EMBOSSING and ENGRAVING. Because of the high price of the precious metals, many methods have been evolved for giving base (inferior) metals a thin plating of gold or silver. Base metals, and silver, can be gilded by mixing gold with mercury, applying this mixture to the metal, and heating it to evaporate the mercury. A

piece was tested for its contents of precious metal, the year of testing and the maker. It is named after Goldsmiths' Hall, London, an assay (testing) office. Plate is assayed in some other European countries, but not in the United States.
Hard paste is true PORCELAIN made from china clay (kaolin) and china stone (petuntse). Chinese porcelain is made from this recipe, which was rediscovered in Europe by Johann BÖTTGER.

Imari ware was PORCELAIN made at Arita, in

Kyushu, Japan, for export to Europe. Much of it was richly patterned in blue, gold and red, and it was widely imitated in factories throughout Europe.

K Kaendler, Joahann Joachim (1706–75) was the chief modeller and sculptor at the Meissen factory in Germany from 1731 until his death. His porcelain figures and models are delicate and lively.
Kakiemon style is a very simple, asymmetrical way of decorating PORCELAIN. It was evolved by the Japanese

potter family of Kakiemon, in about 1650.
Knitting is looping a con-

Lace made on pillow, Brussels 1600s

tinuous length of thread (often wool) together to make a fabric. Knitting is carried out by hand with knitting pins, or needles, or by machine. The fabric is very elastic.

L Lace is a delicate, open-work fabric, made by twisting or knotting threads together. Linen is the most usual thread, but cotton and silk are also used. There are 2 types: pillow or bobbin lace, in which threads wound on bobbins are worked around pins stuck into a pillow; and needle-point lace, made with needle and thread on net or a lattice of threads.

Above: A selection of copper and brass ware, displayed in the kitchen of Saltram House, in Devon, England. It includes scales with ceramic weights.

Below: A cut-steel nocturnal, an instrument used for finding the time by night from the position of the stars. It was designed to be used with the stars of either the Great Bear or the Little Bear constellations.

is very much stronger than pure copper and flows more easily for casting. Nickel silver and its variants are white in colour and are often used as cheap substitutes for silver, or as a base which can be electroplated with silver.

Pure copper has tended to be used mainly for household articles, which often have a simple beauty of line that appeals to modern collectors. Bronze is employed largely in sculpture and ORMOLU (*see pages 6 and 46*). Pewter, because of its colour, was for a long time regarded as a substitute for silver. It was used for plates, jugs and other household vessels, and for cutlery. Most domestic utensils were pewterware in poorer European households until cheap pottery became readily available, in the early 1700s.

Brass is the copper alloy most used for making fine articles, again as a substitute for silver or gold. In the days when candles provided the chief source of artificial light, brass candlesticks were widely used all over Europe. Flemish and Dutch brassfounders were particularly known for their production. The pillar-shaped candlestick on a square or round base was designed in the 1700s. Large church candlesticks were also made of brass. Another feature of church brasswork is the lectern (stand for holding a bible) in the form of an eagle, a design in use in Europe for at least 700 years.

substitute for silver was SHEFFIELD PLATE, which was used from about 1765 until the invention of ELECTROPLATING in the 1840s.

Skill in silver and gold evolved independently in Mexico and Peru before the arrival of the Europeans in the 1500s. A great deal of it was melted down by the Spanish conquerors of those regions in their greed for treasure, but enough survives to show that the American Indians had little to learn in the way of craftsmanship.

Copper and its alloys

Copper, which has been in use about as long as gold, is one of the most versatile metals. Many articles are made from the pure metal, but copper is also used with other metals to make a number of useful alloys. The most important alloys of copper are: brass (copper and zinc); Britannia metal (copper, antimony and tin); bronze (copper and tin); nickel silver or German silver (copper, nickel and zinc). There are many variations of these basic alloys depending on the proportions of the metals in them, with names such as bell metal, Dutch metal, gun metal, paktong, pinchbeck and Mannheim gold. Pewter is mostly tin, with a little copper and antimony (and formerly some lead as well).

Like gold and silver, copper and most of its alloys can be worked by hammering sheets into various shapes. It can also be cast in moulds. The choice of which alloy to use is governed by two considerations: colour and hardness. Bronze

Iron and steel

The Iron Age began about 5,000 years ago, and still continues today. Its harder form, steel, has been made for around 3,500 years. Although iron and steel are the most utilitarian of all metals, they have produced some distinctive art forms of their own. For centuries the blacksmith was one of the leading craftsmen.

Decorative ironwork is of two kinds, wrought and cast. Wrought iron is made by heating rods or bars until they are red-hot and hammering them to the shapes required. Gates, railings and screens are commonly made of wrought iron. The various parts are joined by riveting, welding (hammering two pieces of iron together when very hot so that they fuse) or gripping them with small iron clips. Cast iron is made by pouring liquid iron in moulds. The original design is made in wood or plaster, and a mould is produced by pressing the original into special sand.

The mould is destroyed when it is removed from the casting. Cast iron has been made for at least 3,000 years, but it became popular in the 1700s and 1800s, when it was used as a structural material that could also be ornamental.

Steel reached its height of popularity in the manufacture of arms and armour, which were decorated by ENGRAVING, DAMASCENING and cut-work.

Calligraphy and printing

Before the invention of printing all books had to be copied out by hand. It was a slow and laborious business, and because a high proportion of books were religious much of the copying was done by monks. Perhaps because such work was for them a labour of love, most of these handwritten books were examples of fine calligraphy – literally, beautiful writing. Many of the

Right: A fine example of wrought iron work: the gates of Chirk Castle, in Wales, picked out in colours.

Right: A blacksmith and his assistant at work. A skilled smith can make anything from a horseshoe to a sharp, tempered scythe blade. In the illustration one smith is heating an iron rod which is then held in a vice on the anvil and hammered into shape while still hot.

tion, it is sometimes called 'Sandwich glass' after one of its chief makers, the Boston and Sandwich Glass Company, but it was first made by Bakewell, Page and Bakewell of Pittsburgh in 1825.

R Revere, Paul (1735–1818) was a skilled silversmith and engraver of Boston, Massachusetts. He was the son of a French Huguenot refugee, Apollos Rivoire. At the start of the American War of Independence he rode through the night in April, 1775, to warn

fellow-colonists of the approach of British soldiers.

S Sand-blasting is a process used for engraving glass. The sand is forced in a jet against the glass, and cuts away the surface. Parts which are not affected are protected by stencil plates. The process is also used for cleaning stone and metal.

Sans-serif type has all the strokes the same thickness and no tiny finishing lines at the ends of the strokes. (The sans-serif type can be seen in the captions and reference sections of this volume). It

first came into use early in the 1800s.

Schaper, Johann (1621–70) was a German glass painter. he worked at Nuremberg, where he developed the technique known as *Schwarzlot*, in which the decoration is in black enamel, sometimes relieved by a little red or gold.

Sèvres is France's national PORCELAIN factory. It was set up in Vincennes about 1738 in a former royal palace, and was moved to Sèvres in 1756. Both places are suburbs of Paris. The factory was bought by King Louis

XV in 1759, and under his ownership the factory enjoyed privileges which

Sevres porcelain plate 1784

curbed competition. Sèvres porcelain is noted for fine painting, particularly of panels portraying flowers, birds, landscapes and other pictorial subjects, and for its beautiful, vivid colours, especially shades of blue.

Sheffield plate was the predecessor of ELECTROPLATING as a substitute for solid silver. The process was invented by an English cutler, Thomas Boulsover of Sheffield, about 1743. Boulsover fused a copper ingot to a thinner one of silver, then rolled the combined ingot out, forming a thin

Left: A page from a book before the days of printing. This is a Flemish Book of Hours (a form of prayer book), and the floral border and rich initials are thought to be the work of Alexander Bening, a Flemish book illustrator of the 1400s and 1500s.

Venetian printer Aldus MANUTIUS, who based it on a style of handwriting used in Italy at that time. On these three basic designs – the 'gothic' of Germany, roman and italic – all later type faces have been based, even SANS-SERIF.

The early printers, like the copyists they replaced, were artists as well as craftsmen. There was a great decline in the artistic side of printing in the 1800s, partly due to mechanization. However, the work of William MORRIS (*see page 46*) and others led to a revival of interest in typefaces and book design. Many fine artists, such as Pablo PICASSO (*see page 23*), Gustav DORE and Aubrey BEARDSLEY have illustrated books; some, such as 'PHIZ', owed their reputations to such work.

Below: This 'improved' printing press was in use in 1786 – more than 300 years after Gutenberg invented printing from movable type. Yet despite a few refinements it was basically little altered from the press that Gutenberg used.

Left: A modern book illustration by Edmund Dulac (1882–1953), a French-born British artist. It is 'Aladdin and the Genie', from the *Arabian Nights Entertainment*.

manuscripts were illuminated with pictures, elaborate borders, and decorative initials.

The first printing from inked woodblocks was carried out by the Chinese, Japanese and Koreans more than 1200 years ago. Printing in the modern sense, from movable type (letters which can be used over and over again) was invented in Germany in the 1440s. Its creator was a Mainz goldsmith, Johannes Gensfleisch, known as GUTENBERG. Gutenberg's books, and those of his immediate successors, were designed to copy as closely as possible the work of the calligraphers they were replacing. So the earliest typefaces were copied from the black-letter or 'Old English' hand commonly used in northern European books.

In Italy, where the study of the Greek and Roman classics was well under way in that burst of learning called the Renaissance, scribes tended to use a different script based on the alphabet of the Romans. From this came the so-called 'roman' type (like the type on this page). Its companion type, *italic*, was introduced by the

---

plate, silver on one side. From about 1770 the copper was silvered on both sides. Sheffield plate was extensively used until the invention of electroplating, but by 1851 the process was no longer in use.

Soft paste is an imitation form of PORCELAIN made in Europe before the secret of true HARD-PASTE porcelain was generally known.

Stoneware is an extremely hard form of pottery which has undergone VITRIFICATION, thus becoming waterproof.

Storr, Paul (1771–1844) was an English silversmith who

helped to create in silver a REGENCY style (*see page 47*).

T **Transfer printing** is a process for decorating ceramics quickly and cheaply. It was invented in England about 1750. A print is taken from an ENGRAVED copper plate on special paper, which is then laid on the BISCUIT-fired ceramic article while the ink is still wet. It is fixed by FIRING and then undergoes GLAZING.

V **Vitrification** is the process of becoming glass or glass-like; china clays all

vitrify at very high temperatures.

W **Weaving** is the process of making cloth on a loom. Lengthways threads (the warp) are stretched on a frame, and cross threads (the weft or woof) are woven through them.

Wedgwood, Josiah (1730–95), was one of the greatest English potters and the grandfather of the naturalist Charles Darwin. From his factory in Staffordshire he became one of the leaders of the Industrial Revolution. He invented creamware, a fine

cream-coloured pottery; basaltes, an unglazed black STONEWARE; and jasperware,

Willowpattern china

a fine stoneware in blue, green, yellow and black with applied white decorations. The factory, and these wares, are still flourishing.

Willow pattern is one of the most popular 'Chinese' patterns used on ceramics. It was invented in England about 1780 by Thomas Turner of Caughley, Staffordshire. Later a 'Chinese legend' was also invented to explain the design.

Because of lending libraries, literature has become one of the most accessible of the arts.
A good novel can transport the reader into another time and place, while poetry can
encapsulate human emotions.

Literature

Above: *La Mort d'Arthur* by the pre-Raphaelite artist of the 1800s, James Archer, is a fanciful interpretation of the Arthurian legends which were popular in medieval times.

The word 'literature' is often used to mean anything that is written, from sales pamphlets to poetry. But literature is strictly that branch of writing which forms one of the fine arts. More than just a method of conveying information, it is an appeal to the mind and the emotions. Although people also talk of the literature of a particular language, or even of an individual country, true literature is international and appeals to everyone, whether in translation or in the original. There are various branches of literature (drama being one not dealt with here), of which fiction and poetry could be said to be the most important.

Fiction

The art of story-telling is almost as old as the use of language. Before the invention of writing, stories were passed on by word of mouth, forming a traditional oral literature. A few stories from the distant past have come down to us in written form, such as the story of Susanna and the Elders, from the *Apocrypha* of the Bible. Some stories blended fiction with dim memories of historical events, such as the story of Noah and the Flood or its Sumerian equivalent, the Epic of Gilgamesh.

Much early fiction was in the form of poetry, including the epics of HOMER, and the later

Reference

A **Alliteration** is repetition of the same initial sound in a succession of words.

Andersen, Hans Christian (1805–75), a shoemaker's son, became a writer and won international fame for his fairy stories. He also wrote some sketches inspired by travel abroad.

Aristotle (384–322 BC) was a Greek philosopher and scientist. After acting as tutor to Alexander the Great he founded a school in Athens. Aristotle's work dominated European scholarship until the Renaissance.

Assonance occurs when 2 or more words have the same vowel sound, but different consonants, as in *sane, late.*

Austen, Jane (1775–1817) was an English novelist. Although she led an uneventful life, her 6 famous books display a remarkable psychological insight into the lives of ordinary people. She poked gentle fun at the manners of her time and the sensational novels then popular. *Pride and Prejudice* (1813) is perhaps her masterpiece.

Jane Austen c. 1810

B **Boccaccio,** Giovani (c. 1313–75) was an Italian author who was the first great modern prose writer. He is most famous for *The Decameron* (1348–53) a collection of 100 short stories.

Boswell, James (1740–95), a Scottish lawyer, is best known for his *Life* of the writer Dr Samuel Johnson, which appeared in 1791, but in his own lifetime was famous for his book in support of Corsican independence. His private *Journals* were discovered in the 1920s and 1930s.

Bunyan, John (1628–88), an English tinker and lay preacher, was jailed for preaching without a licence. While in prison he wrote *The Pilgrim's Progress* (1678) a lively allegory of the journey of man's soul to salvation.

C **Camoens,** Luis de (1524–80), was Portugal's greatest poet. (In Portuguese his name is spelt *Camoes*). His finest work is *Os Lusiadas* (The Lusitanians, 1572) which celebrates Portuguese history. He had an adventurous life, spent partly in India.

Left: A detail from the frontispiece of the first edition of John Bunyan's *The Pilgrim's Progress,* which was first published in 1678.

medieval romances, such as the Arthurian legends or the equally fanciful stories woven around the historical figure of Frankish emperor Charlemagne. The Arthurian legends were given a more permanent form and an epic unity as literature in *Morte d'Arthur* by Sir Thomas MALORY in the 1400s. The earliest great prose fiction author of the modern age was the Italian Giovanni BOCCACCIO, who flourished a century earlier. His *Decameron*, a collection of 100 stories (the first short stories) inspired later writers, such as William SHAKESPEARE.

Medieval romances were the inspiration of the Spanish writer Miguel de CERVANTES, whose *Don Quixote* (1605–15), a satire on romances, was the world's first great novel. Spain was the origin of the picaresque tale, in which the hero is a *picarón*, a rogue and vagabond. Romances and picaresque stories were the stock-in-trade of most fiction writers in the 1600s, until the advent in 1678 of John BUNYAN's allegorical *Pilgrim's Progress*. In contrast to his predecessors, Bunyan wrote simple and direct prose, which owed much to the Authorized Version of the Bible, published in 1611. Bunyan and the Bible, between them, had an enormous influence on English-speaking readers for more than two centuries. The only influence as great was that of the dramatic poet William SHAKESPEARE. Although drama could justifiably be classed as fiction, its story belongs in another place, as part and parcel of the theatre. It is noticeable that the rise of the novel

followed the decline of drama as a main means of literary expression.

The novel as we know it came into existence in the 1700s. A major early work was *Robinson Crusoe* (1719) by Daniel Defoe (1660–1731). But Defoe's novels were episodic and a minor English author, Samuel RICHARDSON, is credited with writing the first 'modern' novel with his *Pamela* (1740). This has a continuous plot and characters and actions representative of real life. Its successor, *Clarissa* (1747–8), became famous all over Europe. Richardson was writing at the start of the romantic movement, whose German manifestation was the *Sturm und Drang* (storm and stress) movement. A leader of *Sturm und Drang* was Johann von GOETHE, whose novel *Die Leiden des jungen Werthers* (*The Sorrows of Young Werther*, 1774) caused a sensation because of its highly romantic story. A flood of imitations followed its publication.

Goethe's novel was partly autobiographical, and so were two masterpieces by STENDHAL, one of the French novelists of the early 1800s. They were *Le Rouge et le Noir* (*Scarlet and Black*, 1831) and *La Chartreuse de Palme* (*The Charterhouse of*

Right: For hundreds of years stories were passed on by word of mouth. Most so-called fairy stories were transmitted in this way. The brothers Jakob and Wilhelm Grimm, who worked in the 1800s, put many of these stories down on paper. This Arthur Rackham illustration shows a scene from one of them, the story of Hansel and Gretel.

Carroll, Lewis, (1832–98), was an Oxford University lecturer in mathematics, whose real name was Charles Lutwidge Dodgson. He is best known for his two children's fantasies, *Alice's Adventures in Wonderland* (1865) and *Through the Looking Glass* (1872).
Cervantes, Miguel de (1547–1616) was Spain's finest prose writer, best known for his novel *Don Quixote* (1605–15). He spent 5 years in the army, was captured by pirates and was then a slave for 5 years.
Chaucer, Geoffrey (c. 1340–

1400) was a civil servant, diplomat and politician in the service of the English

Carroll's Alice in Wonderland

kings Edward III and Richard II. He was the first great British poet. His *Canterbury Tales* (begun in 1386) owes much to BOCCACCIO.
Churchill, Sir Winston S. (1874–1965) was a soldier turned statesman who became Britain's prime minister during World War II. His work as a writer brought him the Nobel Prize for literature in 1953. Among his works are personal narratives of the 2 world wars, in which he played a leading role, and a *History of the English-Speaking Peoples* (1956–58).

D **Dante** Alighieri (1265–1321), a Florentine writer, was one of the leading poets of the Middle Ages. His finest works are the *Vita Nuova* (New Life, 1292) and the *Divina Commedia* (Divine Comedy, which he began in 1307) a vision of Hell, Purgatory and Heaven.
Descartes, René (1596–1650), a French philosopher and mathematician, based all philosophical thought on reason. His basic philosophical conclusion was 'Cogito ergo sum' (I think therefore I am).

Dickens, Charles (1812–70) was the most popular English novelist of the 1800s. He was a notable creator of characters, and campaigner against poverty and injustice. His 20 novels include *The Pickwick Papers* (1836–37), *A Tale of Two Cities* (1859) and *Great Expectations* (1861).

Dickinson, Emily (1830–86) ranks as one of the finest American poets of the 1800s. She lived a secluded life and almost all her poems were discovered after her death.
Dostoevsky, Fyodor (1821–

Right: A scene from the film of Leo Tolstoy's great novel *War and Peace*. The book tells the story of the Napoleonic invasion of Russia in 1812, and the disaster which overtook the French forces.

Above: Honoré Daumier's illustration to one of the greatest of Spanish works of fiction – Miguel de Cervantes's satire *Don Quixote*. In this picture the Don is in the background, followed by his faithful servant, Sancho Panza.

Palma, 1839). These books are romantic, yet they have intense political overtones and are commentaries on life as Stendhal found it. In this they look back to the satire of Jonathan SWIFT's *Gulliver's Travels* (1726) and forward to the strongly sociological works of Charles DICKENS and Harriet Beecher STOWE in English, and Stendhal's fellow-countryman Victor HUGO.

Dickens, in such novels as *David Copperfield* (1859–50) and *Oliver Twist* (1837–39), exposed the evils of the Industrial Revolution, while Mrs Stowe's *Uncle Tom's Cabin* (1852) was an indictment of slavery in the United States. These works were in complete contrast to other kinds of novels, such as the study of manners as exemplified in the brilliant works of Jane AUSTEN, or the historical romances of Sir Walter SCOTT and Alexandre DUMAS. A more serious treatment of historical subject is Leo TOLSTOY's *War and Peace* (1866), a study of life in the Napoleonic Wars. Tolstoy, together with Stendhal and Gustave Flaubert (1821–80) in France, George ELIOT in Britain, and Fyodor DOSTOYEVSKY in Russia, were among the great realistic novelists of the 1800s.

Dostoyevsky is sometimes said to be the father of the modern novel. His *Brothers Karamazov* (1879–80) probes deeply into human emotions. Research into psychology and the subconscious mind influenced such writers as James JOYCE, D. H. LAWRENCE, Marcel PROUST and the Australian Patrick WHITE. American literature produced a masterpiece in *Moby Dick* (1851) by Hermann Melville (1819–91). Leading American writers of the 1900s included F. Scott Fitzgerald (1896–1940), Ernest Hemingway (1898–1961) and William Faulkner (1897–1962), while Russia has Boris Pasternak (1890–1960) and Alexander Solzhenitsyn (1919–   ).

Large numbers of novels of a less serious nature, including romances, detective stories, science fiction tales and books which exploit sex and violence, are published every year and they are read by millions for pleasure. But popular fiction can also be good literature. For example, Raymond Chandler (1885–1959) wrote detective novels that portray superbly urban life in the United States and science fiction is the chosen subject of another fine American writer, Ray Bradbury (1920–   ).

81) was one of Russia's greatest novelists. The powerful realism of such books as *Crime and Punishment* (1866) stems partly from his own imprisonment for political activities, which was followed by years of grinding poverty, domestic trials and ill health.

Dumas, Alexander (1802–70), a French author, wrote an enormous number of novels and plays on historical themes, among the most famous of which were *The Three Musketeers* (1844) and *The Count of Monte Cristo* (1844–45).

Dumas, The Three Musketeers

E Eliot, George (1819–80) was the pseudonym of Mary Ann Evans, one of Britain's greatest writers.

Her novels, including *Mill on the Floss* (1860) and *Middlemarch* (1872), show great psychological insight.

Eliot, Thomas Stearns (1888–1965), one of the leading poets of the 1900s, was born in the United States and became a British subject. He was a critic and publisher as well as a poet. His works included *The Waste Land* (1922) and the verse play *Murder in the Cathedral* (1935).

Emerson, Ralph Waldo (1803–82), an American writer and philosopher, is best remembered for a few of his poems and for his essays.

F Free Verse is poetry with the irregular rythms of ordinary speech, and often with no rhyme.

G Gibbon, Edward (1737–94) was the son of an English country gentleman of private means and spent a large part of his life writing his history of *the Decline and Fall of the Roman Empire* (1776–88).

Goethe, Johann Wolfgang von (1749–1832) was a German writer, scientist and statesman. For some years he helped run the government of the Duchy of Weimar. The masterpiece of his large output of plays, poems and novels was the verse-drama *Faust* (1808–32).

Grass, Günter (1927–   ), a German author, is noted for his bitter, satirical novels, such as *The Tin Drum* (1959).

Grimm, Jakob (1785–1863) and Wilhelm (1786–1859) were the first editors of the *Deutsches Wörterbuch*, a dictionary which took 106 years to finish. They are best known for their fairy tales.

Above: A reciter, from a picture on a Greek vase. The Greeks called such men *rhapsodes*, a name which means 'song stitcher'. They recited poetry at public festivals.

Right: A Chinese poem, delicately painted on a scroll in the 1600s. The Chinese make the most of the beautiful outlines of their writing.

Poetry

Poetry has been found on clay tablets made in ancient Sumeria and on the walls of buildings in ancient Egypt. It has been transcribed and handed on to future generations from Greece and Rome, China and Japan. Because it uses language in a musical way, with such devices as RHYTHM, rhyme, ASSONANCE, ALLITERATION and repetition, it seldom translates well.

Greek and, in particular, Latin were the languages of scholarship in Europe for hundreds of years. As a result, poetry in those languages has greatly influenced later poets. The vivid imagery of Homer's epics – the *Iliad* and the *Odyssey* – inspired the Roman poet VIRGIL to write the *Aeneid* in the same vein. The highly personalized songs of SAPPHO, an early woman poet, led to the lyrics of HORACE and his imitators.

The composition of Latin verses persisted into the Middle Ages, but at the same time there was a steady growth of vernacular poetry, written in languages people actually spoke. Much of it was epic in the Homeric vein, such as the Scandinavian sagas with their tales of the gods, or the Anglo-Saxon legend of *Beowulf*. Vernacular poetry came into full flower in the 1200s and 1300s, almost as a prelude to that rebirth of learning called the Renaissance, with the works of such poets as DANTE and PETRARCH in Italy, Geoffrey CHAUCER in England, and François VILLON in France. Villon took his inspiration from the songs of wandering troubadours or minstrels. Petrarch drew not only from the troubadours but also from the Latin classics and he is justly remembered for perfecting a number of poetic forms, among them the SONNET.

The Renaissance poets produced some of the world's finest verses. Outstanding poets of the time included Luis de CAMOENS in Portugal and Edmund SPENSER in England. Poets were often musicians, too, and in Italy and England in particular they produced many madrigals and similar songs. Renaissance influence lasted well into the 1600s. John Milton (1608–74) has been called the 'last Renaissance man' and his *Paradise Lost* is one of the greatest poems of all time.

With the 1700s came the Age of Reason, a time when scientific thought and discoveries dominated men's minds, to the exclusion of imagination and superstition. Not surprisingly, it was a mostly arid period for poetry, although it did produce two great English poets, John Dryden (1631–1700) and Alexander Pope (1688–1744).

The change came with the Romantic movement, as it did with the novel. Writers, such as GOETHE and Friedrich von SCHILLER in Germany, Alfred de MUSSETT in France, John KEATS and Percy SHELLEY in England, wrote emotionally charged poetry, beginning a movement that was carried on through the 1800s by such poets as Emily DICKINSON, William WORDSWORTH and Alfred Lord TENNYSON.

There was inevitably a reaction against romanticism in the late 1800s and the 1900s. In France poets adopted symbolism, filling their verses with imagery. Among them was Stephane MALLARME, who had an influence on other artists, such as the composer Claude Debussy. English-language poets, anxious to express the feelings of the modern world, broke away from what they considered the fetters of conventional poetic form to write FREE VERSE, of which Walt WHITMAN was a pioneer. The foremost writer of free verse was T. S. ELIOT, who often used harsh images taken

---

Heredotus (c. 484–424 BC), the first Greek historian, spent his youth in travel, then settled down to write a history of the world.
Homer was by tradition the author of 2 Greek epics, *The Iliad* and *The Odyssey*, but some scholars doubt if there was such a person.
Horace (65–8 BC), a Roman soldier and civil servant (Latin name Quintus Horatius Flaccus), was the great lyric poet of his day.
Hugo, Victor (1802–85), a French writer, was one of the main romantic authors of his time. Novelist, playwright

and poet, his best known works are the novels *Notre Dame de Paris* (1831) and *Les Miserables* (1862).

Joyce James (1882–1941), an Irish novelist, used a style known as 'stream of consciousness' to express the inner thoughts of his characters, notably in *Ulysses* (1922) and *Finnegan's Wake* (1939).

Keats, John (1795–1821) was one of the leading English poets of the Romantic movement. He devoted his short life to writ-

ing poetry, the best of which is collected in *Lamia and Other Poems* (1820).

D. H. Lawrence

Lamb, Charles (1775–1834), an English writer famous for his essays on William SHAKESPEARE called *Tales from Shakespeare* (1807). He wrote under the pen-name *Elia*, and worked all his life as a clerk.
Lawrence, David Herbert (1885–1930) was an English miner's son whose writing provoked either idolatry or fierce criticism. His novels are concerned with the sexual motives behind his characters' actions, and he was prosecuted for obscenity. His most admired novel is *Sons and Lovers* (1913).

Leavis, Frank Raymond (1895–1978), an English lecturer and critic, wrote works important in the study of literature in the 1900s.
Li Po (701–62) was a Chinese poet who spent much of his life wandering. He wrote colourful verses about wine, women and nature.
Locke, John (1632–1704) was an English philosopher, physician and politician. His political theories, in particular his championing of liberal principals and democracy had enormous influence.

Right: Dr Samuel Johnson in the crowded anteroom of the 4th Earl of Chesterfield in 1748. He was waiting to see the earl in connection with his *Dictionary*, having sent Chesterfield the plan of it. Johnson later accused the earl of ignoring him. This picture was painted by the artist Edward Matthew Ward in the 1800s.

from ugly urban life, avoiding romantic clichés.

Of oriental poets, the works of LI PO and other Chinese writers became available to western readers through translations in the 1900s, while the philosophy of Persian writers became familiar through the Rubáiyát of OMAR KHAYYAM, translated in 1859 by Edward Fitzgerald (1809–83). In the second half of the 1900s many African poets in former European colonies began publishing verse, both in their own languages and in European ones.

Biography
Biography involves scholarship and is a matter of research and accuracy. Many important biographies never rise beyond this. But ever since the days of PLUTARCH, considered the 'father' of biography, the finest biographies have combined literary merit with scholarship. Plutarch's *Parallel Lives of Noble Greeks and Romans* drew comparisons between pairs of Greek and Roman leaders. He produced pen-pictures of the men rather than straight history. A similar anecdotal technique was used by the Renaissance artist Giorgio VASARI in his *Lives of the Painters, Sculptors and Architects* (1568), which tried to show how art had progressed.

Modern biography begins with James BOSWELL's monumental *Life of Samuel Johnson* (1791), Boswell was fortunate in that he knew his subject personally. But in his quotations from letters and conversations, he set a subsequently unequalled standard of excellence, matched by a flair for good writing.

Boswell's own *Journals*, discovered and published 150 years after his death, provide an exceptional example of an extremely frank autobiography. Autobiography at first tended to be more of a commentary on life around the subject, rather than an account of the subject's own career, or – in the 1900s – an attempt to justify the subject's actions in that career. Boswell's *Journals* and the *Diary* (1660–69) of Samuel PEPYS are personal because they were not written for publication. They are also entertaining, a quality shown in recent times in the many biographies by André MAUROIS.

History
As with biography, the writing of history is all too often a dry if scholarly narration of facts, perhaps coupled with interpretations of certain incidents in similar vein. Yet the first historian, HERODOTUS, combined an ability to present facts

---

M **Macaulay,** Thomas Babington (1800–59) was an English lawyer who had a brilliant political and literary career. His *History of England* (1848–61) is still read and so are some of his poems.

Madrigal is a lyric set to music for unaccompanied voices, mostly about love, popular in the 1500s and 1600s.

Mallarmé, Stephane (1842–98), a French poet, led the Symbolist movement in writing, relying on suggestion rather than statement. His best known poem is *L'après-midi d'un faune* (The Faun's Afternoon) (1876)

Mann, Thomas (1875–1955) has been described as Germany's greatest modern novelist. His early masterpiece *Buddenbrooks* (1901) is a family saga spanning 4 generations. It contains one of his recurrent themes: conservatism as opposed to artistic sensibilities.

Maurois, André (1885–1967) was a French novelist and biographer from Alsace whose real name was Emile Herzog. His novels are elegant and witty, but he is best remembered for his biographies and his critical studies.

Montaigne, Michel de (1533–92) was a French land-owner active in local government, who channelled his energies into his writing. His most important works are his 107 essays, a form which he created.

O **Omar Khayyám** (c. 1050–1123) was a Persian astronomer and mathematician who revised the Muslim calendar. His *Rubáiyát*, a collection of 4-line verses, became famous when it was translated into English in 1859 by Edward FitzGerald (1809–83).

Samuel Pepys, diarist

P **Paine,** Thomas (1737–1809) was an English-born political agitator who became in turn an American citizen and a French citizen, and took part in both revolutions. His pamphlets, the most famous of which is *The Rights of Man* (1792), helped to inspire people to fight for freedom.

Pepys, Samuel (1633–1703) was a government official who worked to establish the British navy. His *Diary* (1660–69), written in code, is a vivid record of his times.

Petrarch (1304–74) was an Italian poet, whose name in

with a gift for story-telling which has stood as a standard for 2,400 years. He influenced other Greek and Roman historians, among them THUCYDIDES and TACITUS, whose histories are dramatic and colourful.

This then has been the characteristic of historical writing as literature through the ages. Many famous works of history, such as the *Anglo-Saxon Chronicle*, are records of the times set down as their writers saw them. Edward GIBBONS' *The History of the Decline and Fall of the Roman Empire* (1776–88) is a great literary landmark in historical writing. It is a masterpiece of narration and interpretation, written in a stately prose that has served as an example to countless authors since. As gripping, and more brilliant, is the *History of England* (1848–61) by Thomas Babington MACAULAY. He has been criticised for 'bending' facts slightly for effect, but his history is superb as literature. The books by W. H. PRESCOTT on Spain and its empire combine literary skill with historical aptitude.

Another kind of historical writing is the first-hand account by someone who has played a part on the world stage of great events. Such works

Above: A French manuscript illustration of the late 1400s showing an episode from the *Chronicles* of Sir John Froissart. It was the Joust of St Inglevère, near Calais, in which 3 knights took on allcomers for a week.

are more history than autobiography. Winston CHURCHILL's volumes on the two World Wars are an outstanding example.

Essays and Other Works

There is a large body of other non-fiction writing which deserves, for its style and content, to rank as literature. It includes essays, philosophy, volumes of letters and books on special subjects, such as travel, music, religion, art and even science, providing that they are more than just books of reference or textbooks.

The essay is a particularly 'literary' form of writing. It is usually short and is always a personal statement by its author about its subject. As Michel de MONTAIGNE, who created the essay and its name, wrote: *'C'est moi que je peins'* – 'It is myself I portray'. Although French in origin, the essay became a particularly English language form and two of its greatest exponents were Charles LAMB in England and Ralph Waldo EMERSON in the United States.

By their very nature, essays often tend to be philosophical and many philosophers, such as VOLTAIRE, were also major essayists. The works of some philosophers, such as René DESCARTES, John LOCKE and, more recently, Jean-Paul SARTRE, have had a great influence on the ways that we think and also rank among the greatest works of literature. The revolutionary philosophy and outspoken views of Thomas PAINE were expressed with a simple vigour which immed-

Right: A bust of Herodotus, who is regarded as the first important historian. He wrote his 9 books of history in the 400s BC, basing them largely on his own travels and personal research.

Italian was Francesco Petracco. He is known chiefly for his sonnets or *Canzioniere*, almost all inspired by unrequited love for a lady called Laura.
Plutarch (c. AD 64–120) was a Greek historian, biographer and philosopher. He was chief magistrate at Chaeronea in Boetia, where he also taught, and was a priest of Apollo at Delphi.
Prescott, William Hickling (1796–1859) was an American historian who made himself a master of the history of Spain and its colonies. His finest books are

the *History of the Conquest of Mexico* (1843) followed by the *Conquest of Peru* (1847).
Proust, Marcel (1871–1922), a French novelist. *A La Recherche du Temps Perdu* (1913–17) which is a brilliant study of French society revealing deep psychological insight.

R Rhythm, in poetry, is the regular or partly regular beat of stressed and unstressed syllables.
Richardson, Samuel (1689–1761) was an English printer and publisher whose 3 novels written in his last 20

years, set a standard for the future in terms of plot and general construction.

S Sappho (born 650 BC) was a Greek poet born in Lesbos. She was the greatest woman poet of antiquity and wrote poems full of passion and feeling.
Sartre, Jean-Paul (1905–80), dramatist and novelist, a French philosopher who was the leading exponent of the existentialist movement, which held that a man's fate is controlled by his own actions not by outside forces. His views are most

clearly expressed in *L'Etre et le Néant* (Being and Nothingness, 1943).

Illustration from Walter Scott novel

Schiller, Friedrich von (1759–1805) was a German army surgeon who became a leading poet, historian and dramatist. His most famous works of poetry are *An Die Freude* (to Joy) and the great ballads which include *Lied von der Glocke* (Song of the bell) (1787–98).
Scott, Sir Walter (1771–1832) was a Scottish lawyer and romantic poet and novelist. His fast-moving epic poems include *Marmion* (1808) while his 28 novels, beginning with *Waverley* (1814), virtually created the historical novel.

iately appealed to his readers' hearts and minds.

Many literary works have been written in the form of letters – Richardson's novel *Pamela* was an early example – but some collections of real letters are notable contributions to literature. For example, those of the Marquise de Sévigné (1626–96) give a vivid picture of French society.

Books of travel form another class of literature. Perhaps the most famous is that of the Venetian merchant Marco Polo (1254–1324), who wrote an account of his journey to China and service with the Great Khan, Kublai. Not all great explorers have written well and their accounts are often of interest for their content only and in spite of their style. But when a traveller is also a born writer, he can vividly portray an alien culture in a book like *Arabia Felix*, in which the British diplomat Bertram Thomas (1892–1950) described his journey across the Rub'al Khali, the Empty Quarter of Arabia

High standards in literature and other arts is not only the result of the skill and genius of the individual artists, but also the product of people who criticise their work. Critical works are often good literature. Criticism goes back to the days of

Right: This cartoon of Thomas Paine, with its reference to his early days as a tailor, was drawn in 1791 by the English caricaturist James Gillray.

Below: The theme of Edward Gibbon's masterpiece *The Decline and Fall of the Roman Empire* is vividly illustrated by this dawn view of the Forum at Rome. It shows the ruins of the Temple of Castor and Pollux, the Arch of Titus, and in the background the shattered relic of the Colosseum.

Shelley, Percy Bysshe (1792–1822), perhaps the most romantic of all the English Romantic poets, was a libertarian and a revolutionary at heart. He used many poetical forms, over which he displayed equal mastery. His love poems show exceptional lyricism.

Shakespeare, William (1564–1616) has been called the world's greatest playwright. In addition to the dramatic poetry in his plays he also wrote over 150 SONNETS which reflect the sensual mythological imagery of the Renaissance.

Sonnet is a 14-line poem, with fixed metre and rhyme. Devised in Italy, it has been a popular medium for expressing the highest poetic thoughts.

Spenser, Edmund (c. 1552–99), an English poet, served as secretary to the Governor of Ireland. His greatest work is the unfinished *The Faerie Queene*, a series of epic adventures embodying virtues such as chastity and friendship.

Stendhal (1783–1842) was the pen-name of Marie Henri Beyle, a French soldier and diplomat. He is regarded as one of the creators of the psychological novel in French psychological novel of which the best known is *Le Rouge et Le Noir* (1831).

Stowe, Harriet Beecher (1811–96) was the daughter of a congregational minister and wife of a theological professor. Besides *Uncle Tom's Cabin* (1852), she wrote many books about life in New England.

Swift, Jonathan (1667–1745), an English author, spent more than 30 years as dean of St Patrick's Cathedral, Dublin. He was a champion of the Irish peo-ple, and in his many satires attacked some of the hypocrisies of his age.

Jonathan Swift's Gulliver's Travels

Tacitus, Publius Cornelius (c. AD 55–120), a Roman historian, spent a large part of his life in public service. He is our main source for many areas of Roman history.

Tennyson, Alfred Lord (1809–92) was one of the leading poets of Victorian England. His most notable works include *In Memoriam* (1850) in which he mourned a dead friend, and the verse novelette *Maud* (1855).

Thucydides (c. 460–400 BC) was a Greek historian who chronicled the Peloponnesian War, in which he

Below: The philosopher Plato teaching his pupils. His school stood in a grove which formerly belonged to a hero named Academus, and for this reason it was called the Academy.

ancient Greece where the outstanding figure was the philosopher ARISTOTLE. In his *Poetics* he examined the nature of tragedy and comedy. His section on comedy has been lost but his views on tragedy influenced other writers for hundreds of years.

By their critical writings, many authors have helped to advance the movements of which they themselves were a main part. For example, the cause of Romanticism was aided by critical writing from Goethe and Samuel Taylor Coleridge (1792–1834) and the cause of Impressionism in art was furthered by critical essays by Charles Baudelaire (1821–67), the French poet and critic. In more recent times some major critics have been detached from the work they criticise. An outstanding example is F. R. LEAVIS.

Literature for Children

The writing of books specifically for children is a comparatively modern development. Children once read only what interested them among adult works. They were brought up to read the Greek and Roman classics in their original tongues. They also read the medieval romances, of which the King Arthur stories, put together by Mallory, remain popular to this day. Children also took readily to such exciting stories as *The Pilgrim's Progress* (1678) and *Gulliver's Travels* (1726).

The founder of children's book publishing was the bookseller John Newbery (1713–67) who began issuing books especially for children in 1744. They included books of nursery rhymes and stories written particularly to appeal to young readers. Their authors are unknown. By the end of the 1700s, the production of books for children was booming throughout Europe.

A great body of folk stories, which are now classified as 'fairy tales', already existed. Two major collections of these, one by the brothers GRIMM and the other by Hans Christian ANDERSEN, were issued in the 1800s. Many of Andersen's tales were actually his own inventions. Since then there has been a flood of works for children, some by adult authors such as Dickens, but many by specialist writers. Among the most famous are the 'Alice' books by Lewis CARROLL. They were unusual among works in the 1800s, because they did not have a moral standpoint or a religious flavour.

played a part as a squadron leader of ships. His writing aimed at being impartial.

Tolstoy, Count Leo (1828–1910), writer, philosopher, novelist and mystic, was a master of the psychological novel. Having spent his early years in dissolute living and then playing gentleman-farmer he became an ascetic. His masterpieces are *War and Peace* (1866) and *Anna Karenina* (1877).

V Vasari, Georgio (1511–74) an Italian painter and architect, studied with Michaelangelo. He is remembered for his art history *Lives* (1550) rather than his art or architecture.

Villon, François, a French poet, led a wild life in the 1400s, becoming involved in theft, murder and other crimes. His lyrics include bawdy jests and moments of great tenderness.

Virgil (70–19 BC) was a Latin poet who was able to follow his craft because he was supported by a patron, the wealthy Gaius Maecenas. His full name was Publius Vergilius Maro. His work has been admired and imitated ever since he died.

Voltaire (1694–1778), whose real name was François Marie Arouet, was the most distinguished French writer of the Age of Reason. His keen satire brought him imprisonment and then exile, but later made him both famous and popular as a philosopher and dramatist. *Candide* (1759), his best known work, is a philosophical work disguised as a novel.

W White, Patrick (born 1912), an English-born Australian, won the Nobel Prize for literature in 1973. His novels include *The Tree of Man* (1955), *Voss* (1957) and *The Solid Mandala* (1966).

Walt Whitman, American poet

Whitman, Walt (1819–1892) was an American printer, journalist and civil servant whose poems praise democracy and his country. His poems were published under the title *Leaves of Grass* (1855), and are mostly in FREE VERSE style.

Wordsworth, William (1770–1850) was a leader of the Romantic movement in England. He believed poets should use ordinary language, rather than the pseudo-classical style favoured in the 1700s.

The Performing Arts

Jean Cooke

David Sharp

Introduction

The Performing Arts describes the most universal of all the arts, music, which has the extraordinary power to stimulate the emotions and refresh the spirit. Music takes many forms, from 'pop' songs to symphonies and it has also found expression in the theatre – in opera, musicals and dance. Theatre, variety, including the circus and the music hall, and the cinema have all declined in recent times because of competition from the radio and, especially, television. In the western world, television is, for good or ill, the most popular and potent of all the media of entertainment. Creative artists in television have a responsibility to prevent their industry being dominated by the mediocre. Instead, like artists throughout history, they are striving to find ways of artistic expression which are unique to their chosen medium.

The division between 'popular' and 'serious' music is often exaggerated. If popular music is music that stands the test of time, then Mozart and Beethoven are two of the most successful popular composers.

Music

Music is an art with many strands, and its appeal in one form or another is universal. The biggest division is probably between Western and Eastern music. For centuries the music of southern and eastern Asia, particularly that of China, India and Japan, grew up completely separately from that of Europe and countries colonized or dominated by Europe. The music of Africa also had a separate existence. Since the late 1800s, however, there has been a world-wide interchange of musical ideas.

Another important division is between music as an art form – what is often called 'serious' or 'classical' music – and popular music. Here the dividing lines are less clear. So called 'popular' music is as much an art form as any other, and a great deal of 'serious' music has a wide popular appeal. The two kinds of music borrow freely from each other, both in the area of ideas and in techniques.

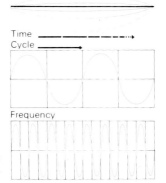

Above: Sound is produced by vibrations in the air. This diagram shows one such source of sound, a vibrating string. The distance between vibrations determines pitch, the size of the vibrations the loudness.

Above: A group of musicians, from a Flemish illuminated manuscript of the 1400s. Among the instruments are (from left to right), pipe and tabor, triangle, shawm (an early oboe), trumpet, harp, 2 lutes, more shawms, bagpipe, psaltery, cornett, and a portative organ (whose player is seated on the steps).

Left: A group of folk musicians at Bukhara, in the Soviet republic of Uzbekistan. They are playing traditional instruments.

Reference

A **Adam de la Halle** (c. 1240–c. 1306) was a French *trouvère* (minstrel). He spent some time in the service of Count Robert II of Artois. He was the first *trouvère* to write simple part-songs. His best-known work is a drama, *Le Jeu de Robin et de Marion*.

B **Bach,** Carl Philipp Emanuel (1714–88) was the second surviving son of Johann Sebastian BACH.

From 1740–67 he was official accompanist to King Frederick the Great of Prussia, a keen flute player. Then he moved to Hamburg

Johann Sebastian Bach

to coordinate the music of 5 churches.
Bach, Johann Christian (1735–82) was the youngest son of Johann Sebastian BACH. He spent the last 20 years of his life in England, so he is often called the 'English Bach'. He wrote elegant, tuneful music, much admired by Wolfgang Amadeus MOZART when he visited London as a boy.
Bach, Johann Sebastian (1685–1750) was a supremely gifted musician and composer and the most important member of a family which contained

nearly 40 musicians. He held musical appointments at Weimar, Coethen and Leipzig and gained a wide reputation as an organist, as a large part of his work involved him in writing much music for church services and festivals. His famous works include the 'Brandenburg' Concertos and the 'Goldberg Variations' both written for patrons.
Bartók, Béla (1881–1945) was a Hungarian pianist and composer. He was intensely nationalist in outlook, but his modernism was more admired outside Hungary.

For political reasons he emigrated to the United States in 1940, where he died in poverty.
Basie, Count (1904–) a pianist and band leader, became a leading player of swing during the 1930s and 1940s. His real name is William Basie. His band played with a particularly bouncing rhythm called 'jump'.
Beatles, The, an English pop group, was the leading pop group of the 1960s. They began playing in Liverpool clubs in about 1960, and achieved international

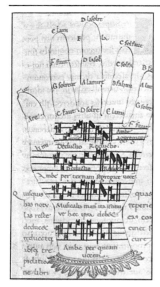

Above: The 'Guidonian Hand', a device for teaching understanding of the hexachord, or first 6 notes of the scale. It was named after Guido d'Arezzo, a Benedictine monk who lived from about 990 to 1050, and invented the musical stave which is still in use today.

Folk music

The term 'folk music' was coined in the late 1800s to describe one particular kind of popular music; the traditional music of a country. Folk music is generally defined as music that is passed on from one generation to another without being written down. Most of it is song or dance music. Originally each tune must have been composed by somebody, like any other kind of music. Because of the way it has been passed on, folk music changes gradually over a long period of time, so it can be described as a product of evolution, rather than the brainchild of one person.

In this way folk music acquires a distinctive sound for each country or racial group. For example, the folk music of England, Scotland and Ireland, although those countries are so close, is recognisably different, one from another. So are the various folk musics of other related groups, such as the Slav countries of eastern Europe.

Under the pressures of modern civilization, folk music was in danger of disappearing, but it has been recorded and written down thanks to the activities of scholars such as Cecil SHARP and Ralph VAUGHAN WILLIAMS in England, Béla BARTÓK and Zoltán KODÁLY in Hungary, among many others. Folk tunes have provided inspiration for a number of 'concert hall' composers.

Early Western music

Although we know – from remains of instruments that have been dug up by archaeologists – that music played a significant part in the lives of the ancient peoples of the Middle East, Egypt, Greece and Rome, we know next to nothing about how that music sounded. The story of Western music as we know it begins in the late Middle Ages, about a thousand years ago. It developed along two parallel lines. One was the music of the Christian Church, which had as its foundation the traditional hymns and psalms of the Jews. The other was the popular, secular music of the time, much of it the work of the wandering minstrels who moved about Europe,

Right: Musical evenings in the home were a feature of life in the educated classes up until the early 1900s. This combination of voice, violin, lute and cello in 'Musicians at Home', a painting made in 1880 by the artist Adolphe Alexandre Lestrel was typical of a much earlier period than Lestrel's own.

fame by 1964. The group broke up in 1970. Its members were: George Harrison (1943–), John Lennon (1940–80), Paul McCartney (1942–) and Ringo Starr (Richard Starkey 1940–). After 1970 they performed individually.

Beethoven, Ludwig van (1770–1827) was German born of Flemish ancestry and is considered as one of the most brilliant composers of all time. He spent most of his life in Vienna, and was making a reputation as a pianist and composer when he began to go deaf. Despite this handicap he continued to compose for the next 25 years. His piano SONATAS such as the 'Moonlight', his 9 symphonies and string quartets are important and innovative.

Berg, Alban (1885–1935) was an Austrian composer, a pupil of Arnold SCHOENBERG, whose TONE ROW system he adapted freely. His best-known works are his operas *Wozzeck* and *Lulu*. Much of his music is highly romantic and full of symbolism.

Berlioz, Hector (1803–1869), a French Romantic composer, was a master of orchestration and large-scale works. His compositions include operas, symphonies, and religious works, his most representative piece being the oratorio *La Damnation de Faust*.

Borodin, Aleksandr (1833–87), Russian composer and scientist, was a professor of chemistry at St Petersburg (Leningrad) who made time in his teaching life to write music, including 3 symphonies and the opera *Prince Igor*.

Boulanger, Nadia (1887–1979), a French music teacher, had a far-reaching influence on American music. Many distinguished US composers attended her music school near Paris in their youth.

Hector Berlioz

Boulez, Pierre (1925–), a French composer, developed the TONE ROW method of composition still further by applying it not just to PITCH but to rhythm, length of notes, and orchestration. He is a distinguished conductor and head of an institute for accoustical research in music in Paris.

Brahms, Johannes (1833–97) made his early reputation as a pianist. Robert SCHUMANN and his wife Clara helped Brahms to become established as a composer in the symphonic tradition of BEETHOVEN.

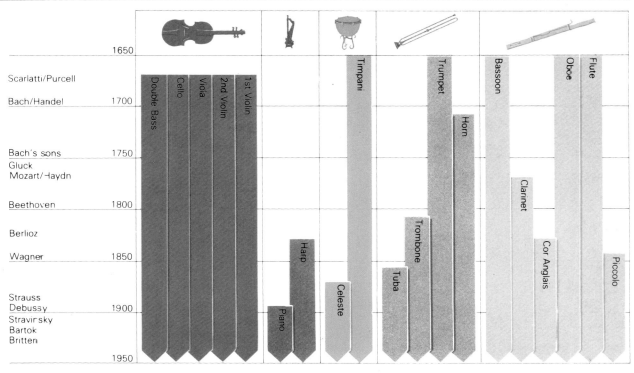

Right: The orchestra has developed slowly over the past 300 years. Some early bands consisted mainly of trumpets, timpani and woodwind, but the growth of the modern orchestra came after the establishment of the 5-part string orchestra in the late 1500s. The harpsichord was part of the orchestra until the late 1700s.

singing and playing. These minstrels were variously known as troubadours, *trouvères*, or *Minnesingers*. One of the most famous of these minstrels was ADAM DE LA HALLE, of Arras in Picardy, a musician of the 1200s some of whose compositions still survive.

The survival of music, apart from folk music, depends on its being written down. Various systems were employed, from the time of the Greeks onwards, but most of them were either aids to memory or depended on the performer interpreting the signs more or less freely. The present system of notation evolved from about the 1300s onwards. But practice varied so much that decoding exactly what was intended, even up to the end of the 1600s, is very difficult.

The backbone of Church music for a long time was plainsong, a simple, melodic way of chanting hymns, psalms, and various ritual parts of the Mass, the Church's supreme act of faith and communion. From very early times it was often accompanied by an organ. From about 1000 onwards the singers themselves took to adding a second melody line to the main plainsong tune. In this way two of the main elements of present-day music grew up: harmony and counterpoint. Harmony is two or more notes sounded together to form a chord. Counterpoint is two or more tunes sung or played together – incidentally producing harmony. It is also called polyphony, literally 'many voices'.

The two strands of music, religious and secular, merged during the 1400s and 1500s. This was because very often the same composers wrote both kinds of music – for example the Belgians Guillermus DUFAY, who sang in the choir at the Vatican, and ORLANDO DI LASSO, and the Englishman John DUNSTABLE, who spent some time in France. Another link was provided by the Reformation. Under the leadership of Martin Luther, the former monk who did more than perhaps anyone else to reform the Church he served, the ordinary worshippers were drawn more closely into the music of the services. The hymns that Luther introduced, sung not in Latin (then the universal language of the Church) but in the everyday language of the people, were musically closer to the popular songs of the time than to the plainsong tradition.

The 1500s saw the rise of the madrigal, a secular song usually on a theme of love or nature, for several unaccompanied voices. Its ancestor was the *chanson*, a French term for a song, which in turn was derived from the songs of the min-

Britten, Benjamin (1913–76), a leading British composer, founded an annual music festival at Aldeburgh, a fishing village where he lived. He was helped in this by his lifelong friend, the tenor Peter Pears. He is renowned for his operas, church music and songs.
Bruckner, Anton (1824–96) was an Austrian organist and teacher at the Vienna Conservatory. He is best known for his 9 large-scale symphonies.
Byrd, William (c. 1543–1623) was the most important English composer of the Elizabethan age. He wrote music for the Protestant church though he himself was a Roman Catholic. He and a fellow musician, Thomas Tallis (c. 1505–85), held a monopoly for printing music.

C **Cadenza** is a flowery passage for a soloist in a CONCERTO often just before the close of a movement. Originally the soloist was expected to improvise his cadenzas, but today most cadenzas are composed and learned beforehand.

Cage, John (1912–) is an American composer and teacher. He was a pioneer of using unusual sounds in music, and of *musique concrète*.

Frederick Chopin

Chopin, Frédéric (1810–49), pianist and composer, was born in Poland of a French father and a Polish mother. At the age of 20 he settled in Paris. On a base of Slavonic rhythms he built up music of exuberant fancy and romance. He wrote almost exclusively for the piano and works include mazurkas, nocturnes, waltzes, sonatas, concertos and a funeral march.
Concerto is a work for a soloist or group of soloists with orchestra. Before the time of Wolfgang Amadeus MOZART the word had a much wider and less specific meaning.
Copland, Aaron (1900–) became the leading American composer of the 1900s. He was a pupil of Nadia BOULANGER. He combined modern harmonic ideas with American folk traditions to produce a distinctive style.
Corelli, Archangelo (1653–1713), founded the modern school of violin playing. He was the first outstanding violin composer/teacher. He spent most of his life in the service of Cardinal Pietro Ottoboni in Rome.
Crescendo means gradu-

strels. Clément JANNEQUIN, Josquin DES PRÉS and Lasso were among the greatest of the *chanson* writers. The madrigal was devised in Italy, where its principal exponents were Andrea GABRIELI, Carlo GESUALDO and Claudio MONTEVERDI. From Italy the madrigal travelled to England, where a whole host of composers in and around the court of the Tudor monarchs poured out a flood of beautiful compositions. The outstanding names of this movement were probably William BYRD, Orlando GIBBONS and Thomas MORLEY.

The 1600s saw the rise of opera (*see pages 81–8*) and also the development of instrumental music. Monteverdi is often credited with the 'invention' of the orchestra of mixed instruments. Earlier instrumental groups tended to be all of a kind – a wind band, a string band, a group of brass instruments. It was at this time, too, that the violin and its fellows (viola, cello, double-bass) began to rise to prominence. The strings for serious music in the 1500s and for much of the 1600s were the viols, the reedy-sounding, fretted, bowed instruments played on the knee. The violin was a more vulgar instrument, used for popular music. But gradually its brilliance and agility led it to take over from the viols, which had largely gone out of use by the 1700s.

Many composers, such as Henry PURCELL,

wrote for both kinds of instruments. The violin itself received a boost from a group of virtuoso players and composers in the land of its birth, Italy. Outstanding among them was Archangelo CORELLI, often described as the 'father' of modern violin playing.

Western music: Baroque and Classical

Two men, born the same year, dominate the first half of the 1700s. They belong to a style we now call 'Baroque'. The music of Johann Sebastian BACH marks the high point of polyphonic composition, while that of George Frideric HANDEL looks forward to the next generation of composers. Bach wrote almost exclusively for the Protestant Church, while Handel wrote many operas and oratorios – which might be described as religious operas with no scenery or action. Both were outstanding keyboard players, particularly of the organ. Bach also pioneered what is known as 'equal temperament' – that is, tuning keyboard instruments so that all keys are equally in tune. If an instrument is tuned 'perfectly', as most were before Bach's time, some keys are in tune and others badly out.

The 1700s saw some of the most dramatic developments in instrumental music of all kinds. One of J. S. Bach's sons, Carl Philipp Emanuel BACH, helped to lead the way with the develop-

ment of SONATA FORM. This is a type of construction which composers use to shape certain sections of their larger compositions to give the maximum variety and interest. Up to the 1700s instrumental music was remarkably flexible in the way it could be performed. Parts for some instruments could be omitted or doubled, and the choice of instruments was decided partly by what was available: for example, the same part might be played by a violin, an oboe or a flute.

During the 1700s composers began to write more precisely for instruments, and most of the types of composition we know today – SONATA, SYMPHONY, OVERTURE, STRING QUARTET, for example – took their present shape. Many of these terms had very imprecise meanings until that time. C. P. E. Bach and his younger brother Johann Christian BACH helped to give the symphony its modern form. An even greater influence was that of the orchestra at Mannheim, in Germany. Its director, Johann STAMITZ, trained it until it was far superior to any other of the time. Stamitz also introduced the 'Mannheim sound' – the use of CRESCENDO and decrescendo, instead of alternate loud and soft playing – and incorporated clarinets as regular members of the orchestra.

Stamitz wrote 45 symphonies, but the greatest output came from Franz Joseph HAYDN, who wrote 104, and probably did more than any other composer to bring the symphony to perfection. Some of his early symphonies are highly inventive but some were routine affairs, composed as part of Haydn's duties as a court musician. Then Haydn became a close friend of the much younger Wolfgang Amadeus MOZART, who wrote more than 40 symphonies. The two men learned a great deal from one another. Mozart's last three symphonies, written in as many months in the summer of 1788, were incomparably finer than anything either man had written previously. Haydn then wrote 12 more symphonies, finally establishing the grandeur of the form.

Early pieces in the 1700s for string orchestra and those for string quartet (two violins, viola and cello) were very similar in style. Some of Haydn's first quartets could be equally well performed as orchestral works. Over nearly 50 years Haydn wrote about 30 string quartets, and perfected the form. Again, he and Mozart learned from each other.

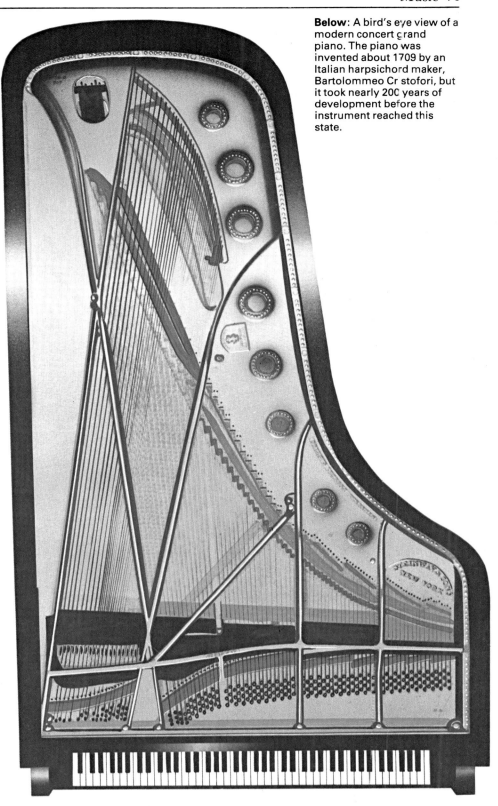

Below: A bird's eye view of a modern concert grand piano. The piano was invented about 1709 by an Italian harpsichord maker, Bartolommeo Cristofori, but it took nearly 200 years of development before the instrument reached this state.

F Foster, Stephen (1826–64), was America's leading composer of popular songs in the 1800s. His 175 songs included such evergreen favourites as *The Old Folks at Home* and *Jeanie With the Light Brown Hair*.

G Gabrieli, Andrea (c. 1510–86), was a Venetian organist and composer. He wrote many madrigals and part songs. Among his pupils was his nephew Giovanni Gabrieli (1557–1612), who wrote some of the first works especially for instruments rather than voices.

Gershwin, George (1898–1937), an American jazz pianist, wrote a jazz concerto for piano and orchestra in 1924, *Rhapsody in Blue*. It linked jazz and 'serious' music. He also wrote the opera *Porgy and Bess* and many musicals.

Gesualdo Carlo (c. 1560–1613) was Prince of Venosa. He wrote 6 sets of madrigals whose harmonies and emotional intensity were far in advance of their time.

Gibbons, Orlando (1583–

1625), an English organist in royal service, was the finest keyboard player of his day. His works include madrigals,

Dizzy Gillespie, jazz musician

church anthems, string music and pieces for keyboard instruments.

Gillespie, Dizzy (1917–), an American jazz trumpeter, helped to start the bebop movement in jazz. He is a composer, and has led several big bands. His real name is John Birks Gillespie.

Glinka, Mikhail (1804–57), a Russian civil servant, gave up his post to devote his life to music. He is regarded as the first outstanding Russian composer and his *Russlan and Ludmilla* pioneered the style of the Russian national school of composers.

G Grainger, Percy (1882–1961), an Australian pianist and composer, made extensive use of folk music in his compositions. He was a highly extrovert person, known on occasions to vault over the piano before starting a concert recital.

H Haley, Bill (1925–81) began his musical career with a form of hillbilly music – a version of Country and Western. He formed his group, The Comets, in 1952 and introduced rock with the record *Rock Around the Clock*.

important in musical history as the growth of Romanticism in art and literature. Up to the end of the 1700s musicians were largely in the pay of rich and important people, and were treated as servants. Even Mozart describes eating at table with his employer's valets, who were more highly regarded than he was, and wearing livery, the household uniform. Beethoven contended that an artist was the equal of anybody.

Beethoven occupies a unique position in music, because he was much more than just a Classical or a Romantic composer. His later music, especially his last few string quartets, explores complexities of musical emotional thought which challenge the listener. He was followed closely by Franz SCHUBERT, whose early death came before his full potential had shown itself. Schubert was a master of melody, and his 600 songs are among the finest ever composed.

True Romanticism is often said to have begun with Beethoven's contemporary Carl Maria von WEBER, and it was carried on by – among others

The work of Haydn, Mozart and their contemporaries is often referred to as the 'Classical' period of music. Much of it is light and elegant, which has earned it the name of *style galant* (polite style). However, in poetry and other arts a new, more subjective style was evolving, which is known as Romantic. This outwardly emotional approach to art was already apparent in the later works of Haydn and Mozart, and it was developed largely by the work of one man: Ludwig van BEETHOVEN. Beethoven may be thought of as the last great Classical composer or the first great Romantic.

At this time, too, the CONCERTO and the sonata were developed to the forms we know today. The concerto as an opportunity for a solo instrument to play with (or against) an orchestra evolved in the Baroque period, but really came into its own as a means of displaying the talents of the soloist with the concertos of Mozart and Beethoven. For the same reason the CADENZA came into being. The keyboard sonata settled into the same general form as the symphony, and with the development of the piano the less expressive harpsichord dropped out of favour.

Above: *A Schubert Evening at the House of Josef von Spaun* – an unfinished painting by Moritz von Schwind, who was a close friend of the composer.

Right: The statue of Ludwig van Beethoven in Vienna by the sculptor Denkmal. Although Vienna was not Beethoven's native city, it was where he spent his most productive years.

Western music: the Romantics

Beethoven led the way in a development as

– Hector BERLIOZ, Felix MENDELSSOHN, Frédéric CHOPIN, Robert SCHUMANN, Franz LISZT and Richard WAGNER. These composers were all strongly influenced by the sister arts of literature and painting, and also by the spirit of nationalism, then spreading rapidly over Europe. The nationalistic feeling was probably strongest in Chopin, sorrowing over the fact that his beloved Poland was partitioned between Prussia and Russia; in Liszt, anxious to stress the musical heritage of Hungary by using its folk tunes in his works; and in Wagner, absorbed in the ancient legends of Germany.

Traditionally many composers have also been noted as performers. For example, Bach was best known in his own time as an organist, while Mozart and Beethoven were outstanding as pianists. But in the 1800s a new phenomenon arose; the virtuoso composer, a player of exceptional brilliance who wrote largely for his own instrument, extending the techniques of performance. Chopin and Liszt were dazzling pianists, while

Niccolò PAGANINI raised the standards of violin-playing to heights other players had not dreamed of. Europe was full of such virtuosos, touring from one city to another and usually playing only their own works, but most of them are largely forgotten except by students who play their pieces for study and technical exercise.

The 1800s saw the development of 'serious' music in Russia. Russia had a rich heritage of folk and church music, but relied on music from other lands, particularly Italy, for the entertainment of the court and aristocracy. Strong nationalist feelings were produced as a result of the French invasion of Russia during the Napoleonic Wars. An independent Russian line of music was founded in 1836 by Mikhail GLINKA, with his opera *Ivan Susanin* (English title, *A Life for the Tsar*). Its Russian theme, with melodies based on folk tunes, caught the imagination of other Russian musicians. It is a remarkable fact that the pioneers of this new Russian music – Glinka, Aleksandr BORODIN, Modeste MOUSSORG-

Below right: The general layout of a modern symphony orchestra. This is the most usual arrangement, though some conductors prefer slightly different seating plans.

Right: The horn is one of the most beautiful of the brass instruments, though because of its tone quality it is often grouped musically with the woodwind.

Horn

Oboe

Left: The oboe is a woodwind instrument in which the air is made to vibrate by a double reed held in the player's mouth.

Harp

Percussion

Piano

Harp

Horns

Clarinets

Flutes

Trumpets

Bassoons

Oboes

Trombones

Tubas

Second violins

Violas

Double basses

First violins

Cellos

Cello

Left: The harp today is an elaborate instrument, largely the work of a French maker, Sébastien Erard, in the early 1800s. He invented the pedal system so the harp can play in any key.

Percussion / Percussion strings

Brass

Wind

Strings

Right: The cello is the bass member of the violin family. In the orchestra it is usually reinforced by the double-bass, which sounds even lower.

---

one ballet. His music became popular again in the 1970s.

K Kodály, Zoltán (1882–1967), a Hungarian composer, was an authority on his country's folk music, and helped to develop a purely Hungarian style of music. His best-known work is the opera *Háry János*, and the orchestral suite he compiled from it.

L Liszt, Franz (1811–86) was a Hungarian pianist who dominated European music in the mid-1800s. He

gave up a career in the Church to become a virtuoso pianist, but took minor orders late in life. He was a

Franz Liszt

prolific composer, especially for the piano, and explored new ideas of HARMONY. He was generous with money and influential in helping other musicians.

M Mahler, Gustav (1860–1911), a Czech-Austrian composer, is remembered for his 9 large-scale SYMPHONIES. No. 8 is called 'The Symphony of a Thousand' because it requires 1,004 singers and players. He is the bridge between the late Romantic style and the new-style works of SCHOENBERG.

Mendelssohn(-Bartholdy), Felix (1809–47) was a German composer, a member of a wealthy Jewish-Christian family. At the age of 20 he began a revival of the music of Johann Sebastian BACH, which had become neglected. His popularity as a pianist and conductor led to a series of concert tours all over Europe, which tired him and hastened his early death. His best-known works include his violin CONCERTO and the Symphony in C Minor.
Messiaen, Olivier (1908–), a French com-

poser and teacher, experimented with unusual sounds in his works, and also with unusual RHYTHMS involving intricate mathematical systems. He has been an organist in Paris since he was 23, and many of his most important works are for the organ.
Milhaud, Darius (1892–1974) was one of the group of French composers called *Les Six*. He lived in the United States from 1940 to 1947. He is best known for his stage works, including ballets such as *La Création du Monde* and operas.

SKY, Nikolai RIMSKY-KORSAKOV and others were amateurs for whom music was either a hobby or who later changed to it as a profession. This Russian music was to have a great influence on composers in Western Europe.

A great deal of the story of Russian music in the 1800s is that of opera (*see pages 81–8*). However, one of the mightiest of Russian composers, Petr TCHAIKOVSKY, is better known as one of the five symphonists who dominated the second half of the century. The others were Johannes BRAHMS, whom some people hailed as Beethoven's natural successor, the Czech Antonín DVOŘÁK, and two Austrians, Anton BRUCKNER and Gustav MAHLER.

An enormous influence on music of all kinds was exerted by Wagner. His own music is almost all opera (*see page 81*), but his constant search for a new richness of sound led him to a sensuous, chromatic HARMONY that sounded very strange to most of his contemporaries. In this he was following a path taken by Liszt in his later works. The musical world became divided into the supporters of Wagner and those of the more conventional Brahms. Wagner's natural successor was Richard STRAUSS, who wrote SYMPHONIC POEMS rather than symphonies, orchestral pieces with a

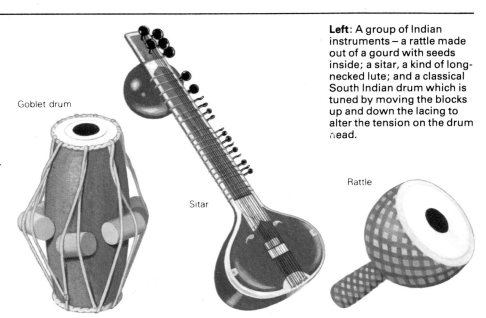

Goblet drum

Sitar

Rattle

Left: A group of Indian instruments – a rattle made out of a gourd with seeds inside; a sitar, a kind of long-necked lute; and a classical South Indian drum which is tuned by moving the blocks up and down the lacing to alter the tension on the drum head.

Below: A scene from Chinese court life during the T'ang Dynasty (AD 618–907). It was painted on silk, and shows 5 girls with either whistle-type or side-blown flutes.

programme which tried to tell a story in purely musical ways. But the sheer lushness of this kind of music led to a reaction, which was led by three Frenchmen: Claude DEBUSSY, Maurice RAVEL and Eric SATIE.

Asian and African music

The music of Asia is varied, but in general it is founded on melody and rhythm only, the rhythm often being very complex. Chinese and Japanese music uses SCALES similar to those in the West, based on a selection from 12 notes of different PITCH. Often PENTATONIC SCALES are used. The music of India, on the other hand, is derived from 24 notes of different pitch, using quartertones. These notes lie between the smallest INTERVALS in general use in the West, the semitones.

Improvisation, that is, making the music up as it is performed, plays a much larger part in Asian music than it does in the West. For this reason the groups of musicians are often comparatively small. By contrast, the music of Indonesia is centred on the gamelan orchestra, a large body of players performing on a few viols and flutes, backed by a big force of gongs, drums, rattles and similar instruments. The gamelan orchestra was first heard in Europe in 1889, when one performed at the Paris Exhibition. It so impressed Debussy that he at once began to write music influenced by it, particularly in its use of the

---

Monteverdi, Claudio (1567–1643) was an Italian composer who spent most of his life in charge of the music at St Mark's Cathedral in Venice. At 65 he became a priest. For St Mark's he wrote a great deal of church music, including the magnificent *Mass* and *Vespers of the Virgin*, and he was also one of the first composers of operas. He was a master of vocal and instrumental writing.

Morley, Thomas (c. 1557–c. 1603) was an English organist, and court musician to Queen Elizabeth I. He is renowned for his lute songs and for his textbook, *A Plaine and Easie Introduction to Practicall Musicke*.

Morton, Jelly Roll

Claudio Monteverdi

(1885–1941) was a leading jazz pianist, who claimed that he discovered jazz. He was born Ferdinand La Menthe in New Orleans. Morton was a leading jazz figure in the 1920s, but then went into eclipse. He made a brief comeback shortly before he died.

Mozart, Wolfgang Amadeus (1756–1791) was one of the most talented musicians of all time. He was a child prodigy, and his father took him and his sister on a series of tours of Europe. As an adult he returned to his native city, Salzburg, but left as soon as he could to live in Vienna. He was nearly always in debt. Mozart wrote nearly 600 compositions including operas such as *The Magic Flute* and *Don Giovanni*, 41 symphonies and many quartets. He wrote rapidly, but his work is polished to perfection.

Moussorgsky, Modeste (1839–81), was a Russian soldier who gave up his career to write music. Then he lost his private fortune and had to become a civil servant. He wrote several operas, the greatest of which was *Boris Godunov* and a piano suite *Pictures from an Exhibition*. He died partly as a result of excessive drinking.

Orlando di Lasso (c. 1532–94) was a Flemish composer who worked first in Rome and then in Munich. He wrote religious works and bawdy drinking songs with equal enthusiasm.

Overture is a piece of music intended to be played at the beginning of a stage work, such as an opera. Concert overtures are short orchestral works, which may be

pentatonic scale. Through Debussy other musicians also came under the spell of Asian music. Indian music had relatively little influence in the West until the 1950s and 1960s, when large numbers of Indian and Pakistani people emigrated to Britain, taking their music with them. Even then, Indian music had a wider influence on 'popular' music than on 'serious' music.

Geographers speak of two Africas, divided by the Sahara Desert. The separation is more than physical, but amounts to two very different cultures. The music of northern Africa is that of the Arab and Berber peoples who live there. It is close to the music of Asia, where it originated, and is allied through centuries of borrowing and lending with that of Europe – particularly Spain, which was under Moorish rule for hundreds of years.

Africa south of the Sahara is Black Africa; its peoples are largely Negroid in origin, and they have their own music. This music has simple tunes and only the simplest form of harmony. Most African music has a special purpose: songs to which to work or march to war, or for religious ceremonies. Its chief feature is RHYTHM. African rhythm is more complicated than the traditional rhythms of the West, and is very exciting. The beats are hammered out by drums of various kinds, which form the basis of all African music. Other instruments used include xylophones, flutes, horns, bells and rattles. Generally the music is very closely linked to dancing, and dances are used to celebrate all sorts of occasions, including birth, marriage and death.

In the past 50 years Western music has had an influence on traditional African music. The musicians have taken Western instruments, such as piano-accordions and guitars, and adapted them to their own use. But so far this is nothing to the influence that African music has had on the West. It came about because people from West and Central Africa were taken across to America in their thousands as slaves. They took their musical traditions with them, and over the years blended them with those of their White owners. For example, from a mixture of work songs and the Christian religion came the spiritual, a typically African religious song. Most spirituals preserve the African call-and-response kind of song, where the leader sings a phrase to which the rest of the singers then answer. Slaves

Left: Drummers of the Tutsi people of Rwanda playing to accompany dancing.

Below: A group of typical African instruments. The sansa, sometimes called a 'Kaffir piano' from Southern Africa, is made of metal tongues which are plucked with the fingers. The ntenga drum is from Uganda and the rattle is made from a gourd with millet stalks attached.

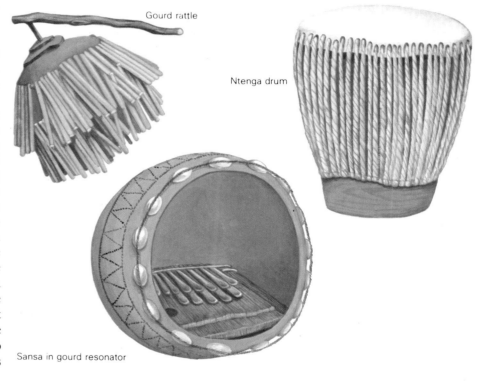

Gourd rattle

Ntenga drum

Sansa in gourd resonator

played at any point in a concert.

Paganini, Niccolò (1782–1840) was the greatest violin virtuoso of his time; he extended the technique of his instrument more than any other player. He spent his life in love affairs, gambling and concert tours. He wrote a few works designed to show off his dazzling skill.

Pentatonic scales are SCALES consisting of only five notes. The best known is the one you can play on the black notes of a piano.

Pitch is the relative deepness or shrillness of a note. Notes are produced by vibrations in the air. A note which has twice as many

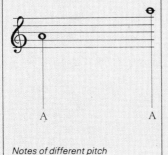

Notes of different pitch

vibrations as another sounds the same but higher. This INTERVAL is called an octave.

Poulenc, Francis (1899–1963) was an outstanding pianist who formed one of the group of French composers known as *Les Six*. He wrote much music, but is best known for his considerable output of songs.

Presley, Elvis (1935–77) was one of the world's most popular rock singers, and did much to make rock an international success. Millions of young people saw

him as a symbol of their revolt against the older generation.

Prokofiev, Sergei (1891–1953) was one of the most important Russian composers of the early 1900s. Unfortunately his early reputation as a musical 'rebel' led the Soviet authorities to regard him with suspicion, and he was censured for writing 'anti-democratic music'. His most popular work is the symphonic tale *Peter and the Wolf*.

Purcell, Henry (1659–95) was one of the finest com-

posers of his day, and probably England's leading composer. He was a musician at the court of England's Stuart monarchs, and wrote much music for special occasions such as royal birthdays. He also wrote music for the theatre, opera, vocal and choral works.

Ravel, Maurice (1875–1937), a French composer, wrote music of very clear texture and with much attention to detail. It includes 2 operas, a ballet, and orchestral and chamber music, but the work which

ORIGINAL NEW ORLEANS JAZZ BAND

Above: The 'Original New Orleans Jazz Band', an early white jazz group which included Jimmy Durante on piano.

Below: This flow chart gives some idea of the way in which jazz developed, and the many influences which helped to make it.

African ritual music

Slavery

Christian church music — European hymns

Work songs — Entertainers: cakewalk — Creole influence

Freed slaves: lyrics

Military bands — Blues — European music

Jazz

St Louis: fast tempo — New York jazz — Scott Joplin: rags

Big bands — Be-Bop — Modern jazz

used this kind of song when working in the cotton plantations or laying new railroads. Solitary workers used the holler, a freely-improvised solo song.

In the late 1800s two forms of music evolved in the United States: the blues and jazz. Blues is basically a holler with an instrumental accompaniment. Jazz has off-beat, African-style rhythms, a comparatively simple harmonic pattern, and a great deal of vitality. The players have scope to improvise. Jazz evolved gradually, but it was preceded by ragtime, a form of off-beat piano playing pioneered by Scott JOPLIN. Jazz itself arose in cities where Blacks were predominant, especially in New Orleans. Jelly Roll MORTON claimed to have invented jazz there in 1902, but it was already well under way by then. It started to spread when a band of White musicians, the Original Dixieland Jazz Band, took it up and made a record in 1918. It spread and developed rapidly during the 1920s and 1930s, under the inspired leadership of such musicians as Duke ELLINGTON, Dizzy GILLESPIE and Count BASIE. In the 1930s it became 'swing', with a more relaxed beat and bigger, more sophisticated bands. After passing through the boogie-woogie phase, a style of piano playing characterized by a strong dotted rhythm in the bass, followed by the instrumental complexities of bebop in the 1940s, it is now at the stage known as 'modern jazz'.

Some jazz musicians, especially George GERSHWIN, used jazz techniques to create 'serious' musical forms. At the same time 'serious' composers borrowed ideas from jazz, among them Aaron COPLAND, Igor STRAVINSKY and Paul HINDEMITH. Even Debussy and Ravel were influenced by rag-time, and this before the jazz age really got under way.

The 'Age of Modernism'

Musically speaking, the 1900s have been called 'The Age of Modernism' and also 'the Age of Experiment'. Musicians everywhere were looking for new sounds, new harmonies, even a new meaning for music. Some of their experiments were successful; some caused a storm. The most famous of these storms occurred in 1913, when the first performance of the ballet *Le Sacre du Printemps* (The Rite of Spring) was given at a new theatre in Paris. The music, strange and barbaric, was by Stravinsky. Protests at the music

brought him international fame was the piano piece *Pavane for a Dead Infanta* [Spanish princess].
Rhythm is the grouping of musical notes into regular or irregular beats. One form of irregular rhythm is called *dotted rhythm*; in it some notes are lengthened and others shortened. Dotted rhythm is characteristic of jazz.
Rimsky-Korsakov, Nikolai (1844–1908) was one of his country's leading composers. A teacher known for his expertise as an orchestrator, he did a lot to help his less

fortunate colleagues, including Aleksandr BORODIN and Modeste MOUSSORGSKY, whose work he rescued from oblivion.

S **Satie,** Eric (1866–1925) was a French composer whose work had considerable influence on his contemporaries such as those forming *Les Six*. His first name is often spelled *Erik*. He gave his compositions strange names such as *Pear-shaped Pieces*, but this whimsicality hid a true vein of originality.
Scales are systems of notes

in order of PITCH, usually with one note regarded as the keynote, or 'home'. The *chromatic scale* consists of

A musical scale, C major

12 notes each a semitone apart (the smallest INTERVAL in general use in the West). Most other scales are combi-

nations of semitones and tones, with 8 notes of different pitch.
Schoenberg, Arnold (1874–1951), an Austrian composer, led the breakaway from conventional music and TONALITY in the early 1900s. He developed the new method of composition based on the TONE ROW. In 1933 he emigrated to the United States to escape persecution by the Nazis.
Schubert, Franz (1797–1828), a Viennese composer, was one of the finest writers of songs. In his short life he wrote over 900 pieces, and

and at the equally barbaric dances which accompanied it led to a free fight in the audience, which almost completely drowned the sound of the orchestra. A year later the same music was performed at a concert: it was immediately popular, and has remained so ever since.

While Debussy, Satie and the Russian-born Stravinsky were experimenting in Paris, a new group of musicians was working away in Vienna. The Austrian capital had seen an earlier, important group of musicians – Mozart, Beethoven and Schubert – who collectively were often referred to as 'the Viennese School'. Now came 'the Second Viennese School', consisting of Arnold SCHOENBERG and his pupils Alban BERG and Anton WEBERN. Schoenberg's early music owed a great deal to Wagner and Strauss, with rich harmonies and flowing melodies. But he came to the conclusion that such music was 'decadent', too overdone, too self-conscious. In an effort to break away from it he evolved a new system of composition. Until then all music had a sense of tonality – that is, the listener expected it to end on a certain chord, regarded as 'home'. Schoenberg did away with tonality, and treated all the 12 notes of the scale as equal. This left him without any framework on which to build his music, so he evolved a new kind of framework, called a TONE ROW. His music was noisy, angular, complicated and difficult both to play and to listen to. Schoenberg followed his new rules very strictly, but his pupils, particularly Berg and Webern, used them much more flexibly, and their music has more immediate appeal.

During the 1920s and 1930s a number of composers wrote music that made use of many of the 'new' techniques, but preserved much of the old. Folk music was the inspiration for many, particularly the Hungarians Bartók and Kodály, and the English composer Vaughan Williams. In England, which had been without a major writer of music for almost two centuries, the leading composer was Edward ELGAR, who carried on the tradition of Brahms. Gustav Holst (1874–1934) and William Walton (1902–) were more revolutionary but had an immediate appeal to audiences. So had much of the work of Benjamin BRITTEN, although he used 'modern' techniques when it suited him. His contemporary Michael TIPPETT was a leader in the movement that used music to express something of the horror people

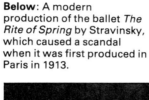

Below: A modern production of the ballet *The Rite of Spring* by Stravinsky, which caused a scandal when it was first produced in Paris in 1913.

felt at the death and suffering caused by two world wars.

American music came to the fore in the 1900s. The United States was a refuge for many European musicians who were forced to flee for political reasons, such as Schoenberg, Hindemith, Bartók, Stravinsky and Kurt WEILL. Many native-born Americans, studied in Paris under an inspired teacher, Nadia BOULANGER. Copland was outstanding and did much to create a truly 'American' style. Others were Roger Sessions (1896–) and Roy Harris (1898–1979). Their fellow-countryman Charles IVES wrote music of an astounding complexity which is only now gaining wide recognition.

Russian music, following the establishment of Communist rule, took its own path, political pressure being brought to bear on composers whose music was too unconventional. Under these handicaps such men as Dmitri SHOSTAKOVICH and Sergei PROKOFIEV produced outstanding works. In France, a group of musicians known as *Les Six* dominated the 1920s and 1930s, though only three – Darius MILHAUD, Arthur HONEGGER and Francis POULENC – wrote really memorable works. Several other countries each produced a few outstanding musicians, such as Finland's Jean SIBELIUS, who like Wagner used his country's folk tales as the themes for his pieces, and Heitor VILLA-LOBOS of Brazil, who wrote music also based on his country's folklore.

---

the tunefulness of his work has made him a popular composer.

Schumann, Robert (1810–56), a German composer, spent a large part of his life as a musical journalist, and encouraged new and original work by others. He was helped by his wife Clara, a brilliant pianist, and their friend Johannes BRAHMS. He was primarily a composer for the piano. He suffered from mental instability and died in an asylum.

Sharp, Cecil (1859–1924) was an English music teacher who devoted his life

Jean Sibelius

to discovering and recording English folk music, then in danger of being forgotten. He also found many old tunes in America, where they had been kept alive by the descendants of English settlers.

Shostakovich, Dmitri (1906–75) was a Russian composer who showed great skill in reconciling his own originality with the more sedate ideas of his country's Communist rulers. His 7th and 10th symphonies and his violin concerto gained him fame outside Russia.

Sibelius, Jean (1865–1957) was Finland's greatest composer. His finest works include his 7 symphonies. He was a fierce nationalist and based much of his music on Finnish sagas.

Sonata is a composition for one or 2 instruments, usually in several movements (sections). The word has changed several times and many early sonatas are different in form and scope from those of today.

Sonata form is a way of writing a movement (section) of a piece of music. Very basically it consists of a

statement of 2 themes or ideas, a development section in which the composer 'plays around' with the 2 ideas and probably some fresh material, and then a recapitulation of the themes.

Stamitz, Johann (1717–57) was a German composer who revolutionized orchestral writing and playing, and helped to create the modern SYMPHONY and to introduce the clarinet as an orchestral instrument. His own compositions, which include 74 symphonies, are largely neglected.

Stockhausen, Karlheinz

Above: A Moog synthesiser, an electronic instrument for composing music by translating ideas into electronically produced synthetic sound. It can make many different types of sound.

The electronic age

The new sounds created by composers in the early part of the 1900s were made with conventional instruments. For many composers, to whom TIMBRE was more important than melody, harmony or TONALITY, such instruments were not adequate to express their music. Satie and others experimented with typewriters and car horns in their compositions. Then inventors began producing instruments in which electricity was used to produce the sound. One of the most successful was the Ondes Martenot, invented in 1928, which was played with a piano-like keyboard. Several composers, especially Olivier MESSIAEN and Milhaud, wrote for it.

These early electrical devices could be played like conventional instruments to produce sounds of a definite pitch. Composers then became anxious to break away from this notion completely. Among the leaders of this movement was Edgar VARÈSE. He sought for sound generators which would give him a completely new way of constructing audible patterns. Using conventional instruments, he juxtaposed blocks of contrasting percussive sounds of no definite pitch to 'build up' his compositions. It was not until near the

end of his life that the electronic instruments he had dreamed of were available.

Three ways of producing electronic music came into being in the years following the end of World War II (1945). *Musique concrète* was devised in Paris. It made use of natural sounds which were then altered by electronic equipment such as tape recorders. Pierre BOULEZ was one of the pioneers of this technique. Tape music was produced at electronic studios in New York City, where one compilation was named *Music for magnetic tape*. One of the practitioners of this process was John CAGE, who had already made a name with his music for 'prepared piano'. Cage prepared his piano by inserting pieces of wood, metal and other substances between the strings so that some of them produced unfamiliar buzzes and twangs. The *Elektronische Musik* produced in Cologne by Karlheinz STOCKHAUSEN and others relied on generating basic sounds by electronic means, and then modifying them electronically to produce the desired quality.

The ultimate in electronic musical wizardry so far is the synthesizer, which manipulates sounds by electronic means in infinite variety. It can be coupled to a computer, when it can produce any

Right: A small electronic studio used for composition. Its basis is a synthesiser, (**13**), and sound is also originated through microphones (**1**), tape decks (**3, 5**) and a record player (**4**). All these signals pass through mixers (**2, 6**), a filter (**11**) and reverberation units (**12**) to a patch board (**7**), where they are collected and fed by way of an amplifier (**8**) to twin loudspeakers (**9, 10**).

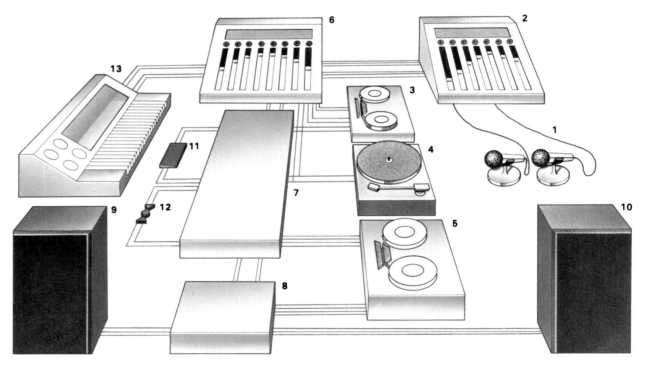

(1928–), a German composer, is one of the leaders in writing electronic music, for which he uses the full resources of a modern sound studio. His work has helped to create a whole new world of sounds.
Strauss, Richard (1864–1949) was the last great German Romantic composer. He was influenced by the work of Richard WAGNER, and was one of a group of composers who concentrated on what they called 'expressionism'. He was known as a composer of opera and his works include

Salome and *Der Rosenkavalier*.
Stravinsky Igor (1882–1971) was a Russian composer who became an American citizen in 1945. His early works aroused fierce controversy because of his bold and unconventional use of HARMONY and RHYTHM. He wrote a great deal of music for the ballet and theatre, and had an enormous influence on the next generation of musicians.
String quartet is a composition for 4 stringed instruments – 2 violins, viola and cello – which may be

The Amadeus string quartet

described as a SONATA for this particular combination.
Symphonic poems are large-scale orchestral works which attempt to tell a story in music. They are sometimes called *tone-poems*.
Symphony is a SONATA for orchestra. It is usually a large-scale work with a serious aim, in 4 movements (sections).

T Tchaikovsky, Petr Ilyich (1840–93), a Russian composer, combined a Romantic turn of mind with beautiful melodies and a mastery of orchestration. His

kind of music that the computer tells it to. It can imitate a wide variety of instruments, including the standard orchestral ones such as violins. Such an instrument would have appealed very strongly to Varèse, who felt that the composer should communicate directly with the listener, without the aid of a performer.

Composers have also experimented with music in which the performer is given some freedom of choice in what he does. Some composers ask the performer to throw dice to decide in what order to perform a group of pieces. Others indicate that the performer can begin anywhere in the piece, providing he goes right through it, back to his starting point. Many composers combine live performance on conventional instruments with pre-recorded music on tape. Such music has up until now a fairly limited audience, though its performers claim that it is exciting and rewarding to play.

The age of pop

Popular music has always existed side by side with 'serious' music. Folk music was an earlier form of it. In the 1800s songs from the music halls (see pages 113–16) and light, sentimental ballads formed the basis of popular music of the time, together with songs from musical comedies and other shows. Before the days of radio, television and recordings, people made their own music at home, and composers such as Stephen FOSTER wrote ballads which sold – as sheet music – in their thousands. This trend continued into the early 1900s, with, from the 1930s onwards, songs from films outstripping all others in popularity, and gramophone records selling as well as sheet music.

The popular music of today has several ancestors. One of them is country and western music, which is a form of folk music that grew up among the White peoples of the southern United States. It was based partly on the folk music of the British Isles which had been taken to America by settlers and there preserved, and partly on religion, which gave it a strong moral flavour. Country music, as it is generally known, reflected the everyday life of pioneering people, riding the range, homesteading, or building railways.

The growth of radio in the 1920s led to regular broadcasts of country music, which gained in this

Above: A performance of Benjamin Britten's Church drama *The Burning Fiery Furnace*, written in 1966. It is an example of the more 'traditional' music which co-exists with the electronic music of the mid-1900s.

way a much wider audience. The most important of these radio programmes, which began in 1925 and is still broadcast from Tennessee, is called 'Grand Old Opry'. The growth of radio and, after World War II, the development of the light, cheap long-playing record, did a great deal to aid the development of modern 'pop', as popular music soon became known.

Swing, the 1930s development of jazz, was popular as music for dancing because of its strong catchy beat. In the 1950s the fusion of swing with the blues and country and western music produced rock 'n' roll, later shortened to rock. The main instrument for rock was the newly-developed electric guitar. Small groups sprang up, producing music with a strong, dominating beat. The first famous rock band was Bill HALEY and his Comets, and Elvis PRESLEY led the way as a rock singer.

Rock music started in the United States where as with country music, regular broadcasts of records made it popular. It soon spread to Europe, where small groups performed to enthusiastic audiences of teenagers. In England

---

Petr Tchaikovsky

most popular works are the 4th, 5th and 6th (*Pathétique*), symphonies and the ballets *Swan Lake* and *Nutcracker*.
Timbre is the quality and character of an instrument's sound. For example, a trumpet has a different timbre from a violin.
Tippett, Michael (1905–) is one of England's leading composers, and one of the most original. He writes the texts for most of his operas and vocal works. He combines traditional melodic lines with modern harmony and sound quality. He was knighted in 1966.

Tonality is the feeling that a piece of music belongs to a particular key – that is, harmonically, it has a sense of 'home', on which it ends. Atonality, largely a phenomenon of the 1900s, is having no established home key.
Tone row, also called note row, is a system of composition devised by Arnold Schoenberg in about 1924. In this system all 12 notes of the chromatic scale are treated as equals, and are arranged in a fixed order to serve as the 'theme' of the work.

Varèse, Edgar (1885–1965) was a French-born American musician who settled in the United States in 1916. In his quest for music that was 'just sound', free from all other associations, he produced such works as *Ionisation*, for 41 percussion instruments and 2 sirens. Later he wrote pure electronic music.
Vaughan Williams, Ralph (1872–1958) was with William Walton (1902–) the most important British composer of his era. He was nearly 30 before he

began serious composition. He was a collector of folk tunes, and used these tunes and original melodies of similar character to create a truly English style of composition in his numerous choral works, operas, ballets and symphonies.
Villa-Lobos, Heitor (1887–1959), Brazil's leading composer, was for many years in charge of his country's musical education. He produced a large number of compositions, and was influenced by his country's folk music, of which he was a keen collector.

Right: Many influences have affected the development of popular music. Although pop and rock, its best-known manifestations, are still with us, popular music has already explored many new fields – and development is still going on.

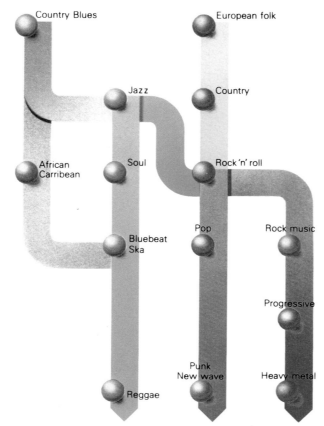

Country Blues

European folk

Jazz

Country

African Carribean

Soul

Rock 'n' roll

Bluebeat Ska

Pop

Rock music

Progressive

Punk New wave

Heavy metal

Reggae

Below: A huge open-air pop music festival, held in Texas. Festivals like this draw young people from a wide area.

its leading exponents were the BEATLES, a young, bright foursome who wrote witty words for their songs, and experimented with more complicated harmonies than had been usual in popular music. They and other groups performed to ever larger audiences, producing eventually the phenomenon of the rock festival, an open-air event lasting several days with audiences of thousands. The creators of rock music have made even more use of electronics than 'serious' musicians, using amplified instruments and synthesizers.

With the advanced composers of 'serious' music becoming ever more remote from their audiences, it was small wonder that millions of younger folk should regard pop music as the music of the people. In time the concern many young people felt for the social issues of the day came to be reflected in 'protest' songs, a move in which Bob DYLAN was a pioneer. However, as has happened many times in the past, in some respects the borderline between the two kinds of music is vague. The use of classical skills and forms, such as opera and the symphony, has been explored by rock composers and performers. Such cross-fertilization helps to revitalize both forms.

Wagner, Richard (1813–83), a German composer, mainly composed operas, in which he wrote his own text and supervised all aspects of the production. But he had an enormous influence on the music of his time, through his bold use of harmony and his use of the *Leitmotiv* – a short musical phrase associated with a particular character or idea. He was always in debt though he was befriended and financed by King Ludwig II of Bavaria.
Weber, Carl Maria von (1786–1826) helped to

Scene from Das Rheingold

establish a truly German national opera (earlier German operas had Italian texts and themes). He was also an important writer for the clarinet as a solo instrument.
Webern, Anton (1883–1945), was a follower of Arnold SCHOENBERG and the TONE ROW system of composition. he wrote only 31 pieces, all small and short in form. Some last only 2 or 3 minutes. He spent most of his life in Vienna, where he was accidentally shot and killed by an American sentry at the end of World War II.
Weill, Kurt (1900–50) was

one of the many German composers who emigrated to the United States to escape from the Nazi rulers of his own country. He did his best to bridge the gap between 'serious' and popular music – so successfully that records of the song 'Mack the Knife' from his *The Threepenny Opera* sold more than 10,000,000 copies.

Grand opera is an art form born in Italy in the late 1500s. It has spawned several other forms of musical theatre, including the Viennese operetta and the virile American musical.

Music on Stage

Music as we know it today grew from the rhythms of dance. Movement and music were fused as words and music are in song today. The dance led slowly to the development of drama. In the West, this occurred through the separation of the dancing and singing chorus from the protagonist in the Greek hymn to Dionysius, the *dithyramb* (see page 97). Music remained part of drama throughout the Classical period (*see page 106*). In the East, dance and drama have never divided. Today, the classical stages of Asia present fully integrated musical, danced dramas. The unity of music with other arts of the stage is ancient, and any division occurred only in the late 1500s. Even then, music continued to be a part of most stage entertainments.

Most people accept that music engages the emotions and heightens the effects of drama. Many have advanced theories on how music reaches into listeners' minds to produce this effect, but none is generally satisfactory. In fully integrated forms of music drama, such as the operas of Richard WAGNER, Benjamin BRITTEN and Michael TIPPETT, the music contributes more than a strictly emotional effect. It plays a vital part in the intellectual and artistic unity of the opera.

Opera

Opera is a drama expressed through music, acting, and the art of stage design, costume and lighting. There are many kinds of opera. They fall into two groups: those sung throughout and those that are sung and spoken. The latter consist of songs and choruses linked by spoken dialogue. There are various forms of this style: COMIC OPERA, OPERA BOUFFE, OPERA COMIQUE, OPERETTA and SINGSPIEL. Operas which are sung throughout have ARIAS and choruses linked by RECITATIVE, a form of sung dialogue which is not primarily melodic and which normally enhances

the natural intonations of speech. Operas of this kind are grand operas. There are two main forms: OPERA SERIA and OPERA BUFFA, although spoken dialogue is used in some operas in this form. Operas written for few singers and small orchestras were meant for presentation to audiences in large rooms, private theatres or small concert halls. These works are generally called chamber operas.

Making an opera

To write an opera, a librettist and a composer are needed (although they can be the same person). The librettist writes the book, which usually consists of dialogue and lyrics. He may work from an existing story as Arrigo Boito (1842-1918) did when writing librettos for VERDI's *Otello* and *Falstaff*, which he based on plays by William SHAKESPEARE (*see page 112*). In these cases, the

Above: Many operas in the first half of the 1700s included extensive dance sequences, fanciful costumes and static tableaux. The music and lyrics performed most of the function of transmitting the story and mood of the piece to its audience. It was not until the reforms of Christoph Willibald Glück that the intention of creating a unified music-drama approached its goal.

Reference

A **Aria** is an air or song. In opera, an aria is a lyrical expression of a character's feelings. From the 1700s onwards, opera composers usually wrote arias in 3 sections, the last one like the first, with the middle section as a contrast. This form, called a *da capo aria*, declined from the mid-1800s.

B **Bellini,** Vincenzo (1801–35) wrote in a style that placed great demands on the singer's sense of style and vocal control. His best-known operas are *Norma* and *La Sonnambula* (both 1831) and, in the French grand opera tradition, *I Puritani* (1835).

Bizet, Georges (1838–75) only won operatic acclaim with his last opera, and this really only after his death. His earlier operas are revived occasionally, but do not match the standards of his last work, *Carmen* (1875), a story of gypsy love and revenge. His early operas were *Les Pêcheurs de Perles*

Carmen *by Bizet*

(1863) and *La Jolie Fille de Perth* (1867).

Borodin, Aleksandr Porfirovitch (1833–87) was one of a group of 5 Russian composers who joined forces, in an endeavour to compose music that expressed their sense of nationalism. His one opera, *Prince Igor*, he left unfinished. His compatriots, RIMSKY-KORSAKOV (*see page 76*) and Alexander Glazunov (1865–1936) completed it for him.

Britten, Benjamin (1913–76) an English composer wrote 11 operas. One of his many gifts was the ability to write simply without loss of dramatic effectiveness, thus making his operas accessible to amateur performers. His second opera, *Peter Grimes* (1945), is widely

acclaimed as his best. Like all of his operas, except *A Midsummer Night's Dream* (1960), *Peter Grimes* explored themes of good and evil. Among Britten's other operas are: *The Rape of Lucretia* (1946), *The Turn of the Screw* (1954), *Albert Herring* (1947), *Billy Budd* (1951), *Gloriana* (1953), *Noye's Flood* (1958), *Curlew River* (1964) and *Death in Venice* (1973).

C **Callas,** Maria Meneghini (1923–72) was born of Greek parents in the United States. She was a

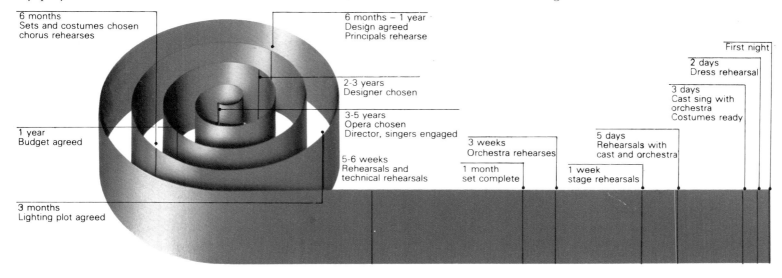

atmosphere that the opera needs. One of the composer's greatest challenges is to form an artistic unity from the opera's separate elements. He must create the characters and express the action and changing moods of the work in music related to an overall concept.

Staging an opera

The staging of opera raises several problems not experienced in conventional playhouses. One such problem is the difficulty of bringing together a full cast for rehearsal and performances. Singers cannot perform the most demanding roles on consecutive nights, and if they are to sing one opera in the evening they cannot rehearse during the day: their voices would fail. This makes the planning of schedules complicated. The difficulty is increased by the fact that most opera houses commonly change the opera performed night by night. The planning of technical rehearsals in between striking (taking down) one set of scenery and raising another, is fraught with pitfalls.

The opera company's directors and planning committee, having decided on a new production, appoint a conductor, director, designer and singers for the main roles. In some opera houses there is a resident designer, but many companies choose an outside artist whose style they believe will be suitable for the work. Some distinguished directors design their own costumes and sets. The Italian theatre and film director Luchino Visconti (*see page 125*) for example has fulfilled this dual role with brilliance.

The designer makes sketches of the sets after

librettist translated the plays, cut and reshaped them to fit the form that Verdi required for an opera of recitative, arias and ENSEMBLES. A librettist may work from an idea of his own or one that is suggested to him. In a modern libretto, there is usually less division between the dialogue and sung pieces of an opera so the librettist may write the libretto much as he would write a play, except that he must write words that are suitable for singing.

An opera composer must write music that allows the singers to fully express the characters they play. The music must create the dramatic

Above: Verdi's opera, *Aida*, received its premiere in Cairo in 1871. It had been commissioned for the opening celebrations planned for the completion of the Suez Canal. The opera is a tragedy in which the daughter of a captive Ethiopian king falls in love with a prince of Egypt. The couple die rather than submit to the pain of parting. The opera is one of Verdi's most spectacular, and includes music for dances and processions.

6 months
Sets and costumes chosen
chorus rehearses

6 months – 1 year
Design agreed
Principals rehearse

First night

2 days
Dress rehearsal

2-3 years
Designer chosen

3 days
Cast sing with
orchestra
Costumes ready

1 year
Budget agreed

3-5 years
Opera chosen
Director, singers engaged

5 days
Rehearsals with
cast and orchestra

3 weeks
Orchestra rehearses

5-6 weeks
Rehearsals and
technical rehearsals

1 month
set complete

1 week
stage rehearsals

3 months
Lighting plot agreed

dramatic soprano capable of the most intense portrayals of the great roles in Italian opera of the 1800s and early 1900s. She excelled in the title roles in BELLINI's *Norma* and PUCCINI's *Tosca*.
Caruso, Enrico (1873–1921) won greater and more lasting fame than any other operatic tenor. The power and purity of his voice with its exciting range and colour, together with his ability as an actor, made him ideal for many of the roles in VERDI and PUCCINI operas. His finest role was the clown in LEONCAVALLO's *I Pagliacci*.

Comic opera, as the name suggests, is opera based on humorous, lighthearted themes. Most comic operas have spoken dialogue, as in those by GILBERT and SULLIVAN. Many light operas may be grouped under the heading comic opera, but the term does not include OPERA COMIQUE.

D **Donizetti,** Gaetano (1797–1848) wrote over 60 operas. The early compositions show an indebtedness to ROSSINI, but he quickly developed his gift of melody along lines that were

characteristically his own. He wrote arias with runs, trills and florid decorations which required an accomplished technique from singers, especially lyric soprano's with a high range known as *coloratura*. His best-known operas still in the repertory are: *Lucia di Lammermoor* (1835), *La Fille du Régiment* (1840), *L'Elisir d'Amore* (1832) and *Don Pasquale* (1843).

E **Ensembles** are sections of an opera or NUMBERS composed for a group of singers, when 3 or more characters sing together.

F **Flagstad,** Kirsten (1895–1962) was a Norwegian

Maria Stuarda by Donizetti

soprano who made a name for herself as the greatest Wagnerian soprano of her time. Her voice was unusually pure and true throughout its range for so powerful an instrument. She first sang at the Bayreuth Festivals of WAGNER operas in 1934, and made her debut at the Metropolitan Opera House, New York City, the next year.
Folk opera is composed around themes drawn from folk stories and includes music derived from folksong. *The Bartered Bride* by Bedrich Smetana (1824-84) falls into this category.

Left: In the stage rehearsals of an opera, the producer checks the timing of the stage moves, lighting, costumes and make-up. The conductor rehearses cast and orchestra. Stage staff go through the changes of set, while the scene painters put finishing touches.

Scene painter

Stage hands

Stage manager

Chorus

Properties manager

Producers assistant at prompt desk

Producer

Principals

Musical director

Wardrobe mistress

Left: The complex forces required for the performance of an opera demand a long planning period. This slow gestation is mostly caused by the difficulty of bringing together the international soloists for the main roles, and making space in the opera-house's programme for rehearsals and stage set construction. Despite the length of the planning period, the last weeks of rehearsal are always a race towards opening night.

discussions with the director. Together, they develop the visual style of the opera. When these plans are advanced, the designer may build a model of the sets on a model stage, and light them to test their appearance in three dimensions. The producer uses the model to check and modify his plans for the movements of the characters and chorus. The stage manager sits in on these meetings to plan the scene changes and make a plot or planned schedule for the lighting. He also plans the schedule with the designer for the making of costumes and building and painting of scenery.

Singers, if the production is of a well-known opera, may already know their parts; but if the opera is little known or new, they will rehearse with a *répétiteur* or coach. The *répétiteur* will also help the singers with the language of the opera if it is one with which they are unfamiliar. The chorus master trains his chorus in their parts. The solo singers meet to learn to sing any ensemble sections (parts sung together) of the opera, gradually acquiring vocal balance as they grow accustomed to the quality and strength of each other's voices. As these rehearsals proceed, the conductor may join the soloists and chorus to bring them to the correct tempo. The director will also join them occasionally to discuss points of dramatic interpretation.

After some weeks of work, the solo singers and chorus should be word and note perfect, and the conductor polishes the musical aspect of the singers' performance. If the opera is a new one, the conductor may rehearse the orchestra in

Gershwin, George (1898–1937) the American composer, spanned both jazz and popular music, and classical music. His brother Ira Gershwin (1896–1937) wrote lyrics for many of his musicals, including 5 George White *Scandals* (1920–24), *Fancy Free* (1927), *Show Girl* (1929), *Strike up the Band* (1930) and *Girl Crazy* (1930). George Gershwin's Black opera *Porgy and Bess* was first done in 1935.
Gilbert, William Schwenck (1836–1911) was an English librettist and dramatist who collaborated with Arthur SULLIVAN on a series of 14 light comic operas.
Gluck, Christoph Willibald von (1714–87) an Austro-German composer, wrote his first operas in the Italian style. He later felt strongly that opera was losing its way, and should return to the principles of musical and dramatic unity that were its motivating force when it was developed. *Orfeo* is the earliest work that has a regular place in the international operatic repertory. Among his other operas, *Armide* (1777) and *Iphigenie en Tauride* (1779) are still seen.

Intermezzo is a musical interlude played during a break in an opera's action. Some composers call the piece an interlude. They commonly introduced them in operas of the 1700s. A recent example of this occurs in Benjamin BRITTEN's *Peter Grimes* (1945).

Leitmotiv is a musical theme which a composer uses to identify a particular character, mood, object or idea. He can also use a *leitmotiv* to tell the audience that a character is remembering something

that has been introduced earlier in the opera, when the actual singer is silent.
Lehár, Franz (originally Ferencz, 1870–1948) composed operettas in Vienna.

The Merry Widow *by Lehar*

Their tuneful frivolity captured popular acclaim. His operettas include: *The Count of Luxembourg* (1909), *Frederica* (1928) and *The Merry Widow* (1905).
Leoncavallo, Ruggiero (1858–1919) composed only one successful opera. His short *verismo* (realistic) opera, *I Pagliacci* brought him lasting fame. It is usually performed with *Cavalliera Rusticana* by Pietro Mascagni (1863–1945) in one programme.
Light opera is an English term for operetta. The 2 are interchangeable.

sections, choosing, perhaps, the woodwind section for special rehearsals of difficult material. When his players have learned their parts, he brings them together for full orchestral rehearsals. In preparing a new opera, the composer may attend rehearsals to advise the cast and director of his views.

Finally, the director brings the parts of the new production together. The singers and orchestra meet for a *sitzprobe*, in which they play and sing their way through the opera while sitting on the stage or in the auditorium. The director takes his soloists and chorus to a rehearsal room where they learn their moves, and adjust them to the timing of the music. They sing lightly at these rehearsals, saving their voices for performance. As the opera production progresses, the technical rehearsals begin. The stage manager rehearses the stage staff in complex scene changes, tests the PROPERTIES (*see page 111*) and effects in position, tries out the lighting. The singers try on their costumes and wigs, and the wardrobe department makes necessary changes.

The stage rehearsals are worked act by act before about three general stage rehearsals at which the singers work through the opera. The orchestra usually plays for only the first of these rehearsals, the others being accompanied by piano. Then the cast, orchestra and stage staff launch the first performance.

Musicals

Musical comedies at the end of the 1800s usually consisted of a skimpy plot that connected a series of catchy songs and dances such as *The Quaker Girl* by Lionel Monckton (1861-1924). These entertainments often showed an underlying satirical theme, but the aim was light-hearted entertainment. Artists working in the United States in the 1920s and 30s raised the standard of musicals and their production to a level comparable with that of opera and ballet with shows like *Porgy and Bess* in 1935. Theatre directors, composers and librettists from all over the Western world started to give the medium serious attention.

A modern musical such as *West Side Story* may be for an intimate performance or it may be as

Left: *My Fair Lady*, one of the most successful musicals of the 1950s, was the product of a collaboration between the lyricist Alan Jay Lerner and the composer Frederick Loewe. They based their musical on a play, *Pygmalion*, by George Bernard Shaw. This is the opening of the show, set in Covent Garden Market.

Massenet, Jules Émile Frédéric (1842–1912) wrote 27 operas, of which 5 are well-known. His style was tuneful, and romantic. His best work is *Manon* (1884) in which he wrote music of moving tenderness. He followed this opera with others including: *Werther* (1892), *Thaïs* (1894), *Cendrillon* (1899) and *Le Jongleur de Notre Dame* (1902).

Mozart, Wolfgang Amadeus (1756–91) was described by WAGNER as the 'greatest and most divine genius': an opinion shared by many lovers of opera. Mozart's early stage works were written in the form of

Werther by Massenet

SINGSPIEL, but perhaps his compositions in the OPERA BUFFA style are the ones in which his genius is most evident. These include *Le Nozze di Figaro* (1786), *Don Giovanni* (1787) and *Cosi Fan Tutti* (1790). He was fortunate in his main librettist, Lorenzo da Ponte (1749–1838). Mozart's OPERA SERIA compositions include *Idomineo* (1781) and *La Clemenza di Tito* (1791), his last opera.

Moussorgsky, Modeste Petrovitch (1839–81) was one of the most fervently nationalistic composers of the group of Russians known as 'the Five' *see also* BORODIN). His melodies are strongly influenced by the folk music of his country, and his operas are based on Russian historical themes. His opera on Pushkin's drama about *Boris Godunov*, a Russian tsar who reigned between 1598 and 1605, is a lavishly dramatic work, full of insight into the tsar's tortured mind. RIMSKY-KORSAKOV (*see page 76*) later re-orchestrated and edited it. Moussorgsky's second opera, *Khovantchina* (1886), was first produced after the composer's death, and Rimsky-Korsakov provided the score.

Number is jargon used by musicians to quickly refer to an ARIA, ENSEMBLE or chorus in a large-scale work, such as an opera. Each of these sections of a work has a number printed near the beginning, so when a conductor calls a number, the cast and orchestra can turn rapidly to the correct place in the score.

Offenbach, Jacques (1819–80) was born at

Left: Mozart's *singspiel, Die Zauberflöte (The Magic Flute)* is a work of humanist symbolism, but the composer and his librettist thread it through with a delightful humour. The librettist, E Schikaneder, was the first to play Papageno the birdcatcher, the principal character of the comedy element. He traditionally has a costume of feathers, and carries his magic pipes and a birdcage.

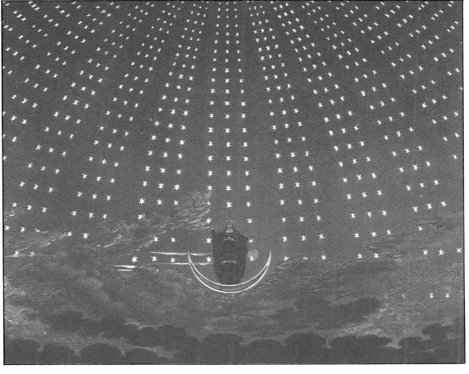

Above: In this magnificent set for *Die Zauberflöte* (The Magic Flute), Karl Schinkel has created a canopy of stars for the Queen of the Night, the evil character of the *singspiel*. She makes her appearance in a moon which can be drawn out of sight.

Left: Erté's costume designs for *Der Rosenkavalier*, by Richard Strauss, caught the opera's style beautifully. They have a sensuous mixture of elegance and opulence.

demanding in its forces as grand opera. Because there is often a fair amount of dance in a musical, the part played by the choreographer is usually greater than in opera. The production is planned on lines similar to those of opera, but scheduling of rehearsals, and the set and wardrobe making is simplified by the fact that musicals are usually performed as a continuous run and not as part of a repertory.

Stage music down the years

In the late 1500s in Italy, a group of scholars, poets and musicians sought to emulate the Ancient Greek dramatists in a form of drama which included music, poetry and dance. The group, centred in Florence, called themselves *camarata* (comrades). They abandoned the style of most composers of the day, who sometimes strung madrigals together to form an entertainment on stage. The *camarata* took themes from Classical mythology and history, and set them to music which followed the declamatory inflexions of the actor's voice. In this way, they hoped to recreate the atmosphere of the Greek theatre in its heyday.

The first opera which has survived is *Eurydice*, by Jacopo Peri (1561–1633) with additions by Giulio Caccini (c. 1558–c. 1615). They staged it for the marriage of Marie de Medici to Henry IV of France in 1600. With little doubt, the greatest Italian composer of opera of the next hundred years was Claudio MONTEVERDI (*see page 74*). In

---

Offenbach-am-Main in Germany, but spent most of his boyhood and the rest of his

Offenbach's Contes D'Hoffmann

life in Paris. His operettas, nearly 90 of them, brought him great fame in France, Great Britain and the United States in his lifetime. His *Orphée aux Enfer* (1858), *La Belle Hélène* (1864), *La Vie Parisienne* (1866), *La Grande Duchesse de Gerolstein* (1867) and *La Périchole* (1868) all contain vivid satirical portraits of life in France during the reign of Napoleon III (1852–70) known as the 'Second Empire'. Offenbach died before the first performance of *Les Contes d'Hoffmann* (1881), his one foray into more substantial opera.

Opera buffa evolved from the INTERMEZZO. It was a common practice, in the early 1700s, to insert a short comedy between the acts of a tragic opera. These comedy intermezzi became independent of the main opera, and took the name *opera buffa* (comic opera). The first of these is usually thought to be *La Serva Padrona* (1733) by Giovanni Pergolesi (1710–36). Later composers enriched the form, and most conformed to the tradition of ending the opera with a concerted ENSEMBLE.

Opéra bouffe is the French version of *opera buffa* in *opéra bouffe* of the 1800s, the style becomes more farcical than is generally found in the Italian *buffa*.

Opéra comique is a confusing term. In 1715, it was first used to announce a satirical entertainment in which the grand opera style was parodied. The term at first included only comedies with spoken dialogue, but later encompassed such works as *Carmen* by BIZET.

Opéra seria was the main operatic form of the 1600s and 1700s. It used classical and mythological subjects in a highly stylized way. There was a reaction to this rigid style in OPERA BUFFA.

Operetta is a sung drama of a lighthearted character, frequently farcical. Most operettas have spoken dialogue. It is often difficult to distinguish operetta from musical comedy. *See also* LIGHT OPERA.

Orchestra pit is the area in front of and usually below the stage, which holds the orchestra.

Overture is a term for the passage of orchestral music played before the performance of musical drama and

Right: The settings for musical comedies of the early decades of this century were usually lavish. Here, the designer has created the magic world of the Arabian Nights for *Chu Chin Chow*, which for some years held the record for the number of performances in London.

Below: *The Mikado* was probably the most successful of the operettas written by W. S. Gilbert and Sir Arthur Sullivan. The libretto sparkles with fun and gentle satire of governmental bureaucracy, while the music parodies some of the conventions of grand opera in its arias and ensembles.

two of his operas *Orfeo* (1607) and *L'Incoronazione di Poppea* (1642) his use of RECITATIVE was sensitive to the inflexions of the voice, and he developed the ARIOSO passages with masterly, lyrical skill. In his, and later operas, the action had to wait while singers demonstrated the brilliance of their techniques. A composer who followed him, Alessandro Scarlatti (1660–1725), brought the florid aria to the fore in opera.

The Italian born French composer, Jean-Baptiste Lully (1632–87) was a strong influence on the development of the opera in France. He studied the speech of actors working in the declamatory style of the period and from his observations he introduced a recitative which was more suited to the French language. He was followed by the highly gifted Jean Philippe Rameau (1683–1764), who wrote his first opera *Hippolyte et Aricie* at the age of 50. He composed both operas and opera-ballets, where he laid a greater stress on dance than was usual in opera.

In the 1700s operas consisted of a succession of florid arias linked by recitative. Occasionally, singers joined forces in ensembles, and a composer might introduce a chorus. The form had lost the sense of dramatic purpose envisaged by the *camarata*. One of the great exponents of the form of opera which flourished especially in Naples was the German, HANDEL (*see page 72*). His early operas show influences from the composers of German opera, which had a well developed tradition in Hamburg. The principal composer there was Reinhard Keiser (1674–1739), whose best-known surviving opera was *Croesus* (1711).

In England, opera developed from the masque, a form of dramatic spectacle. Only one opera by an English composer ranked with those produced by the Italians and French. This was *Dido and Aeneas* (1689) by Henry PURCELL (*see page 75*). Purcell died six years later at the age of

musicals, which usually encapsulates the mood of the following performance. In the earliest days of opera, there was no overture, only a fanfare or a few chords or bangs on the drums to catch the audience's attention. Gradually 2 types of overture developed, the Italian and the French. The Italian style consisted of 3 movements: a quick one, a slow one, and a quick finale. The French began with a slow movement repeated, a quick movement, and a dignified dance movement. This was the form adopted by many composers of the 1700s. MOZART overtures are in a modified SONATA FORM (*see page 77*). From WAGNER onwards, the overture either uses integrated themes from the opera or disappears altogether. Some overtures are written purely as orchestral pieces.

P Patter song is a comic song delivered at great speed. The most famous of these is probably 'Largo al factotum' from *Il Barbiere di Siviglia* by ROSSINI. There are several in the operas of GILBERT and SULLIVAN.

Prima donna is a leading soprano in an opera company.

Puccini, Giacomo (1858–1924) was one of the most successful composers of opera. His powerful sense of drama and his gifts as a composer of sensuous, lyrical music won the devotion of audiences all over Europe and the United States. His operas include: *La Bohème* (1896), *La Tosca* (1900), *Madame Butterfly* (1904), the one-act *Gianni Schicchi* (1918) and *Turandot* unfinished at his death was completed by a friend.

R Recitative is a form of sung dialogue in which melody and regular rhythm are discarded so that the music may follow the natural sounds of speech.

Scene from Madame Butterfly

36, leaving English opera in an underdeveloped state. The arrival of Handel, composing in the Italian style, brought opera to life again in England with operas such as *Rinaldo* (1711) and *Serse* (1738). At this time, a ballad-opera – a light form of opera, incorporating popular tunes with spoken dialogue – *The Beggar's Opera* (1728), by John Gay (1685–1732), swept London audiences off their feet.

The opera was ripe for reform at this period. Drama had taken second place to the showpiece arias required by star singers, and librettos had become banal and foolish. The reformer was Christoph GLUCK. He wrote a preface to his opera *Alcestis* (1767) in which he proclaimed that music should be servant of the drama, that the course of the action should not stop for a vocal showpiece, that there should be more unity between aria and recitative, and that the OVERTURE should set the mood for an opera. Gluck's manifesto, and the success of his expressive operatic compositions, caused his ideas to be shared by many German and Austrian composers.

MOZART, one of the supreme composers of opera, carried the spirit of Gluck's ideals into his own work. Most of Mozart's best work is in the *opera buffa* style, but he also excelled in *singspiel* (a form that had grown from translations of English ballad-operas performed in Germany) such as *Entführung aus dem Serail* (1782).

In Mozart's mystical *singspiel*, *Die Zauberflöte* (1791), the first signs of a new German Romantic opera style appeared. This found rich expression in Carl WEBER's *Der Frieschütz* much later, in 1821.

The foundation of the present repertoire was laid down by Italian composers of the 1800s. Composers, such as Gioacchino ROSSINI, Gaetano DONIZETTI, Vincenzo BELLINI and Giuseppe VERDI, wrote full-blooded, dramatic music, rich in melody.

Reacting to their Romanticism, a group of *verismo* (realistic) composers, working in Italy at the turn of the century, brought opera away from heroic stories, and drew on plots about people on a more everyday scale. Ruggiero LEONCAVALLO's *I Pagliacci* (1892) is about travelling players, PUCCINI's *La Bohème* (1896) is set among struggling artists in Paris, and his *Il Tabarro* (1918) is about bargees.

The ideal of opera which fused all the elements of musical and stage drama found one of its great champions in Richard WAGNER. He used LEIT-MOTIVES to identify characters and moods. He worked these with subtlety and great dramatic effect into the texture of the opera to weld it into a united whole. His most massive concept, *Das Ring des Nibelungen*, a series of four related operas is the fullest exploration of his ideas about the dramatic and musical unity of opera. It is also the culmination of the German Romantic opera style.

National styles of opera spread through Europe in the 1800s. In Russia, it began with the work of Mikhail Ivanovitch GLINKA *(see page 71)*. It was carried forward by Aleksandr BORODIN's *Prince Igor* (1890), Modeste MOUSSORGSKY's *Boris Godunov* (1874), Petr TCHAIKOVSKY's *Eugene Onegin* (1879) and *Sadko* (1898) by RIMSKY-KORSAKOV *(see page 76)*.

The grand operas of the early part of the century appeared mainly in France. Many of these, such as *Les Huguenots* (1836) by Giacomo Meyerbeer (1791–1864), are now seen only rarely. Georges BIZET, composer of *Carmen* (1875), wrote operas in a less grand manner, leading to the growth of OPERA COMIQUE, one branch of which produced OPERETTA.

Wagner's influence extended far into the twentieth century. His ideas may be traced in *Pelléas et Mélisande* (1902) by Claude DEBUSSY *(see page 70)* and *Der Rosenkavalier* (1911) by Richard STRAUSS.

Below: David Hockney designed the sets for Stravinsky's opera *The Rake's Progress* in a British production in 1977. In American and British opera houses, it is fairly common to bring in well-known artists as designers. In Europe it is unusual.

In Germany, Alban BERG (*see page 68*) adapted older structural forms used by earlier composers into new and exciting forms using twelve-tone harmonies (*see* TONE ROW, *page 79*), in one of the period's most important operas, *Wozzek* (1925). Other composers returned to classical styles. Perhaps the most performed of operas in this neo-classical style is *The Rake's Progress* (1951) by Igor STRAVINSKY (*see page 78*).

The English ballad-opera form revived in Germany in the new *zeitoper*, a kind of operetta. The use of this topical form in which the author might comment on issues of the day, proved extremely popular in the 1920s. *The Threepenny Opera* (1928) by Kurt WEILL (*see page 80*) with libretto by the playwright Bertolt Brecht, is frequently revived. In general, composers in the 1900s have moulded their operas by a symphonic (*see* SYMPHONY *page 78*) use of music, always working towards greater unity of music and drama. The opening of such new media as radio, cinema and television has attracted some composers. *Amahl and the Night Visitors* (1951) by Gian-Carlo Menotti (1911–), specially composed for television, has been screened several times.

Operetta, a type of musical stage entertainment which seeks only to amuse, produced much delightful theatre from about 1870 onwards. Its main centres were Vienna, where Franz LEHAR held sway, Paris, under Jacques OFFENBACH's voluptuous melodic touch, and London, where W.S. GILBERT and Arthur SULLIVAN teased and amused their audiences with 30 years of comic operas.

The simplicity and lightness of the musical comedy lost favour in late 1930s. Composers of the calibre of George GERSHWIN made the line between opera and the musical hard to define. The plot, in such musicals as RODGERS AND HAMMERSTEIN's *Oklahoma* (1943), was more intricate than earlier musicals had required. The dance, music and drama fused into an operatic unity. By the time Leonard Bernstein (1918–) wrote *West Side Story* (1957), the musical had moved into tragedy and social comment, and is no longer intended merely to amuse. In recent years, there has been a resurgence of popular music on stage in such rock 'n roll musicals as *Hair* (1967) by Gault MacDermot (1928–), while the more conventional musical thrives by its side in works such as *Evita* by Andrew Lloyd Webber (1948–).

Below: *A Chorus Line*, an American hit musical of the mid-1970s brought the 'backstage musical' back into the limelight. Telling the stories of a group of people auditioning for parts in a musical, it shows the individuality and talents of the faceless men and women who find the drive to keep on dancing even when they seldom reach stardom. The final routine shows all the individuals finally as one in a dazzle of music costume and spectacle. The set is stark and the best possible effects are achieved with the aid of imaginative lighting and the use of mirrors.

Sullivan, Arthur Seymour (1842–1900) was a British composer of light comic operas written with William GILBERT. They included *H.M.S. Pinafore* (1878), *The Pirates of Penzance* (1879) and *The Mikado* (1885).

Tchaikovsky, Petr Ilych (1840–93) composed music for his operas which, although Russian in character, is more Western in its tradition than that of his contemporary Russian nationalist composers. Of his 11 operas, *Eugene Onegin* (1879) and *The Queen of Spades* (1890) are frequently seen. *See also page 78.*

Tippett, Michael (1905–) is an English composer of many works which include several operas. He had great success with the operas *The Midsummer Marriage* (1952), *King Priam* (1961) and *The Knot Garden* (1970). *See also page 79.*

Verdi, Giuseppe (1813–1901) was probably the most prominent composer of opera in Italy during the 1800s. His first successful opera, was *Nabucco* (1842). This was followed by a string of international favourites, including *Rigoletto* (1851), *Il Trovatore* (1853), *La Traviata* (1853), *Un Ballo in Maschera* (1859), *La Forza del Destino* (1862), *Aïda* (1871), *Otello* (1887) and *Falstaff* (1893).

Wagner, Richard (1813–83) German composer, brought a new intensity to the ideal of the unity of drama and music. He abandoned the use of RECITATIVE and ARIA. He employed instead 'endless melody', rarely making formal breaks to begin an aria. His first successful opera was *Rienzi* (1840), followed by *Der Fliegende Holländer* (1843) and *Tannhäuser* (1845). *Lohengrin* (1848) and *Tristan und Isolde* eventually reached an audience in 1859, and *Die Meistersinger von*

Theatre at Bayreuth

Nürnberg in 1867. Wagner built a theatre at Bayreuth in which he gave a performance of his series of 4 operas, *Der Ring des Nibelungen* (1876). His last opera was *Parsifal* (1882). *See also page 80.*

Weber, Carl Maria Friedrich Ernst von (1786–1826) a German nationalist composer. Of his 10 operas, 2 have stood the test of time: *Der Freischutz* (1821) and *Oberon* (1826). *See also page 80.*

Dance has its origin in religious ritual and it still has this function in many Third World countries. However, the most celebrated dance style in the West is ballet, one of the most spectacular forms of theatrical entertainment.

Dance

Dance is a universal phenomenon. People dance in a wide variety of forms in response to many kinds of stimuli. In most parts of the world the early personal and social context is largely lost, especially in Western dances. Among people who have held to an old way of life, such as some Australian Aborigines, the motivation of the dance is more richly and clearly seen. While to such people dancing is often enjoyable, it is something much more important and purposeful: sometimes having magical, religious, socially unifying, informative, celebratory and other meanings.

Over the centuries the social and religious dances separated from spectacular dances. From the former branch grew the folk-dances which, in turn, produced new social dances from the Middle Ages onwards. The spectacular dances and some of the religious ones, with much cross-fertilization from folk dances, provided the stock from which the great dance dramas of the East and the drama and stage dances of the west were to shoot. The forms of dance vary greatly, but its two essentials are found everywhere. These are

Above: Peter Tchaikovsky's *Sleeping Beauty* ballet, set to Marius Petipa's choreography, received its premiere at the magnificent Maryinsky Theatre in St Petersburg, 1890. Since then, it has remained in the repertories of most great companies. After the first performance, Tsar Nicholas II dampened the composer's triumph with the casual response: 'Very nice'. Serge Diaghilev introduced the ballet to audiences outside Russia.
Below: Dance grew from a compulsive urge to respond to the forces implicit in man's experience of life and death. Through ritual dances and social ceremonies, the dances emerged into art forms and entertainments. The ritual, social, art and dramatic dances coexisted through history, and it is easy to find many different kinds danced in all parts of the world today.

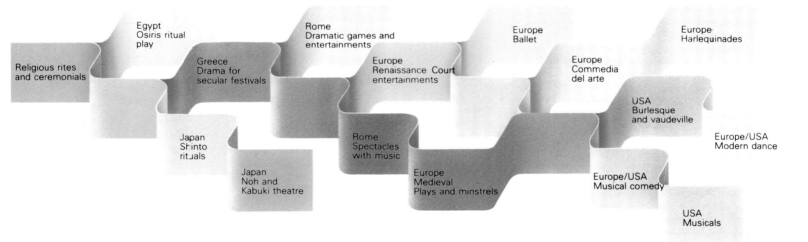

Religious rites and ceremonials

Egypt
Osiris ritual play

Greece
Drama for secular festivals

Japan
Shinto rituals

Japan
Noh and Kabuki theatre

Rome
Dramatic games and entertainments

Europe
Renaissance Court entertainments

Rome
Spectacles with music

Europe
Medieval Plays and minstrels

Europe
Ballet

Europe
Commedia del arte

Europe/USA
Musical comedy

Europe
Harlequinades

USA
Burlesque and vaudeville

Europe/USA
Modern dance

USA
Musicals

Reference

rhythm and movement. In some dances it is hard to appreciate the rhythm, which may be of the simplest and most repetitive kind. In others, as in many from India, it may be brilliantly complex and inventive. Movement too varies greatly. Some people have dances that they perform sitting down. The lightning dance of the Andaman Islanders — for example — requires the medicine man to sit on a stone in the centre of the dance. He moves only his hands and arms to a sung chorus. In other cultures the dance may be violently athletic.

Ancient Dance

The earliest evidence of dancing appears as paintings on the walls of caves. Our stone age ancestors painted dancers, some of whom were dressed in animal disguises. From these and from

Right: The kathkali dances of India are among the most splendid and elaborate of a continent which is rich in the genius of the dance. The performers, all male, dance the drama, dressed in beautiful and extravagant costumes. Their make-up is stylised, and they train for years to increase the expressiveness of their eyes.
Below: Whirling dervishes, in this Indian painting, achieve a trance-like state through their dance. The whirling dervishes are only one form of dance cult which employs the dance as a key to unlock the door to mystical understanding. Voodoo dancers in the West Indies reach states of self-hypnosis in ritual dances.

Grief   Anger   Serenity

the study of cultures at similar stages of development today, anthropologists believe that ancient peoples performed dances to bring them magic prowess in the hunt and to appease the spirits of the animals they hunted. Ancient dances, emerging into history in Ancient Egypt, included both solo and group dances, performed for religious and social purposes.

In many primitive cultures men and women had separate dances, but by the Greek classical period some dances were shared. The Greeks had a chain dance which may have symbolised the male and female relationship. A similar dance was performed by Mexican men and women to the god Huitzilopochtli, the men tied to the women by the hands.

Ritual dance

From its beginnings dance had held a place in man's religious life. The belief that dancing could work sympathetic magic seems to have been widespread, and probably universal. In Madagascar and West Africa, women used to dance a farewell to their departing men, and continued in their absence. They believed that the magic of the dance could reach out to the raiders bring them courage and luck.

Early people's recognition of their dependence on the fertility of crops and animals led to dances to the gods of nature. In north western Australia, a rainmaker dances to a ritual chant round a heap of sand on which he has placed a magic

a founder member and a choreographer of the De Basil Ballet, making *Cotillon* and *La Concurrence* (1922) but left soon for the US where he helped to form the School of American Ballet, out of which grew the American Ballet Theatre. The company with which he has long been identified is the New York City Ballet, was formed in 1948. He has had a long and notable association with the composer STRAVINSKY (*see page 78*) which began with *Apollo* in 1928 (for Diaghilev). He now shares the artistic direc-

torship of his company with Jerome ROBBINS. Some of his many works include *Serenade* (1934), *Concerto Barocco* (1941), *Night Shadow, The Four Temperaments and Symphony in C* (1946), *Orpheus* (1948), *Ivesiana* (1954), *Agon* (1957), *Episodes* (1959), *Bagaku* and *Movements* (1964) *Le Tombeau de Couperin* (1975).
Baryshnikov, Mikhail (1948–) Russian dancer, had reached eminence in Leningrad's Kirov Company when, in 1974, he defected (during a tour of Canada) to become a free-lance in the US and

Western Europe. An outstanding virtuoso, he is regarded as the finest male dancer now in Western ballet. He has become the director of the American Ballet Theatre.

C Camargo, Marie Anne de Cupis de (1710–70), a French ballet dancer, was the supreme virtuoso of the Paris Opéra. She made her Paris debut in 1726, but had already six years experience on stage. She was renowned for the brilliance and daring of her technique.
Corps de ballet is the name

given to those dancers in a ballet (especially a classical one of the 1800s) who perform as a group.
Courante (from the french

Camargo

courir, 'to run') was a rapid, skipping dance of the 1500s–1700s.
Cranko, John (1927–1973) a South African choreographer, had made his reputation with Sadler's Wells Ballet as choreographer of *Pineapple Poll* (1951), *The Shadow* (1953) and *The Lady and the Fool* (1954) when in 1961 he became director of the Stuttgart Ballet, which he then ran for the remainder of his life, making ballets for it; *Romeo and Juliet* (1962), *Onegin* (1965), *The Taming of the Shrew* (1969) and many others, and winning

Right: Men of the Rwanda people perform a dance which has ritual origins and is performed at local festivals. They wear rattles on their ankles to provide some of the musical rhythm.

Below: Many of the dances of India use mime to convey their story and mood – through subtle and graceful movements of the dancer's hands, face and neck. The rhythm of the dance, achieved through movements of the feet principally, is often intricate.

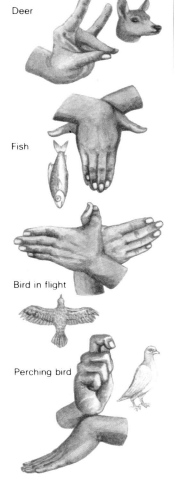

Deer

Fish

Bird in flight

Perching bird

pebble. He circles until he is exhausted. Exhaustion and ecstasy are common features of ritual dances, and may, in part, be their object. The dancer reaches a state of trance in which his mind is ready to receive a mystical experience. Ritual dances of this kind are still found among voodoo cults in the Pacific Islands. Fertility dances survive in many of the world's folkdances. In France and Great Britain, the maypole dances are descendants of the more candid dances of the past, in which our ancestors celebrated and perhaps sanctified procreation. In Japan, women still assume the magic of fertility when they wave branches of cherry blossom in the *azuma asobi* dance.

Dances to the moon and stars are performed all over the world. There is an Angolan dance, for instance, in which people bend to left and right like crescent moons, rising to the centre and waning to the ground. They are creating clear dance images of the lunar month.

Dances for healing the sick vary greatly. In some, the sick person dances to heal himself. In others, a medicine man will dance himself into a trance state in which to make a mystic contact with the demons who cause the patient's illness, and tries to persuade them to relent. The two important elements of ritual dance are the imagery which celebrates what happens in the natural world — as in the Angolan moon dance — and the ecstasy which leads a dancer closer to the spirit world — as in the medicine dance.

Social dance

The roots of dance lie deep in early people's response to natural and supernatural forces beyond their knowledge. While in these early dances they seem to have struggled to understand and control these forces, they also danced to express their position in the world of their fellows. In dance, a person might act out a tribe's history, its young men and women might perform courting dances, and even in the religious dances there was often a strong sense of the community. From

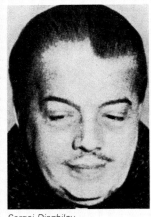

Above: Social and folk dances follow many patterns. The circle dances (**1** and **2**) are one of the oldest forms. When danced around a central object, the dancers may receive power from it, and also return power to it. The serpentine forms of chain dances (**3**) suggest the dancers follow a labyrinthine path towards a goal. The bourée (**4**), a complex social dance, followed an inverted 'S' pattern. Formation dances (**5** and **6**) are of 2 or more straight lines. In some of these, couples dance down the centre of a pair of files.

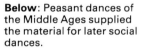

Below: Peasant dances of the Middle Ages supplied the material for later social dances.

these origins, the social dance of historical times developed.

Folkdances today are reflections of the ancient dances. Their meanings are generally obscure, and their forms much altered. National styles evolved over many years to form part of a national heritage as intimate as language. The flamenco dancers of Spain for example, with their graceful arm movements and stamped rhythms, differ remarkably from the light jigs of the Irish, danced with arms pressed to the sides.

Country dances, such as American barn dances developed from European models. National dances performed in national costumes are a much more recent development of regional folkdances.

In the European Middle Ages, courtiers found folkdances of the country people a marvellous raw material from which they wrought a popular art form. Especially in France, courtly dancers took their materials from many nations, bringing the dances home again in barely recogniseable

forms. The earliest of the medieval court dances were probably of the two groups described as *danses hautes* and *danses basses*. The first were slow stepping dances full of dignity and solemn grace. The *danses basses* were brisk skipping dances. Later, the French took a COURANTE and developed their most celebrated dance, the MINUET.

The treasure house of European dance was Spain. The French seized the Spanish *pavana* and, as the pavane, raised it to be one of the most magnificent of all processional dances. The Spanish *alemania*, *zarabanda* and *chacona*, and in the 1700s the *bolero*, *seguidilla* and *fandango* spread far from their native soil. Dance seemed to infect the Spaniards' blood, and Europeans took with delight the product of their genius. But if dancers have often called Spain 'the home of dance', it was in the School of France that the courtiers of Europe learned their dances.

In the ballrooms of the 1800s, the most popular dance was probably the WALTZ. The form was of a form known in France for about four centuries before it appeared in a new guise in Germany from about 1775–1800. After a period of resistance to its intimacy, the dancers touching for the whole period of the dance, the English accepted it when the Prince Regent took the floor in 1816. This 'close hold' set a fashion for many other dances that became popular in the ballroom later.

Dancing was a part of middle class as well as courtly entertainment by the end of the 1700s. In country houses, drawing rooms were cleared to make room for the quadrille, a dance for four couples. The French gave Europe at this time, the polka, originally a Bohemian dance, and the Hungarian galop. In the US, the barn dance tradition was well established. This was a series of dances for groups. Originally, a farmer who called on his neighbours to help him build a new

Duncan, Isadora (1878–1927). American dancer, revolutionised attitudes to modern dance. With her proclamations of freedom (in life and love as in dance movement) she was the embodiment of the reaction against the disciplines and artificialities of ballet. She pursued expressionist ideals, working in bare feet, and costumed in a Greek tunic, adorned with coloured scarves. She had little success in the US, but became a celebrity in Europe. For a time, she taught dancing to children in

post-Revolutionary Moscow. She died, when her scarf caught in a car wheel.

F **Five Positions** , these, are the basic, turned-out positions of the feet in classical ballet. They were codified by Pierre Beauchamp (1636–1705) ballet master to Louis XIV and director of the Royal Academy of Dance.

Fonteyn Margot Peggy (Hookham) (1919–) is the *prima ballerina assoluta* (the supreme ballerina) of the Royal Ballet. She joined the Sadler's Wells Ballet School

when she was 15 years old, and made her debut as a soloist in *The Haunted Bal-*

Margot Fonteyn

lroom in the same year. At 17, when MARKOVA left, she became the young company's leading ballerina; by the time of the war she had danced most of the classics and had had ballets made for her by Frederick ASHTON. After the war when the company moved to The Royal Opera House, Covent Garden, and when, 4 years later, it first visited New York, she was the main attraction. After 1960 the dazzling young Russian defector, Rudolf NUREYEV, became her partner. This partnership — at a time when her dancing

was just past its peak — became the most famous in ballet history. Her career as an unattached star continued very actively till she was 60 — a length of career probably unrivalled in ballet. She could still charm audiences at an age when the skill of a virtuoso would, long since, have withered. Since 1954 she has been president of the Royal Academy of Dancing.

G **Galliard** is an Italian Renaissance dance which was popular in many European countries. It was a

Left: The quadrille was a form of square dance. It grew to popularity in France, and migrated to British drawing rooms in 1816.

Below: Acrobatic disco dancing became a craze in the 1970s.

Below: Ballroom dancers keep alive many forms of dance that derive from early social dances.

barn would thank them for their labours by giving a barn dance in their honour. One of the most popular of the barn dances was the Paul Jones.

At the beginning of the 1900s ballroom programmes were still dominated by the waltz. A gliding slow form of this dance, called the Boston, was one of the developments which led eventually to the smooth, walking steps of the post-1918 'English style'.

In the years between the wars the popularity of public dance halls grew rapidly. There working class and lower middle class couples enjoyed the two-step, fox-trot and sequence dances, comprising simple figures, usually of 16 bar periods. Ballroom dancing of this 'English style' has persisted and become very international and highly competitive. Its rules and discipline have become almost balletic in their exactness. The competitions are controlled by national bodies under the International Council of Ballroom Dancing.

But this competitive 'English style' is for the relatively few — the last graceful offspring, perhaps, of social dance derived from the one-time courts of France and Italy. By the end of the second decade of this century jazz — originating largely among American Blacks — had taken the Western world by storm. In the US waves of new dance-crazes (the Charleston craze being one of the strongest) flowed across the country and on to Europe. There was a seemingly endless series of quickly changing fashions for uninhibited and energetic gyrating dances, including the Lindy hop in the 1930s, the boogie woogie of the 1940s, rock 'n' roll in the 1950s, the 1960's twist, and the discotheque music of the 1970s. In the 1930s the wave of Latin American dances, the rumba, samba, the revived tango, the conga and others, had an influence which has continued ever since.

Stage dance

The relationship of dance and drama is a close one, and nowhere is it so intimate as in the dance dramas of India. In the style called *natya*, the dancer expresses a theme to a sung accompaniment. The *natya* is the true dance drama. The actor-dancer tells the story and recreates the characters of the drama through subtle movements of the head, eyes, neck and hands. The feet form a rhythmic foundation for the dancing upper parts of the body. The gestures used are part of a rich vocabulary of movements, easily interpreted by an audience which has grown up in the tradition.

With the evangelical spread of Buddhism, Indian dance forms travelled through Asia. In some places, the new faith and the culture of its missionaries merged with a strong native tradition, as in Balinese dance theatre.

In a similar way, the emigration of Chinese families to Japan from the AD 1500s strongly

bold, leg-thrusting, leaping dance that took its couples 'both back, and forth, and sidewaies'.

Gavotte was a circular dance of the Renaissance period. It retained its popularity until the 1700s.

Graham, Martha (1893–), an American dancer/choreographer who made her debut in *Xochitl* (1920). She formed her own company in 1929, since when she has produced numerous dance-works. Her influence, particularly in the US but also in Britain and elsewhere, has been far greater than that of

The Galliard

any other modern or 'contemporary' dancer. Unlike almost every other modern choreographer she has made brilliant use of decor and costumes. Among the finest of her many works are *Primitive Mysteries* (1931), *Appalachian Spring* (1944), *Deaths and Entrances* (1943), *El Penitente* (1940), *Diversion of Angels* (1948).

MacMillan, Kenneth (1929–) British dancer and choreographer, whose career has been very largely in the Royal Ballet. He specialises in full-length works (*Romeo and Juliet*, (1965), *Anastasia* (1971) and *Manon* (1974). Among his finest works are *The Invitation* (1960), *Le Sacre du Printemps* (1962), *Las Mermanas* (1963, *Song of the Earth* (1965), *My Brother, My Sisters* (1978) and *Gloria* (1980). He directed the Ballet of the West Berlin Opera 1966–69, directed the Royal Ballet 1970–77 and is now the Royal Ballet's resident choreographer.

Makarova, Natalia (1940–) Russian dancer of Leningrad's Kirov Company. She was the leading ballerina in the West during the 1970s. She was already well known as a brilliant and poetic classicist when she defected in 1960), *Le Sacre du Printemps* (1962), *Las Mermanas* (1963, *Song of the Earth* (1965), *My Brother, My Sisters* (1978) and *Gloria* (1980). He directed the Ballet of the West Berlin Opera 1966–69, directed the Royal Ballet 1970–77 and is now the Royal Ballet's resident choreographer.

London in 1970; her career since then has been mainly with the American Ballet Theatre but she has often appeared with the Royal Ballet and other companies.

Markova, Dame Alicia (Alice Marks 1910–) British dancer and teacher, joined the DIAGHILEV Company aged 14, was rapidly promoted and was on verge of stardom when Diaghilev died in 1929. As guest ballerina, with Anton DOLIN, she greatly helped the Vic-Wells Ballet in its first years, formed the Markova-Dolin Company in 1935 and later,

influenced the Japanese dance. The emperor Ashigaka Shogun (1375–95) founded a school of dance, and Japanese traditions were formally established. When Kan-ami Kiyotsugu (1333–84) worked out the principles of the Nō play (1406), he and his son, Zeami Motokiyo (1362–1443) interpreted the plays with dramatic dance and music. The ritualistic severities of Nō were later modified by the more popular dance-drama, Kabuki, about the end of the 1500s.

The highest form of stage-dance in the West is ballet. As it has evolved, it is a form requiring an elaborate, difficult technique which produced a singular beauty of line and musicality. It can be dramatic, narrative, poetic or 'abstract'. It has long been regarded by its disciples as being the mainstream of Western theatrical dance and this claim has been repeatedly justified by its tendency and ability to absorb other forms of dance — social, folk and theatrical.

Its origins may be traced to the court ballets of the Italian Renaissance princes, in which the distinguished guests themselves were the performers. From Italy the court ballets came to France, where in the reign of Louis XIV (1638–1715) they achieved their greatest splendour. *Le roi soleil* (Sun King) himself (the title came from a role taken by him in one such ballet) was an eager and frequent participator. When he retired from dancing, the technique of court ballets was becoming too difficult for the courtier-amateurs. Male professionals began to take over. Jean Baptiste Lully (*see page 86*) founded the Académie Royale de Musique (1672), which

would become the 'Paris Opera'. Women too began to dance ballet professionally. Ballet had left the court and gone, finally, to the theatre. Its technique had also been codified for the first time and ballet language had become forever French.

The first stars were male, if only because the women dancers' costumes were too cumbersome for virtuosity. Marie CAMARGO and Marie Sallé (1707–1756), rivals for balletic supremacy in Paris (and therefore in all the then world of ballet), introduced lighter, freer costumes and opened the way to the ballerina's eventual domination of ballet's stage, though during the 1700s it was still the male star who shone the brighter. John Weaver (1673–1760) is noteworthy as the British pioneer of the *ballet d'action*, which, under the Frenchman Jean Georges Noverre (1727–1810), ousted the conventional opera-ballet, combining singing and dancing, in favour of a new realism whereby the dance, unaided by song, told all the story. This was the first big revolution in the art of ballet and it was, in effect, intensified early in the 1800s when the romantic movement, so important in music, literature and

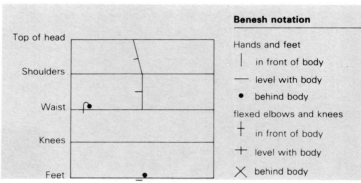

Benesh notation

Top of head	
Shoulders	Hands and feet
	| in front of body
	— level with body
Waist	• behind body
	flexed elbows and knees
Knees	┤ in front of body
	┼ level with body
Feet	✕ behind body

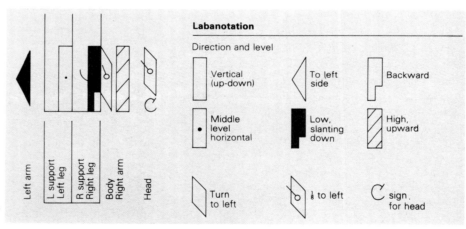

Labanotation

Direction and level

Left arm			
L support Left leg			
R support Right leg	Vertical (up-down)	To left side	Backward
Body Right arm	Middle level horizontal	Low, slanting down	High, upward
Head	Turn to left	⅛ to left	⊂ sign for head

---

was the leading dancer of various companies in the US; she retired in 1962. She was ballet director of the New York Opera 1963–69. Since then she has been a teacher of ballet.

Massine, Léonide (1896–) trained as a ballet dancer at the Imperial Ballet School in Moscow. His training as choreographer for Diaghilev's Ballets Russes began when he was only 16. He stayed with the Diaghilev company till 1920, (rejoining it briefly after 4 years). He helped to form the de Basil Ballet in 1932 and remained

its artistic director and choreographer until the war.

Léonide Massine

For Diaghilev he made, among other works, *The Three Cornered Hat* (1919), *Boutique Fantasque* (1919) and the second version of *Sacre du Printemps* (1920). For de Basil he made the symphonic ballets *Les Presages* and *Choreautin* (1933). As a dancer Massine was incomparable — the supreme character dancer in ballet of the 'twenties and 'thirties.

Mazurka is a Polish national dance that was originally sung as well as danced. It spread to Germany in the mid 1700s and to England

and the US in the following 50 years.

Minuet evolved from a rustic dance of the French province of Poitou. In the hands of the composer Lully (*see page 86*), and probably with the attention of the dancing master to Louis XIV of France, became an elegant, small-stepping dance. It was most popular in the 1700s.

Morris dance is an English folk dance which may have derived from Moorish origins at the time of the crusades. It is danced by men only. The music was usually played on pipe and

drum. The dancers frequently danced from one village to another on May Day.

Nijinska, Bronislava (1891–1972) was a Russian dancer and choreographer for the Ballet Russes. She choreographed among other ballets: *Les Noce* (1923) and *Les Biches* (1924).

Nijinsky, Vaslav (1890–1950) was a Russian ballet dancer of legendary fame. He was the leading male dancer in DIAGHILEV's company and had a more sensational success than any of

painting, began to have important repercussions on the ballet as well. The Romantic Ballet, roughly 1830–50, brought (to an audience now increasingly of the bourgeoisie, rather than of the aristocracy) stories of dryads and witches instead of the Classical gods and beings of the previous century; it brought a much greater freedom and lightness of female costume — the billowy calf-length skirt — and a technique which included more leaping and, for the first time, dancing on tip-toe (on POINT). It also reduced male dancing to a supportive role which was to endure until the present century. The legendary Swedish-Italian Marie Taglioni (1804–84) and her almost equally memorable rival, the Austrian Fanny Elssler (1810–84) were the greatest names in a period which was rich in fine ballerinas; the choreographer Jules Perrot made the ballet *Giselle* (1841), still a favourite in the international repertoire.

By 1850 the map of ballet had altered. Parisian domination, after nearly 2 centuries, was over. The Royal Danish Ballet, under August Bournouville (1805–79), had become distinctive. The

Above: Ballet costumes: (1) the stylised costumes of *Ballet de Cour* (1700s) and (2) Classical simplicity (1800s). (3) Leotards (1900s) liberated dancers movements.

Below: Martha Graham's company brought a personal style to modern dance.

most important development, however, was that of the Imperial Russian Ballet — founded over a century earlier — which between 1850 and 1900 brought ballet to the peak of its purely classical period. This was the period of the tutu, which allowed the ballerina a much greater virtuosity, and of those still famous ballets, *The Sleeping Beauty*, (1890) *Swan Lake* (1895) and *The Nutcracker* (1892), by Marius Petipa (1822–1910), the Marseillais choreographer and balletmaster who presided at St Petersburg for nearly 50 years. Imperial Russian Ballet was a product of Russian temperament plus French and Italian schooling; its most eminent dancers were, for many years, visiting Italians, such as Virginia Zucchi (1847–1930), Pierorá Legnani (1863–1923) and Carlotta Brianza (1867–1930), and it was only in 1900 that Russian dancers really outshone their visitors. This was also the moment when a provincial Russian noble, Serge DIAGHILEV, his painter friends (like Alexander Benois (1870–1960) among them) and the young neo-romantic choreographer Michel Fokine (1880–1942) began to stage a balletic revolution, more thorough and effective than any since the time of Noverre. This revolution was expressed in the repertory and dancing of the Russian company (from St. Petersburg and Moscow) which Diaghilev brought to Western Europe from 1909 onwards. It broadened the art of ballet dancing, retaining the basic classicism but making it much more versatile and expressive; and instead of the previous conventional ballet music and designs, it used the best of contemporary

the ballerinas. His leaps, in particular, were a revelation to Western audiences. The spirit of the rose in *Le Spectre de la Rose* (1911), the slave in *Schéhérazade* (1911), the almost human puppet in *Petroushka* (1911) — these and other roles he danced when they were new in the Diaghilev repertory; and in all of them he was incomparable. Diaghilev tried to make a choreographer of him, to replace Fokine; his *L'Après Midi d'un Faune* (1912) and *Le Sacre du Printemps* (1913) caused an uproar when first

Vaslav Nijinsky

produced in Paris. In 1919 he was declared insane and spent his last 31 years in an asylum.

Nureyev, Rudolf (1938–) Russian dancer, producer, choreographer, became immediately famous when, in 1961, on West European tour with the Kirov Company from Leningrad, he defected. After that he pursued a free-lance career, at first mainly with Britain's Royal Ballet and with Margot FONTEYN in ballet's most famous partnership. He re-made and produced the classics, *Swan Lake, The Sleeping Beauty, The Nutcracker,* and made ballet films e.g. *Don Quixote*.

P Pavlova, Anna Matveyevna, (1882–1931) the most famous ballerina of her day. She made her debut in 1899 in St Petersburg. She danced with NIJINSKY in DIAGHILEV's Ballets Russes in Paris. Subsequently she toured with her own group all over the world. She was remarkable for the perfection of what she did, and her expressiveness. *Giselle* was her greatest role and the short *Dying Swan*, made for her by Fokine, was her signature work.

Point is the term dancers use to describe the tips of

their toes and the movements they perform on them.

R Rambert, Marie (1888–) is a Polish born, British choreographer, dancer and teacher. She was a member of DIAGHILEV's Ballet Russes (1912–13) and founded her own school in London (1920) which became known as the Ballet Rambert in 1935.

Robbins, Jerome (1918–) American dancer, choreographer and director is an exceptionally gifted, versatile and prolific man of the theatre. His works include

work. It amounted to an unprecedented emancipation and exaltation of the art of ballet. Diaghilev's choreographers were successively Fokine, NIJINSKY, MASSINE, NIJINSKA and BALANCHINE and his most famous (and earliest) dancers were Karsavina (1885–1978) and, PAVLOVA, before she formed her own globe-trotting group; but at least equally renowned was Vaslav Nijinsky; he, like Massine and NUREYEV subsequently gave a distinction to male ballet dancing unknown since the 1700s. The Diaghilev Russian Ballet (it remained mainly Russian to the last) endured as an ever touring enterprise till Diaghilev's death in 1929; its example plus that of Pavlova's world-wide dancing enormously increased the international audience for ballet and prompted various nations — notably Britain and the US — who had no ballet companies of their own to start national companies. Hence the development, under the far-sighted Ninette de

Below: Fred Astaire was the most elegant soft shoe and tap dancer.

VALOIS, of Britain's Royal Ballet and, under Balanchine, Diaghilev's last choreographer, of the New York City Ballet. These have become the 2 leading companies outside the USSR, where, ironically, the impact of Diaghilev had been least felt. Soviet ballet continued from where Imperial Russian ballet, without Diaghilev, left off. It has produced great dancers, ULANOVA being the most famous of them, and splendid teachers but its own choreography (that is, apart from the inherited classics) has been acrobatic, stilted and vulgar. Some of the finest Soviet dancers, (MAKAROVA, NUREYEV, BARYSCHNIKOV) have preferred to exchange their privileged position in the USSR for the freedom and hurly-burly of Western ballet. Ballet now has spread round the world, with important new companies emerging in, for instance, Canada, Australia, Japan, Germany, Holland as well as in Britain and (abundantly) in the US. It has also become highly eclectic. This eclecticism dates from — and has greatly increased since — the early days of Fokine and Diaghilev. But, latterly, it has also taken in — or at least come to terms with — a modern or 'contemporary' dance movement which began as a revolt against the conventions and rigours of classical ballet in the 1800s. The driving force of this movement has been mainly American; the famous and unfortunate Isadora DUNCAN (Fokine's contemporary) began it. Its subsequent priestesses have been Martha GRAHAM and Doris Humpry (1895–1958), the former of whom has had a great influence in Britain as well as in the US. There used to be a barbed frontier between ballet and the 'contemporaries' but now there is easy two-way traffic between their respective techniques. Ballet in the 1900s after Diaghilev, has produced its great classical choreographers, Frederick ASHTON for the Royal Ballet, Balanchine (who served a Diaghilevian apprenticeship) for the Americans; it has also produced the remarkably versatile American Jerome ROBBINS and such eclectics as the Dutch Hans Van Manen (1932–) and the American Glenn Tetley (1926–) who are perhaps typical of their times. Theatrical dance, in the 1900s has proliferated into many styles. It is significant that since the death of Pavlova, in 1931, probably the most famous dancer of all has been a tap dancer, known mainly through cinema — Fred ASTAIRE.

Dances at a Gathering, 1969; West Side Story, 1957; Concert, 1956, and Fancy Free, 1944. He is now a co-director of the New York City Ballet. Many of his Broadway productions — including The King and I — were made into films.

T Tudor, Anthony (1908–) British choreographer, very influential in Britain and US, ballet's first 'psychological dramatist'. Identified with the young RAMBERT Ballet, pre-war, when he made Lilac Garden, Dark Elegies etc; then made a great reputation with American Ballet Theatre, (Pillar of Fire, his most famous American work). Principal subsequent ballets include Shadowplay for the Royal Ballet.

U Ulanova , Galina (1910–) is a Russian ballerina aclaimed by many as the greatest danseuse since Pavlova. The lyricism of her style was ideally suited to Swan Lake and Giselle which she performed with the Bolshoi Company in Moscow. She was not seen outside the USSR until 1951, when she achieved immediate success in Western Europe. After her retirement (1962) she became principal ballet mistress to the Bolshoi.

V Valois , Dame Ninette de (Edris Stannus 1898–) choreographer, dancer, founder of the Royal Ballet, joined the Diaghilev Ballets Russes 1923–25 after a young career in revues and pantomime. In 1926 she formed her school, the Acadamy of Choreographic Art. De Valois's life-work became the fostering of Britain's first national ballet, at Sadler's Wells Theatre, London (1931) before World War II, then as a touring company in wartime and from 1946 at the Royal Opera House, Covent Garden, where the Company have been ever since (becoming the Royal Ballet in 1956). She was the Company's pre-war choreographer till ASHTON joined; her main ballets, Job, The Rake's Progress, Checkmate, are still performed. She retired from directorship of Royal Ballet in 1963 to run the Royal Ballet School till 1971. She is still active as producer and advisor to the company and School.

W Waltz is a dance of moderate tempo, performed in 3-in-a-measure time. The waltz reached Vienna fairly late in the 1700s and it was in the 1850s that it was raised to a peak of perfection, encouraged by the music of the STRAUSS (see page 87) family.

Drama, like dance, has its roots in ancient ritual. Modern western theatre, however, derives from the ancient Greeks, whose magnificent open-air theatres still testify to the popularity of classical Greek drama.

Theatre

At its simplest, a theatre is a space in which performers enact a drama, and in which an audience views it. These two functions determine the character of a theatre. The area in which the drama is performed may be a simple platform set in an open space, or it may be an elaborately engineered building containing separate spaces for the players and the audience.

Whatever its form, the arrangement of the theatre acts as a powerful constraint on the drama produced in it. Early theatres developed out of the needs of emerging dramatic forms. Scholars believe that the circular shape of early theatres in Ancient Greece may have been a response to the form of the *dithyramb* (a hymn to the god Dionysus). This was probably chanted by a chorus performing a cyclic dance around a leader. Once built, a permanent theatre has an appetite for dramas that playwrights must fit into its shape and style. In this way, theatres themselves influence dramas written for them.

The stage

Architects of new theatres are usually asked to design stages that can be treated with great flexibility. Theatre companies may plan to stage plays ranging from Greek tragedy, which requires chorus space, to Elizabethan classics, for which an apron stage (*see page 98*) may be a marked advantage. For those plays written in the

Above: Actors in Ancient Greece wore masks. The custom gave the characters a heroic dimension.

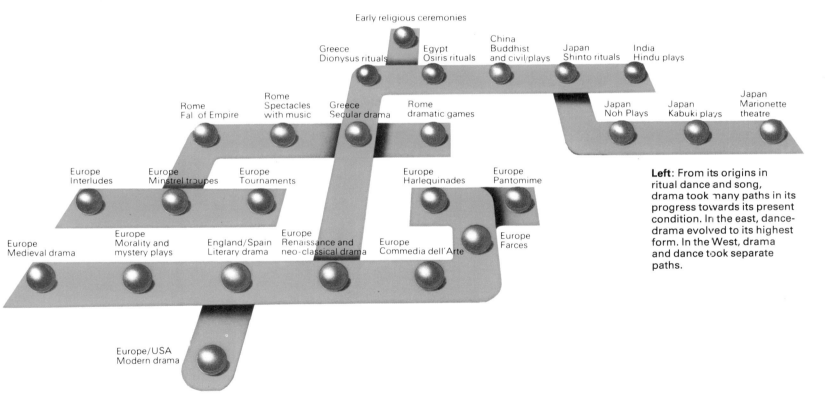

Left: From its origins in ritual dance and song, drama took many paths in its progress towards its present condition. In the east, dance-drama evolved to its highest form. In the West, drama and dance took separate paths.

Early religious ceremonies

Greece Dionysus rituals · Egypt Osiris rituals · China Buddhist and civil/plays · Japan Shinto rituals · India Hindu plays

Rome Fall of Empire · Rome Spectacles with music · Greece Secular drama · Rome dramatic games · Japan Noh Plays · Japan Kabuki plays · Japan Marionette theatre

Europe Interludes · Europe Minstrel troupes · Europe Tournaments · Europe Harlequinades · Europe Pantomime

Europe Medieval drama · Europe Morality and mystery plays · England/Spain Literary drama · Europe Renaissance and neo-classical drama · Europe Commedia dell'Arte · Europe Farces

Europe/USA Modern drama

Reference

A **Abbey Theatre,** Dublin, was founded in 1893, and became an important focal point of the Gaelic renaissance in Ireland. From 1904 the theatre became a home for plays by Irish dramatists. W. B. Yeats (1865–1939), a playwright himself and probably Ireland's greatest poet, was a director from its foundation, and inspired its policy for many years. The new realism of the turn of the century quickly found a place in the theatre, and the naturalistic style of many of its productions attracted dramatists such as Oscar Wilde (1854–1900), George Bernard Shaw (1856–1950), J. M. Synge (1871–1909), Sean O'Casey (1884–1964) and Brendan Behan (1923–64). It was an ideal training ground.

Ariosto, Ludovico (1474–1533) was court poet to the ruler of Ferrara in Italy. His plays imitate closely the styles and forms of the Roman playwrights, Plautus and Terence, but have the vigour of his own time. The first of his surviving plays is *The Casket,* which he wrote in prose (1508) and later composed into verse (1528). *The Counterfeits,* a play similarly written first in prose (1509) and later versified (1529), provided material for Shakespeare's *The Taming of the Shrew.* Ariosto's later plays – *The Bawd* (1529), *The Charlatan* (1520) and *The Academic Comedy* (finished after his death by his brother in 1553) – are accomplished and vivid plays with richly observed characters that are contemporary rather than classical.

B **Battens** are strips of wood bound into the tops and bottoms of scene cloths. The term also refers to strips of overhead flood-lights. The lights are arranged in 3 or 4 alternating circuits so that the electrician can mix colours. In the US they are known as border lights.

Beaumarchais, Pierre Augustin Caron de (1732–99) is remembered for his plays *The Barber of Seville* (1775) and *The Marriage of Figaro* (1784), which both formed the basis for stories of much loved operas (*see page 84*). Common to both plays is the character called Figaro, who is full of good sense and a man of the people, especially in his attitude to aristo-

Pierre Beaumarchais

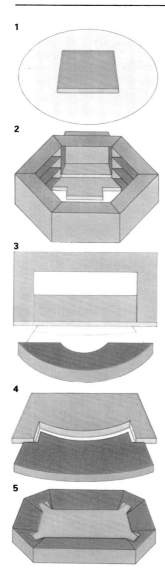

1700s, a proscenium (*see left*) would provide a setting close to the dramatist's original idea. So the architect often has to design an environment which will suit many kinds of drama. Most architects solve the problem by choosing a stage that may be adapted to two or more shapes.

Most stages are one of three types: an arena or theatre-in-the-round; a stage with a deep apron; and a proscenium stage with or without an apron. These are generally enclosed in a building with facilities for players and audience, but some theatres – even in cold climates – are open to the air.

The open air theatre has traditions reaching back to the earliest days of drama, and is particularly well suited to plays that include strong elements of pageantry and spectacle. The ideal site for such a theatre lies in a natural amphitheatre, sloping down to an arena stage. Behind the stage area there is usually a building which the company may adapt as part of the scenery, and which may house dressing rooms. Generally, in open air productions, scenery is kept to a minimum. Many open air theatres in city parks have no building at all. The producer uses the natural shape of the ground, trees and bushes as the setting for the play. Many of these theatres offer rich possibilities to the producer for moving large forces of actors about the stage.

Planners have long been attracted by the advantages of the arena stage, where actors play to an audience that surrounds them – sometimes

Above: Through history the Western stage has assumed many shapes. At first (**1**), people viewed the play from all sides. In the Renaissance, a deep apron stage (**2**) appeared in England. The proscenium stage (**3**) followed, all over Europe. The advantages of proscenium and apron (**4**) were combined in this century, and some designers returned to arena stages (**5**).

entirely, but more often on three sides only. They have built several theatres on this principle in the last few decades, and have described them variously as arena theatres or theatres-in-the-round.

The commonest European theatres are those with a proscenium. These have galleries of seats arranged in a roughly horseshoe-shaped plan, and a rectangular area of groundfloor seating. At the open end of the horseshoe, there is a large arch across which a curtain may be drawn. Behind this frame, called the proscenium, lies the stage. The audience in such a theatre sees a play produced as an illusion, rather in the way it might view a picture in its frame. In order to retrieve some of the contact between actors and audience that is lost with the proscenium, directors frequently add an extension to the stage, carrying it well beyond the proscenium. The extension, known as an apron, may be permanent or temporary.

Many theatres of the last 50 years incorporate the advantages of all these systems. The near-circular auditorium means that each row of seats can hold large numbers. However, the number of rows is kept to a minimum so that the most distant are still quite close to the acting area. The

---

crats. Some people see him as a revolutionary character who heralds the ensuing conflict in France. The plays are comedies of intrigue, a common type of the period, but Beaumarchais had a subtle way with dialogue which raised these dramas to an artistic peak. His humour is darkened by underlying pain, almost threat. In 1767 Beaumarchais published an essay on serious drama concerning the cult of sentiment which was sweeping all forms of literature in Europe at this time. He attacked the lack of

appeal in classical characters and events on the grounds that they were too distant, and claimed that by observing relationships between contemporary people he could move his audience more than the classical revivalists.
Beckett, Samuel (1906–) was born in Dublin, but later settled in Paris. Writing mainly in French, he translated his plays into English. In them he unites wit and humour with the pain of tragedy. In many of his plays, such as *Waiting for Godot* (1952), he expresses

the basic failure of human beings to communicate successfully. Human solitude is a recurring theme in Beckett's plays, and the

Beckett, Waiting for Godot

absurdity of life is a constant source of wonder to the author. His plays *Endgame* (1957) and *Krapp's Last Tape* (1959) have had an international influence on dramatists, but few have gone so far as Beckett in showing the human spirit's capacity to survive pain and torment.
Blank verse was introduced into England in the 1500s and since then has been used by many poets, most notably Shakespeare, in dramatic or epic works. Blank verse, which is unrhymed, is also known as iambic pentameter.

Boom is a pole, similar to a scaffolding pole. The electrician secures his lamps to it and suspends it above the stage.
Box set is scenery consisting of three walls of a room, the fourth wall being open to the audience. The set may include a ceiling to complete the illusion of looking into a room through an open wall.
Brecht, Bertolt (1898–1956) was a German poet and dramatist whose experimental and poetic approach to drama made him a powerful influence in the theatre. From the 1920s onwards he

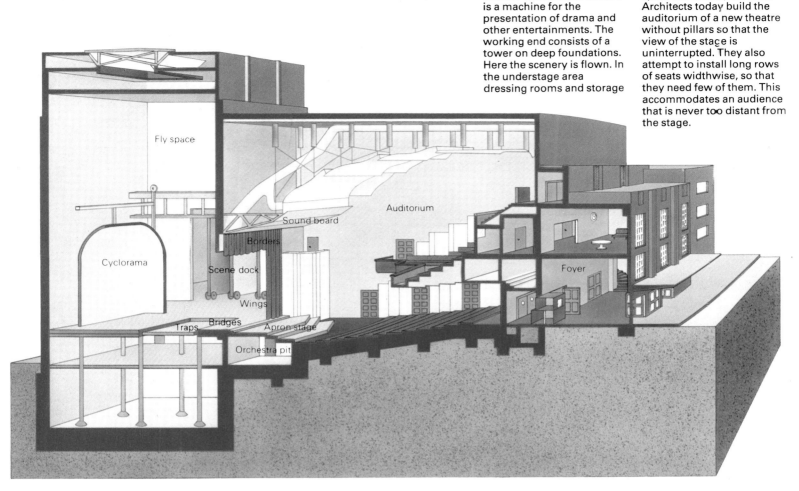

Below: The modern theatre is a machine for the presentation of drama and other entertainments. The working end consists of a tower on deep foundations. Here the scenery is flown. In the understage area dressing rooms and storage space are usually fitted in. Architects today build the auditorium of a new theatre without pillars so that the view of the stage is uninterrupted. They also attempt to install long rows of seats widthwise, so that they need few of them. This accommodates an audience that is never too distant from the stage.

Above left: This modern deeply jutting apron stage almost gives the audience an all-round view of the acting area.

Left: The conventional proscenium stage of this mid 1900s theatre has a small apron at the front to increase the stage area.

stage is generally a little below the playgoer's eye-level, and extended well forward. This type of stage is a compromise between the deep apron stage and the arena, allowing the audience to view the play from three sides, and giving the producer space at the back for creating an illusion with scenery.

The illusion

A director creates settings for a play with the aid of stage designers and their staff, and the stage hands who manipulate the scenery and lighting. During the 1800s and the early 1900s, staging of plays became increasingly elaborate. Some included such extremes as realistic forest fires and waterfall scenes. Scene changes for these extravagant effects held up the play for long periods while stage hands wrestled with scenery

and heavy stage dressing. In the modern theatre, directors usually reduce these interruptions to a minimum by using the ingenuity of designers and stage staff. It has been traditional for much scenery to be painted on canvas stretched across wooden frames called flats. These are usually constructed as tall rectangles reaching up to the borders that cross the stage to mask the BATTENS of lights. Stage hands secure the flats in position by bracing them and weighting the foot of each brace. When several flats are joined, perhaps to make a wall, the stage staff may lash them together with cords that bind round CLEATS or pass through ring screws.

The stage carpenter makes cut-outs for such shapes as tree trunks, and attaches them to frames in much the same way as the painter treats flats. Many sets for conventional pros-

required productions of his plays to show the mechanics of staging, so that the illusion would not sweep the audience 'into another world'. He wanted audiences to use their intellects rather than submit to their imaginations. Brecht wrote songs for many of his plays. *The Threepenny Opera* (1928), based on John Gay's *Beggar's Opera* (1728) has a score by Kurt Weill (1900–1950). Brecht was a Marxist, and in his plays his desire to preach opposition to capitalist society is mixed with sympathy for the

wretchedness of humanity. *Mother Courage* (1941) and *The Good Woman of Setzuan* (1943) are plays that concern dilemmas of moral

Bertolt Brecht

choice. The *Caucasian Chalk Circle* (1955) is the outstanding product of Brecht's search for the form of a modern epic drama. From 1948 he directed the Berliner Ensemble, one of the most vital of European theatres.
Bridge has more than one meaning in theatrical usage. The first describes a catwalk used for access to lighting. It may extend over part of the auditorium as well as across the stage. The second meaning is the floor sections of the stage which the technicians can raise and lower.
Business is the term used to

describe actions performed by actors while playing their roles. For example, an actor may add weight to a pause by removing his spectacles and polishing them before continuing his speech.

C **Calderon de la Barca,** Pedro (1600–81) was one of Spain's most gifted playwrights, working towards the end of its golden age of drama. Calderon was educated as a Jesuit, but left his studies of theology to become poet to the Spanish court. His plays express the stern code of

behaviour demanded of Spanish aristocrats at the time, and some people find his mannered style lacking in humanity. His early plays are of the cloak-and-dagger kind, as in *The Lady Fairy* (c. 1629) which includes 2 duels But the central female character, Lady Angela, brings a fresh and delightful sense of comedy to the play. Of the philosophical plays that follow, perhaps the greatest is *Life's a Dream* (c. 1636), a play which has more universal appeal than much of his writing. After 1651, Calderon took holy

cenium stages include a number of flats set at an angle at the sides of the stage. These mask the actors waiting in the wings, and block the audience's view of off-stage activity. These flats (sometimes curtains are used for the same purpose) are called legs or wings.

The BOX SET is constructed entirely of flats, to reproduce the shape of a room. However, it is less used now than in the past. Instead, designers may arrange their furniture and a couple of walls of flats set at an angle to suggest part of a room. Backgrounds to open air settings are usually painted on backcloths, which can be suspended, or flown (see FLY TOWER) when a change of scene is needed.

Changing the set

In many theatres, a strong grid above the stage supports a number of pulley blocks from which scenery may be flown. Ropes pass through the blocks and are tied to the scenery. The other ends of the ropes are secured to two rows of cleats that are fixed to a rail in the FLY GALLERY. When the stage hands set the scene, they secure the ropes of flown scenery to the lower row of cleats. This row remains tied at all times. When they raise the scene to the flies, the stage hands secure it to the upper row of cleats. In this way, they can lower the scene into position precisely, without repeated checks.

Above: The vogue for classical theatre in the 1600s led to elaborate sets of stately Greek and Roman exteriors.

Right: Some stage effects of the last century were ingenious. Figures were mysteriously revealed or moved, wine spouted from inn signs and smoke swirled on to the stage.

Increasingly, sets are built in rigid sections and secured to trucks (low platforms that run on castors). This method allows stage hands to assemble a scene rapidly, with all the furniture and properties in position. It is a system that demands an off-stage storage space, known as a SCENE DOCK.

For some lavish productions, two or more scenes may be set up on a revolving platform. By using a hand winch or electric power, a stage hand can turn this to reveal a new scene, perhaps with actors already in position. A few large theatres have a mechanized or ELEVATOR STAGE, parts of which can be raised or lowered mechanically. Some of these have so great an area below stage that an entire scene can be prepared there, the platform rolled back, and the scene raised into place. In other theatres, stage hands drive wagon stages (mechanized and enlarged trucks) on stage ready to play.

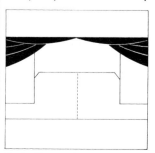

Lighting

The director uses the skills of a lighting engineer to create the impression of the time of day, the atmosphere of the play, and many other aspects of production. Scenes are lit by lights fixed to battens above the stage, and others above the audience. Among the various types of lights used are footlights (or FLOATS) that lie across the front of the stage at foot level, floodlights fixed to stands in the wings, and spotlights for picking out detail from the wings or from the back of the theatre. The lights have frames in front of their lenses, and into these the lighting engineer slips slides (or GELS) of various colours to build the kinds of light the director wants. The engineer can change the lighting's intensity or colour balance at any moment by using a dimmer board. Slides or film can be used to project passing clouds or scenes on to the cyclorama, which is an area of curved plaster at the back of the stage. The director, lighting engineer and stage manager also control the sounds that help to provide the play's audible setting.

Staging a play

There is no one way of staging a play, as the procedure varies with situations. The production sequence for a REPERTORY company playing in its own theatre differs from that of a company which is assembled for one play only, preparing for a theatre strange to the actors and producers.

The play's director first studies the script, to develop his understanding of its characters, the unfolding of the plot, and its setting. The director also consults with the designer, head of the wardrobe staff, and with the stage manager of the theatre in which the play is to be presented. They agree on a visual style for the play. A little later, the director chooses actors and actresses and discusses the production with them. The designer may set up models of the set designs in a miniature theatre and use tufts of dyed material to simulate costumes so that the director can check his plans for movements against the scenery and positions of furniture.

The stage manager should also attend these meetings and carefully note requirements for stage dressing, personal PROPERTIES for the characters, special effects, such as DRY ICE for a misty scene, and anything else needed for the production. Next, the stage manager consults

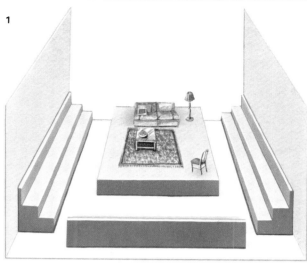

Right: (**1**) The arena stage presents the designer with the problem of creating an illusion without obscuring the audience's view from any angle. The stage has the advantage of bringing the actors close to the audience.

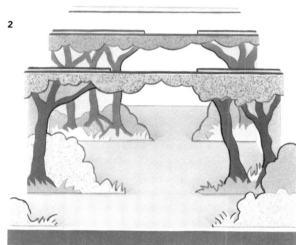

Right: (**2**) On a proscenium stage, the designer may use borders, cut-outs and flats to create a scene. He may 'fly' these for a quick change of set. In a scene, such as the one shown here, he will probably paint a back-cloth.

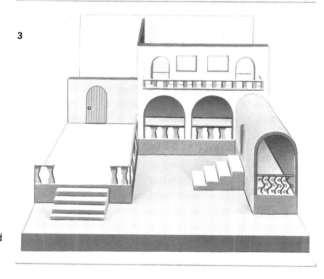

Right: (**3**) Box-sets, consisting of fairly accurate representations of enclosed areas, are common sets for modern plays. They are usually constructed of flats and fibreboard cut-outs. Stage designers often make them sturdy enough to stand up to actors climbing about on them.

---

the first sentimental comedy. However, sentiment had been an element underlying many dramas for nearly a generation. Cibber's book *Apology* (1740), is a valuable source of material on theatre of the period.

Cleat is a double prong of wood or metal that projects from a rail. Stagehands secure rope lines to it when flying scenery or BATTENS. Flats of painted scenery have cleats so that a line may be looped around them, securing the flats to their neighbours.

Cocteau, Jean (1891–1963)

Jean Cocteau

was a French poet, playwright and film director. In his work for the theatre, he revolted against the prevailing realistic style, and his own plays show a variety of styles. Some, such as *The Human Voice* (1937) are even close to realism. His interest in SURREALISM surfaces in *Antigone* (1922), especially in *Orphée* (1926) and in *The Infernal Machine* (1943). Cocteau interested many great artists in designing for the theatre, including Pablo Picasso, Henri Matisse, Max Ernst and Joan Miró.

Comédie Francais, also called *Théâtre Français*, is

the national theatre of France. An earlier name, *La maison de Molière,* also persists. The company has no stars. Roles are distributed among the *sociétaires* (associates) by discussion and agreement. Louis XIV established the theatre in 1680 by merging two troupes of comedians, one led by Molière and the other by Béjart. Its doors closed during the Revolution, but Napoleon reopened them in 1803. The theatre burned down in 1900 and was rebuilt.

Comedy of humours is a

style of comedy seen in the plays of the English dramatist Ben Jonson (1572–1637). His characters are strong, simple concepts which personify a folly or vice. Through his satirical dialogue, Jonson hoped that his audience might laugh as they were confronted by their faults, and that they might learn to rise above them. The ancient doctrine of humours was proposed by the Roman Galen (c. 130–c.200). It stated that a person's temperament resulted from the proportions of the 4 humours (blood, phlegm,

Left: Many play directors find that they must rehearse in rooms away from the stage where the play will appear. They have to make their cast aware of the size of the actual stage so that they can time their moves correctly.

Appoint producer   Choose play   Book theatre

Audition actors   Appoint designer

Learn lines   Agree design

Design programme   Learn moves   Working drawings

Check programme   Make sets   Lighting plot

Print programme   Dress rehearsal   First night

Above: Many of the sequences in the production of a play occur simultaneously. They require the most stringent management if the play is to appear successfully.

with the director to plan a rehearsal schedule for the actors and, later, the lighting and stage staff. The schedules of scene builders must also be co-ordinated with those of the wardrobe staff and the stage manager's assistants who seek suitable stage properties. Rehearsal rooms must be booked and it is also the stage manager's job to make sure that actors have scripts and that they know where and when to attend rehearsals.

At first rehearsals, the director reads through the play with the actors in order to plot their moves. The stage manager attends all rehearsals to make notes in his prompt copy. This copy of the script is used to record all the actors' moves and BUSINESS, as well as the positions of proper-ties, such as a box of matches which an actor may use to light a cigar. All events which involve actors or stage staff are carefully noted down and used to make CUE sheets for the scene shifters, property placing lists for the assistant stage managers, and cue sheets for the lighting man-ager and front of house staff.

Into the theatre

By the day appointed for moving into the theatre,

a director should have brought the actors to a point of readiness without their feeling stale. Sometimes a company has to move into a theatre early on Sunday morning and be ready to play late on Monday night. However, a play that is complex to stage will certainly need a longer time than this, and a few days may be allowed for settling in.

The scenery will have been prepared during rehearsal time, so that it is ready for fit-up on the first morning. During the first five or six hours, the sets should be fixed in position and flown or trucked in preparation for the scene changes. The stage manager marks the positions of scen-ery and furniture on the stage with coloured adhesive tape. For the next few hours, the electri-cian prepares lights with suitable colours, focuses them and tries lighting cues on the control panel. An assistant stage manager, probably the one who will later signal cues from the PROMPT CORNER, joins the director in the auditorium to check the lighting quality.

By about seven o'clock on this first day, the players should be ready for a technical dress rehearsal. The actors walk through their parts,

Right: Early in the planning of a play production, director, stage manager, designer, theatre manager and wardrobe mistress have a meeting.

---

black bile and yellow bile) present in their body. If these were in perfect balance, the personality would be ideal. Because characters in the comedy of humours were drawn on this basis, they leaned towards caricature rather than the rounded characters created by Shakespeare, for example.
Congreve, William (1670–1729) wrote mainly for the stage, and his plays depict the world of fashion-able manners. The poise of Congreve's dialogue, and the agility of his wit raise his

plays to the peak of Restora-tion comedy. His first play, *The Old Bachelor* (1693),

Congreve's The Way of the World

was an immediate success. His last, *The Way of the World*, was produced 7 years later and of its type is hard to match.
Constructivism was a movement that grew in Rus-sia just before World War I. Vladimir Tatlin (1885–1956) established the theory, which architects, painters and sculptors then applied to their arts. Constructivism was applied in the theatre by Alexander Tairov (1885–1950) and Vsevolod Meirhold (1874–1940). Tairov in his Moscow Kamerny Theatre, and

Meirhold in the Moscow Theatre of the Revolution worked with stages set with ladders, suspended plat-forms, scaffolding, ramps and other shapes reminis-cent of factories and build-ing sites. Actors climbed about, swung from and walked among these with varying degrees of acrobatic finesse. In the theatre Con-structivism was part of the revolt against the realistic style, and contributed to-wards EXPRESSIONISM.
Craig, Edward Gordon (1872–1947) was the son of a great English actress, Ellen

Terry (1848–1928). At about 13 years of age, he became an actor with the company of Sir Henry Irving (1838–1905) at the Lyceum Theatre, London. He grew dissatisfied with the style of naturalism that prevailed in the theatre of his time, and turned to stage design in 1900. In his sketches, Craig demonstrated the simple and grand use of space. Craig's system of movable screens and his powerful 'painting' with light was an influence that raced across Europe and the US.
Cue may be the last lines of

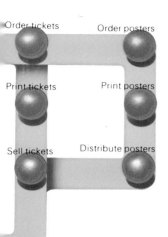

Right: The wardrobe department of a company makes a collection of costumes and materials, but frequently has to create new clothes for each production.

Order tickets Order posters

Print tickets Print posters

Sell tickets Distribute posters

concentrating on making their business work, checking positions of properties and timing costume changes. Meanwhile the director makes further checks on the sensitivity of the lighting, ensures that the sound effects can be heard clearly, that the scene changes will be prompt, and that the actors' make-up is satisfactory. On the following day, the stage staff and designer spend the morning correcting any flaws that the director may have noted in the technical dress rehearsal. By midday, the director meets actors and technical staff to give any further notes on the rehearsal. The dress rehearsal proper lasts throughout the afternoon, with actors and stage staff working almost at full pitch. After a halt for refreshment and press photographs, the players launch the first performance.

The history of drama
The roots of drama lie deep in the rituals of our prehistoric ancestors. Slowly, over many generations, dances and mimes performed in secret ceremonies emerged into public places, and that second element of the theatre – the audience – added its appreciation to the dramatic 'happening'. True drama then germinated. The earliest dramas seem to have included music, mime and dance as well as words. Indeed, words may well have been the last ingredient to be added. The actor frequently separated his own personality from that of the character portrayed by donning a mask. Within the mask, the actor mystically became the animal, god or hero that he played. This was a convention that continued into Ancient Greek and Asian theatre.

The earliest play for which some dialogue still exists is the *Abydos Passion Play*, performed by the ancient Egyptians to celebrate the death and rebirth of the god Osiris. This play may date back as far as 3200 BC and is a fragment of drama at what may have been a point of change, being half ritual and half theatre. Little is known of the earliest forms of Asian drama. Its full flowering occurred at the time of the European Middle Ages.

Drama in the East
The styles of Asian classical theatre are extremely formal. They depend on the common beliefs of the players and their rigorous training. The pursuit of perfection within the limits of his

one actor's speech. These lines will alert another actor to speak his own lines or to make a move. A cue to the stage staff is a signal to change a scene, alter lighting or to supply sound effects.

D **Dadaism** was an artistic movement originated by the poet Tristan Tzara (1896–1963). Its strongest influence was felt between 1916–22. Tzara and his followers rejected existing norms of behaviour and aesthetic standards, and 'spat in the eye of the world'.

In the theatre, Erwin Piscator (1893–1963) used aspects of Dadaism in his 'proletarian theatre' in Germany. His 'happenings' included much

Erwin Piscator

impromptu political and topical material, songs, revues, films, speeches and sketches. Dadaism's influence survived in the chamber theatre productions popular in the mid-1900s. For example, Picasso's farce *Desire Caught by the Tail*, played in an apartment in Paris in 1944, showed marked Dadaist tendencies.

Dips are small, covered sockets in the stage floor. When their lids are raised, they give access to electrical circuits.

Downstage is the part of

the stage nearest the auditorium.

Dress parade is the check made on each player's costumes immediately before the dress rehearsal. The actors don their costumes in correct order of precedence.

Domestic tragedy is characterized by its middle-class behaviour. Most domestic tragedies have sensational plots, and treat their characters – fairly ordinary men and women – with realism. Plays of this kind appeared in England and Spain towards the end of the 1500s, leaving the main-

stream of classical tragedy. Thomas Dekker (c. 1572–c. 1632) and Thomas Heywood (c. 1574–1641) were 2 dramatists who raised the style above the level of most plays of the type. Heywood's *A Woman Killed with Kindness* (1603) is one of the most frequently revived plays of the kind.

Drury Lane Theatre in London is the oldest English theatre still in use. The first theatre on the site was built by Sir Thomas Killigrew in 1663 and was called the Theatre Royal. It was destroyed by fire and rebuilt in

professional ideals and techniques is the ambition of a classical Asian actor. As a Japanese actor said, when advising his son, 'Above all, no originality'.

The inspiration of Indian drama permeates most of the classical theatres of Asia, the stage being populated by gods and heroes of Hindu myths. The principal religions of the sub-continent, Hinduism, Buddhism and Jainism, lend their own cultures to this theatre, providing its demon characters and its declamatory poetry. The Mughal invasions and the teachings of Islam failed to repress the vigour of this drama.

Its main characteristic to a Western audience is the close association of dance and drama. A mysterious figure, Bharata, writing around 100 BC tells all that is now known of early theatre in India. His great work is *Natyashastra*, which contains the essence of the classical theatre.

Indian drama

The ancient Indian dramatists wrote their plays around one dominant mood, and any part of the play which expressed another mood (*rasa*) was subordinated to the main *rasa*. Such a formal convention was also reflected in the rigidly disciplined gestures and vocal delivery of the actors. Their techniques are often indistinguishable

Right: Puppet dramas are popular in many parts of the world. These Balinese shadow puppets are of a fine quality elaborately painted. They are made from thin leather and jointed with rivets so that the puppeteer can make them move. He guides them by means of a stick attached to their backs. Between him and his audience there is a thin screen or a sheet. Behind the puppets, there is a strong light, which throws the puppets' shadows on the screen. The shadow puppet plays are mostly about legendary heroes, gods and comic folk-characters.

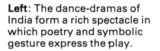

Left: The dance-dramas of India form a rich spectacle in which poetry and symbolic gesture express the play.

from dance, even in literary dramas.

Beside the serious subjects of Indian classical theatre, *prahasana* (forms of farce and satire) are active. In the most popular of these plays, *The Little Clay Cart*, by an unknown author, there is sharp social comment about the false piety of certain strict holy men. As well as the classical theatre, the *jatra* (a form of folk theatre) thrives. This incorporates a chorus which acts like that of Greek tragedy. The *jatra*, unlike the classical theatre, is played by male actors only. Its literary style is cruder than that of the classical theatre, but its subject matter is often similar.

Drama and Islam

In Islamic countries, drama was affected by the fact that the personification of God and the making of masks in human form was prohibited. Perhaps the only play to survive is the *Taziya* passion play, which explores the legends surrounding the succession of the sons of Muhammad. Its performance did not follow the medieval conquests of Islam, but stayed within the borders of Iran. The actors in this play are amateur, often reading from their scripts in performance. They play on a platform or in a courtyard, using the barest suggestion of scenery. Gabriel may step down from a stool to simulate his descent from heaven, and a large waterpot may represent the River Euphrates. An Islamic leader, or *mullah*, raised above the players, narrates parts of the play and comments on the action. All of the roles, including that of the Prophet Muhammad's mother, are played by men.

1674 to plans by Sir Christopher Wren. Since that time, the theatre has been rebuilt twice. The present building is by Benjamin Wyatt who completed it in 1812. Within its walls almost every kind of entertainment has been played, from opera to variety and circus.
Dry Ice is one of the materials used to create a smoke or mist effect on the stage. Chips of dry ice (a solid form of carbon dioxide) are dropped into warm water, and the resulting vapour is blown across the stage by means of an electric fan.

More commonly, stage managers heat a smoke canister, sometimes called a smokepot, on an electric hotplate. The smoke pours out of the canister, and is fanned across the stage. The stagehands must take care that the smoke does not float into the audience, where it might cause outbreaks of coughing and annoyance.

E **Elevator stage** is a mechanical stage. Stage staff can raise sections of it by winches or by electric power.
Eliot, Thomas Stearns

(1888–1965) was probably the most successful of those dramatists who attempted to

T. S. Eliot

revive poetic drama from the 1930s onwards. For his first play in this vein, *Murder in the Cathedral* (1935), Eliot returned to the ancient device of the chorus. His chorus of the common women of Canterbury provides the setting for Thomas à Becket's towering heroism. For his later plays, Eliot took everyday settings, and tried to create a poetic drama in commonplace surroundings. *The Family Reunion* (1939) is a reshaping of the Greek legend of Orestes, but *The Cocktail Party* (1949) is unconnected with legend.

His last play, *The Elder Statesman*, appeared 10 years later.

Existentialism is a movement which flowered in the 1900s, the followers of which are concerned with man's relationship to God or the universe. Most existentialists hold that a man's fate rests with his own actions and is not determined by outside forces. The writer Jean-Paul Sartre (1905–80) was one of its most famous adherents.

Expressionism was an artistic movement which

The puppet plays of Turkey neatly sidestep the Islamic ban on images of humans. The puppets, usually made of camel leather, play in front of a light to throw shadows on a sheet placed between them and their audience. Most of the plays are about the adventures of two Turkish heroes, Karagoz and Hadjeivat. A form of rural theatre, consisting of farcical mimicry of easily recognized stock characters, has provided a base for modern Turkish dramatists to create a national drama.

Drama in China and Japan

In China, an elaborate and refined tradition had developed by the time *The Hundred Yuan Plays* were printed about AD 1600. These were the product of a long history of Chinese theatre, perhaps reaching back to the early Chow dynasty (1122–255BC). Classical forms differed from province to province, but in all there was a unity of music, dance and poetry. This is shown, for example, in the Peking Opera style, which the Emperor Ch'ien Lung (AD 1736–95) first brought to Peking. In this style the actor creates the illusion with very little scenery and props. He uses a finely disciplined technique to express the action and emotions of the play, and the ensemble playing is of a precision rarely matched elsewhere.

From a long history of theatre in Japan, there emerged about the 1400s a classical theatre which took its themes of chivalry from the *samurai* warrior class and aristocratic society. There are about 800 Nō plays, as dramas in this style are called. The actors perform on a stage nearly seven metres square, and wear wooden masks. Musicians sit at the back of the stage, and a chorus sits to the right. Very little scenery is used. Appreciation of a Nō play (Nō means ability) demands a full understanding of its use of intricate symbols and subtle allusions to legend.

The leisured classes enjoyed the Nō play, and the lower classes supported its offshoot, which is called Kabuki. The Kabuki actor, unlike his Nō counterpart, plays with histrionic emphasis. He

Above: (1) Wooden masks of the Nō plays and the stylised make-up of (2) kabuki actors of Japan help to lift the characters into an other-world dimension.

Below: The rich tradition of Chinese street theatre, largely dead on the mainland, survives in Singapore.

arose in the early 1900s, mainly in Germany. It grew in reaction to naturalism and realism and laid emphasis on strong emotion and inner vision. In the theatre, expressionism tried to present emotional reality rather than naturalistic reality, relying heavily on the use of symbols.
Extravaganza and the fairy play were chiefly products of the 1800s. J. R. Planché (1796–1880) discovered the public's taste for fantasy, and wrote burlesques (*see page 113*) of everyday situations and characters, then

set them in fairy isles. W. S. Gilbert (1836–1911), of Gilbert and Sullivan fame, wrote with a delightful, topsy-turvy humour such extravaganzas as *The Palace of Truth* (1870) and *The Wicked World* (1873). His libretti for the operettas written with Sir Arthur Sullivan (1842–1900) had the same humour.

F **Farce** is a form of comic play with lighthearted, broad humour. The form has its roots in the comedies of the Roman playwright Plautus. Early English farces

include Shakespeare's *Comedy of Errors* (c. 1593). Comedies which do not fall into the category may have farcical episodes. Today, farce is

Feydeau farce

a term generally applied to knock-about comedies of the kind written by Georges Feydeau (1863–1921) with such panache.
Floats is the name given to the footlights. They lie in a strip across the front of the stage at the level of the actors' feet.
Fly tower is the tall area above a stage into which stagehands fly the scenery. This means that they suspend the scenery from it and haul it up out of sight when it is not in use.
Fly gallery is the walkway above the stage in the FLY

TOWER. Stagehands secure the scenery to the rail which runs along it.
Forestage is the area in a proscenium theatre between the front curtain and the footlights.

G **Garrick,** David (1717–79) was generally acclaimed the greatest actor of the English stage in the 1700s. His straightforward manner, clear diction and intelligent interpretations of great roles such as Richard III and King Lear drove the prevailing declamatory style of acting from the stage.

Left: Romans made many small statuettes of favourite actors, such as this comedian, which was found in Campania.

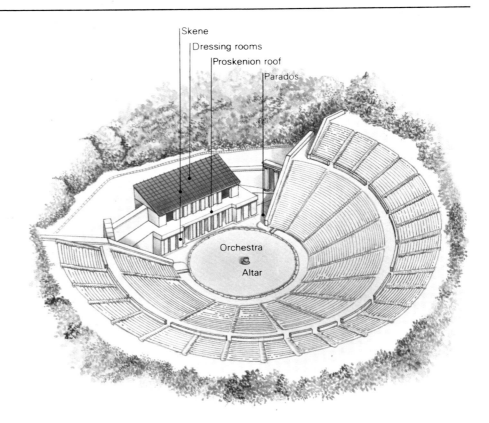

Above: An Ancient Greek theatre consisted of an amphitheatre, around a segment of which the audience sat. Below them, a space for the chorus had an altar at its centre. Beyond this rose the stage building. Actors might play in front of the *proskenion* or from its roof. Painted screens and backcloths attached to the *skene* helped to set the scene.

makes up his face in a bizarre manner to express the character of his role. The Kabuki plays and a form of puppet theatre remain the most popular kinds of Japanese classical theatre.

With the expansion of European cultural influence in Asia during the 1800s – a time when European theatre was not at its best – Western drama made a large and sometimes destructive impact on Asian theatre. In India and Turkey, new playwrights were much influenced by such writers as Henrik IBSEN and wrote for an audience eager to explore themes of social reconstruction. These heralded the birth of national theatre in many parts of Asia. The Western playwrights showed a corresponding interest in Asian theatre, especially in the Japanese classical tradition, and, to a lesser extent, in the Chinese theatre.

Drama in the West

About 490 BC, the curtain rose on theatre in Europe. About this time, Aeschylus (525–456 BC), the first dramatist whose work is known to us, presented his play *The Suppliants* to the citizens of Athens. His play was the result of a long evolution of dramatic rituals, especially the gradual changes which took place in the presentation of the dithyramb (*see page 97*). Some time in the 500s or 600s BC, the choral leader (*exarchos*) separated from the chorus to take up an individual role as protagonist, or main character. The chorus itself acted as antagonist opposite him. This produced a situation in which lay the possibility of conflict, and therefore of drama.

Thespis, who worked about the 530s BC, was the first man known to lead the dithyramb, and so became the first actor, giving the name Thespian to all actors who followed him.

The theatre at this time consisted of rows of rough wooden benches descending a slope to a wide circle below. No buildings would have interrupted the view of the landscape, although a temple might have been seen nearby. Later, the Greeks constructed more formal theatres made of stone, although these were still open to the sky. Beyond the circular area (the *orchestra*) in which the chorus performed about a central altar (*thymele*), a building was added to act as a background and changing rooms for the actors. In the latest theatres, this building (*skene*) had two storeys, the lower one projecting forward to make a stage above the chorus.

In Aeschylus's dramas, the chorus assumed its role as commentator and narrator, while two actors played the protagonist and antagonist. Aeschylus's young contemporary, Sophocles (c. 496–406 BC) added a third actor to the protagonist and antagonist. Each actor might play

Right: The Roman theatre evolved from the Greek. Romans reduced the orchestra, and built a wide, shallow stage. They could also erect an awning above the auditorium to keep the audience dry in wet weather.

From 1747 to 1776 he managed the DRURY LANE THEATRE, where he stopped the practice of seating the privileged members of the audience on stage, and concealed the stage lighting behind reflectors. While at Drury Lane, he trained his cast of actors and wrote plays. In writing his best-known play, *The Clandestine Marriage* (1766), he collaborated with George Colman the elder (1732–94). **Gel** is the name still given to the coloured filters fitted into stage lights. It derives from the fact that once they were manufactured from gelatine.

Goethe, Johann Wolfgang von (1749–1832) was a poet, scientist, novelist and dramatist, and did more to establish a theatre of quality in Germany than any one before him. His first play *Goetz von Berlichingen* (1773) is part of that intensely emotional aspect of the Romantic movement called *sturm und drang* (storm and stress). After a visit to Italy, he was carried away by the classical ideal, and returned to write *Egmont* (1788), a historical drama, and *Iphigenia in Tauris* (1787). His *Faust*

(1808 and 1831) is on so vast a scale and so difficult to produce that it has rarely been performed. Its poetry and scope perhaps serve best as inspiration to other dramatists, encouraging them to attempt extensive themes.

Goldoni, Carlo (1707–93) was a Venetian who began his career as a dramatist by writing for *Commedia del' arte*, but soon felt that he must write for a more realistic stage. He took as his model Molière, and moved to Paris where he wrote for the Italian theatre for several

years. His plays are rich in comic invention, but are without the underlying seri-

Carlo Goldoni

ousness that supports Molière's work. Goldoni's plays, despite his rejection of *Commedia del' arte* are alive with developments of its roles. For example, in *The Family of the Antiquary* (1749), he writes the stock character of Pantalone as a rounded and sentimental man full of good sense and warm-heartedness. Goldoni's best known plays, 16 in all, appeared in one season, 1750–51. These include *The Liar* and *The Pretended Invalid*.

Goldsmith, Oliver (c. 1730–74) was a novelist and play-more than one role, changing costume and mask rapidly in the *skene* building.

All actors in the Greek theatre wore masks to express the heroic or godlike stature of their parts. They wore the long-sleeved robe adopted by Aeschylus, and the *cothurnus*, a high-platformed boot that gave the actor impressive height. The playwright himself often took an acting part in his play, trained the chorus and provided it with music. With Sophocles, these tasks became more specialized, and were divided among several individuals.

Tragedy and comedy

Most of the Greek tragedies are about heroic legends, the gods and fate. The playwrights wrote trilogies (such as the *Oresteia* by Aeschylus,

Above: This wall painting of a Roman theatre was found at Pompeii and shows an earlier form than the one shown below, probably used for gladiatorial contests as well as plays.

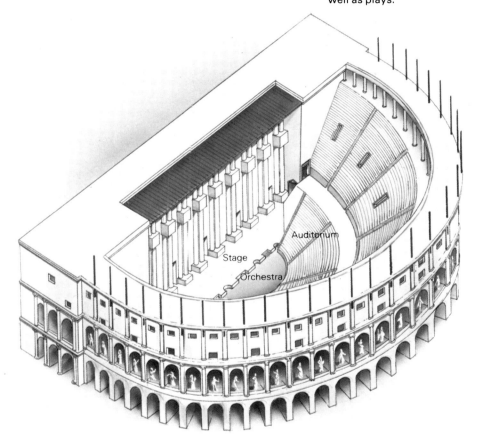

Auditorium
Stage
Orchestra

on the fate of Orestes) often with a fourth play, a satire which was a BURLESQUE (*see page 113*) of the previous three. The plays of Euripides (c.480 –406 BC) are sharp with disillusion, and with this playwright, the real world entered what had been a largely idealized, mystical theatre. Euripides sees all his characters in the light of common day. Not all Greek plays were tragedies, however. The Dionystic festivals in which playwrights competed included comedies after 486 BC. Of these, the greatest are by Aristophanes (c. 448–c.388 BC). He employed his art to express his belief in man's desire for freedom and the moral virtues of his ancestors. The comedies are a rich mixture of crude bawdy and lyric poetry, but their purpose is generally serious and philosophical or political.

There are few surviving plays of the New Comedy, but its most prominent writer may have been Menander (343–292 BC). His plays were more domestic than those of the Old Comedy and, like Euripides, he reduced the role of the chorus, so strengthening the importance of the actors. Women's roles, played by men, received more attention than they did in most earlier plays.

Roman Theatre

Roman theatre at first depended mainly on translations from the Greek. A tradition of mime, based largely on the grotesque characters of the Old Comedy, spread north from Sicily. The first Roman playwright of note was Titus Maccius Plautus (c.254–184 BC), who welded together a

---

wright who wrote his best work in his two fine comedies *The Good Natur'd Man* (1768) and *She Stoops to Conquer* (1773). These plays brought a new breath of realism into the contrived and sentimental theatre of his day.

Gorky, Maxim (1868–1936) was a Russian novelist and playwright who drew on his harsh experience of life as a boy and young man to people his plays with keenly observed and deeply felt characters. His masterpiece, *The Lower Depths* (1903), is filled with a sense of this

hard-won strength. The play has no main plot, but con-

Maxim Gorky

sists of a series of episodes that Gorky skillfully weaves together. It took 30 years for Gorky to reach this peak again, in *Egor Bulichov and Others* (1932). Planned as part of a trilogy, this play shows the writer's powerful sense of theatre.

Gozzi, Count Carlo (1720–1806) was an Italian playwright who immersed himself in the characters and fantasy of the *Commedia del' arte*. He wrote with a sharply satirical pen and his best plays are the *fiabe* (fairytales with a purpose). These were the first Italian

fable plays. They are absurd, humorous, ironic and make cutting attacks on the sentimental dramas of his time. Gozzi left room in such plays as *The Crow* (1761), *Turandot* (1762) and *The Magic Bird* (1765) for actors to improvise.

Green room is a place set aside in a theatre, usually near the stage, where actors may rest, relax and entertain visitors.

H Hauptmann, Gerhart Johann Robert (1862–1946) was a German poet and dramatist who took

his audience by storm with his first play *Before Dawn* (1889). This depicts a group of characters who are, with 2 exceptions, in the deepest state of degradation. *The Weavers* (1892) uses a crowd as the central 'character'. Once again the setting is grim, the subject of the play being revolution. Constantly struggling for something new, Hauptmann entered the theatre of fantasy in his *Schluck and Jau* (1899). The body of his work is concerned with revolution and with portrayals of the working class.

style from the plots and forms of Menander with FARCES from Sicily and Campania. His style included a mixture of naturalistic dialogue and lyric poetry, while his plots are romantic, sentimental and spiced with ribald farce.

Few playwrights have had more influence on other dramatists than Lucius Annaeus Seneca (c.4BC–AD 65), although his plays were probably intended for private reading rather than performance. It was to his tragedies that dramatists of the Renaissance turned for their models. His own plays exaggerated the style of Euripides into sensational MELODRAMA. The form of his plays proved to be very valuable to later dramatists.

Medieval and Renaissance drama

After the fall of the Roman Empire, in the AD 400s, Europe was starved of drama. Only itinerant groups of mimic players kept alive the spark lit in Greece. The Church at first did not approve of these crude pantomimes, but by the 1400s its own liturgy provided a source for medieval drama. Priests acted a few brief lines of the Easter story of the Resurrection during the Latin service. Gradually, the liturgical plays grew beyond the confines of church buildings and were written and acted by ordinary citizens. They performed cycles of Mystery plays, which dramatized biblical episodes. Perhaps the best

Above: The pageant stages of the Middle Ages processed to stations where they paused to perform before continuing. These magnificent pageants were painted in Brussels in 1616.

Below: The popular characters of the Italian *Commedia del' arte* included stock types who appeared in new guises in drama all over Europe.

known of these is the Passion Play of Oberammergau which dates from the 1600s. Other plays took plots that used abstract figures, as, for example, personifications of Fellowship and Everyman. These were Morality plays. FARCES, INTERLUDES, MASQUES and MUMMING PLAYS provided entirely secular drama.

The Renaissance blossomed first in Italy, and writers of this period turned to the plays of Roman dramatists in order to recreate the classical theatre for their aristocratic audiences. At first they staged the plays on wooden platforms in the palaces of noblemen in Rome and Ferrara. The stages were backed by arches, between which hung curtains. After the discovery of the work of the Roman architect Vitruvius and his treatise *De Architectura* (before AD 27), the Italians concentrated on the lavish production of plays. They built such theatres as Teatro Olimpico at Vicenza (1594) with its wide, shallow stage backed by a series of stone arches. The centre arch was large, and revealed a sizeable acting area. The archways could be curtained, or opened to reveal realistically painted scenes of rooms or streets. The spectacular nature of this type of theatre attracted such writers as Niccolo Machiavelli (1469–1527) and Ludovico Ariosto (1474–1533). The Italians' main contribution to theatre of this period was in establishing the shape of the modern European theatre and setting high standards of lavish presentation. Meanwhile, scholars researching into the *Poetics* of the ancient Greek philosopher, Aristotle (384–322 BC) produced a theory of dramatic unity. The 'three unities' as the theory was called,

Coviello

Arlecchino

Pantalone

Ibsen, Henrik (1828–1906) was a Norwegian poet and dramatist in whose work may be seen most of the aims that his contemporaries in the theatre were striving for. Ibsen spent a long theatrical apprenticeship as stage manager and playwright to the National Stage in Bergen. Always one or 2 steps ahead of his age, he was eager to unveil those areas of society that his contemporaries preferred to keep well muffled. His plays were ill received at home, and after 1884 he worked in Italy and Germany

for much of his life. Ibsen's first plays were poetic dramas on historical and folk subjects. He won his audi-

Ibsen, The Dolls House

ence with *Love's Comedy* (1862) and followed it with *Brand* (1866), a tragedy of idealism. The poetic play *Peer Gynt* (1867) ends this phase of his writing. He then launched into a series of plays about society, presented in a realistic form. Perhaps the strongest of these are about the plight of women in his time. These plays include *A Doll's House* (1879) and *Hedda Gabler* (1890). In the last phase of his work, Ibsen wrote with greater use of symbols. This was a strand evident in most of his work, but in plays such

as *When We Dead Awaken* (1900) the symbolism moves to the forefront of the work.

Interlude in English drama developed from the medieval Morality play, and it is sometimes hard to separate the 2 types of play. Perhaps when the play's material was more intellectual than moral in treatment, the term interlude seemed more suitable. Later, short plays performed between acts of a longer one were called interludes, entracts or intermezzi. In Spain, a similar form was explored by Cervantes (1547–1616).

Ionesco, Eugène (b. 1912) is a French playwright, most of whose plays are in one act. He frequently attacks the materialism of Western culture and the importance it attaches to the achievements of science. Among his one-act plays are *The Chairs* (1952) and *The New Tenant* (1957). His best-known full length play is *Rhinoceros* (1959)

Kleist, Heinrich von (1777–1811) was a German playwright whose tortured characters reflect his own unhappy life. He served

Right: In the Middle Ages and into the Renaissance, groups of travelling players entertained aristocracy and common people alike. They travelled on foot and carried their gear in a cart or on packhorses. These companies kept the theatre alive in places where there was no theatre building.

Far right: The Globe Theatre in London was the home of Shakespeare's plays. Its tall wooden sides were a landmark for playgoers. The audience in the balconies were under cover, but the groundlings and actors were exposed to the uncertainties of the weather.

Pulcinella

demanded that one action should take place in one day and in one place. It became a straight-jacket for Italian tragedians, who failed to break its tyranny as Spanish and English writers did.

While Italians at court were struggling to re-establish drama through classical models, companies of professional players set up stages in village squares to perform a popular form of theatre. This drew on the ancient mimes of Rome and Campania, in southern Italy, which had survived the Dark Ages and emerged in the Renaissance as *Commedia del' arte*. It consisted of a number of stock characters, long established stage business and situations. Among the characters were Pantalone, a miserly merchant, married to a young and not notably faithful wife, and the acrobatic, lovesick, childlike Arlecchino. In new guises, these characters appeared in the works of French, Spanish and English playwrights, so that the stock characters of *Commedia del' arte* and the style of its comedy had an enduring influence on western drama.

Drama's 'Golden Age'

In Spain and England, dramatists were less bound by theorists than in Italy. In all European countries, playwrights generally aspired to classical models, but in Spain and England writers drew much from the enquiring spirit of their age

GLOBE . SOUTHWARKE

---

in the Prussian army for 7 years, and his best play, *The Prince of Homburg* (written 1811, but not staged until 1821) is haunted by an atmosphere of Prussian mysticism. Although probably best remembered for his tragedies, Kleist also wrote comedies. *The Broken Pitcher* (1806) is one of these, and he modelled his *Amphitryon* (1807) on a play by MOLIERE.

L **Ladder** is a piece of scaffolding in ladder form, but is not intended for climbing. It is placed at the

side of a stage, and the electrician hangs floods or spot-lights on it.

Lecouvreur, Adrienne (1692–1730) was an actress who joined the Comédie Française in 1717 and for 13 years was idolized by Parisian audiences. With Michel Baron (1653–1729), who had worked under MOLIERE, she introduced a new, simple style of acting that rejected the grandiose delivery of the declamatory school. Their impact on the French stage is comparable to that of CARRICK in England.

Lime is a name used in the

theatre for spotlights that follow an actor on stage. They are more properly cal-led follow spots.

Lope de Vega Carpio, Félix (1562–1635) is said to have written 1,500 plays, of which about 500 survive. The astonishing output of this Spanish playwright ranges over many themes and styles. He refused to be restricted by the classical unities which influenced many European dramatists, and had a gift for creating rounded characters. One of the most loved of these is the comic El Gracioso.

Lope's lyrical verse has its parallel in the BLANK VERSE of his contemporaries in England. Many of his plays are

Christopher Marlowe

realistic, but enriched by a poetic imagination. His treatment of the Romeo and Juliet story in *The Castel-vines and the Monagues* (c. 1608) is full of fun, and ends happily.

M **Marlowe,** Christopher (1564–93) is often called a poet of the theatre rather than a dramatist. In his best plays, such as *Tamburlaine the Great* (1587), *The Tragical History of Dr Faustus* (c. 1588) and *Edward II* (1592), the poetry of his BLANK VERSE is forceful and full of feeling. His heroic

and from a long tradition of medieval theatre. This combination produced a vigorous blend of classical and traditional theatre.

The golden age of Spanish theatre began with the religious plays of Juan del Encina (c.1469–c.1530), which established the first truly national theatre. It was enriched by the work of such outstanding dramatists as Pedro Calderon de la Barca (1600–81), Miguel de Cervantes Saavedra (1547–1616) and Felix LOPE DE VEGA CARPIO.

The Elizabethan dramatists of England wrote for companies of London players. Among these were the Chamberlain's Men, managed by Richard Burbage (c. 1567–1619) who became the first star tragedian of modern times. The theatre buildings were mainly of wood, and loosely based on the new Roman model. The stage was a deep apron which carried the action into the audience who had standing room in the area directly in front of the stage, known as the pit. Never since this time have so many of London's citizens flocked to enjoy the theatre.

Elizabethan dramatists, such as Christopher MARLOWE and Thomas Kyd (1558–94), followed Seneca's taste for the lurid in their revenge tragedies. But equally strong among playgoers was the appreciation of comedy. John Lyly (c.1554–1606) wrote romantic tragi-comedies that paved the way to a kind of comedy unfamiliar to students of classical styles.

English dramatists of the period used BLANK VERSE, which evolved through the plays of Richard Greene (c.1558–92) and found its master craftsman in William SHAKESPEARE, the greatest dramatist of all. His deep perception of human character combined with an astonishing scope of imagination and his gift of poetry raised his best plays to an unsurpassed level.

The leadership in theatre that had previously belonged to the national dramas of Spain and England passed to France in the mid-1600s. This period of glory for French drama was heralded by the work of Pierre Corneille (1606–84), whose plays set Paris alight with enthusiasm for the theatre. His tragedy *Le Cid* (1637), written within the rules of the 'three unities', yet straining their restrictions, is a play of great force and fine poetry. It pointed the direction for French dramatists to follow with success, and led to the works of the great playwrights Jean Racine (1639–99) and Jean Baptiste Poquelin MOLIERE (1622–73). In tragedy and comedy respectively these writers raised the classical type of drama to its greatest achievements. Racine's noble verse and the realism of his characters made his

Left: In the last quarter of the 1600s, the French Comédie Italienne won many enthusiastic followers in a Paris that boasted several active theatres staging the Neoclassical dramas of such playrights as Molière and Racine. Italian Comedia dell' arte characters, Pulcīnella, Arlecchino and Colombina with their many extravagant companions, enchanted Parisian audiences with the lively gaiety of their antics.Their characters were stock, but the had evolved with a freedom that lent them the *élan* to carry them into the hearts of their audience. Their influence permeated drama all over Europe, from Scandinavia to Italy itself.

characters have a human stature not commonly found in heroic tragedies of the period until Shakespeare's *Macbeth* and *King Lear*. Marlowe's Tamburlaine became an emperor, but was born a peasant, and Faustus and Edward both have the fears and weaknesses of common men.

Masque is a form of courtly revelry. It may have evolved from MUMMING PLAYS in the 1500s, when guests might burst into a party, carrying presents and dancing in disguise before their hosts. In the early 1600s, the masque

Masque, design Inigo Jones

grew into a spectacular entertainment for the nobility. The masque reached its finest form in the Stuart period, when Ben Jonson wrote the *Masque of Blacknesse* (1605) and 4 years later *The Masque of Queenes*. This latter masque included a dance of 'anticks', leading to a development called an antimasque.

Melodrama has come to mean plays with extravagant plots, overblown emotional display and exaggerated characterization. Earlier, the term described a play spoken to background music. In the 1700s such dramas were popular. Later, the term applied to plays which had songs, such as John Gay's *Beggar's Opera*. More recently, revivals of the form include Arnold Schönberg's *Pierrot Lunaire* (1912).

Molière, stage name of Jean Baptiste Poquelin (1622–73) was a French playwright who was one of the world's greatest masters of satire, wit and comedy. Of some 30 plays, the best known include: *Les Précieuses Ridicules* (1659), *Le Misanthrope* (1666), *Tartuffe* (1667) and *Le Malade Imaginaire* (1673).

Moscow Art Theatre was founded in 1898 by Constantin Stanislavsky and Vladimir Nemirovich-Danchenko. It set its sights on achieving a theatre of reality, in its acting and presentation. A policy of seeking plays of high literary merit succeeded when they produced most of Chekhov's plays, many of Tolstoy's and Gorky's *Lower Depths*. The ensemble has produced a superlative quality in the playing of Chekhov especially, and its international tours have carried its style across the world.

Mumming plays were a common Christmas or Easter entertainment in England, from the Middle Ages up until the 1800s. They cele-

Left: Classical plays staged in the late 1800s were frequently extravagantly elaborate. In this painting of the church scene from Shakespeare's *Much Ado About Nothing*, the stars of the day – Ellen Terry, Sir Henry Irving and Forbes Robertson – play in a sumptuous set that must have taken many hours to set up and take down.

tragedies the most praised of their day. He frequently based his plays on contemporary scandals, but his greatest works take as their theme the passion of love. Molière's greatest gifts lay in stimulating 'thoughtful laughter', as his audience enjoyed his rich gallery of characters. His plays are among the finest of the kind known as 'comedy of manners', which is concerned with the artificial world of polished wit and the opposition of the aristocratic and middle classes.

The stage used by Racine and Molière was of the Italian proscenium type, with panels of scenery at the sides and backcloths.

Restoration theatre

During 1642–60 all theatres in Great Britain were closed by the Puritans. When the monarchy was restored, Charles II encouraged the playing of female roles by women instead of boys, which had been the usual practice. At the same time players began to use stage make-up.

The comedy of manners and heroic tragedy were written by the English playwrights William Wycherley (1640–1715), William CONGREVE and John Dryden (1631–1700). Some of their plays were scurrilous, but many sparkled with wit. At this time, audiences often overflowed from the auditorium onto chairs on the stage, and the audiences expressed approval or disapproval in loud and sometimes violent terms.

As the 1700s advanced, the style of British theatre became more histrionic. Richard Brinsley Sheridan (1751–1816) and Oliver Goldsmith (1728–74) wrote comedies, many based on the comic observation of fashionable society. Great actors and acresses, such as David GARRICK, Sarah Kemble Siddons (1755–1831) and other members of the Kemble family, established an outstanding national tradition of acting. Their

Below: *The Cherry Orchard* by Anton Chekhov is a play that is rich in complex emotions. For its characters, the orchard represents many things: the lost joys and innocence of childhood, and a symbol of a Russia that teeters on the brink of revolutionary but hopeful change.

---

brated the passing of winter and the triumph of good over evil. The texts were secret and handed down by word of mouth from father to son. As part of the ritual the mummers had to wear masks or have sooted faces.

O O'Neill, Eugene Gladstone (1888–1953) is widely acknowledged as the greatest American dramatist. After a period of illness in 1912, he began to write plays. A number of these were of one-act, and several were produced by the Provincetown Players, a group with whom he developed a valuable relationship. His first great play is probably *Desire Under the Elms* (1924), followed in 1926 by man's relationship with nature.

P Pastorals were, in the theatre, entertainments set in idyllic countryside and peopled by shepherds and shepherdesses. The pastoral already had a long history in poetry by the time that theatre pastorals appeared in the Renaissance. One of the earliest of these was *Orfeo* (1471) by Angelo Poliziano. Shakespeare's pastoral *As You Like It* (c. 1600) is more ironic than most earlier examples.

Prompt corner is on the

A property master

left-hand side of the stage as an actor faces the audience. It is here that the prompter sits during each performance, ready to supply an actor with any forgotten cues or lines.

Properties, normally known as 'props', are any objects that the actors need to use on stage, such as pens, walking sticks, spectacles, or articles of furniture.

R Reinhardt, Max (originally named Max Goldmann: 1873–1943) was an Austrian producer and director whose grand vision startled the audiences of his time. For example, his brilliant use of crowds, often pouring them through the auditorium, had an electrifying effect. He made excellent use of CRAIG's ideas about stage design, working with simple, massive decor and dramatic lighting effects. Reinhardt was quick to appreciate new ideas, and was among the first to stage Expressionist drama (see EXPRESSIONISM).

Repertory theatre is one where a permanent company presents one play while rehearsing another.

reforms of acting and production standards had an influence on French theatre where they were supported by Francois Marie Arouet de Voltaire (1694–1778) who for example insisted on historically accurate costumes in the theatre.

The rise of modern theatre

In Germany, where a national form of broad comedy had hitherto dominated the stage, Karoline Neuber (1697–1760) introduced translations of French plays. Her work opened the way to the production of plays by Johann Cristoph Friedrich von Schiller (1759–1805) and his friend Johann Wolfgang von GOETHE who opened an influential theatre in Weimar in 1791.

The Romantic movement that swept the arts of Europe was seized by the theatre as a means of expressing the poetic and mystical aspirations of man's spirit. Dramatists threw aside classical forms to give free rein to their poetry, and though many of the resulting melodramas now seem absurd, some survive well. Heinrich von KLEIST's *The Prince of Homburg* (1811) has a strange, mystical plot made credible through its humour and perceptive psychology. More and more the theatre of this period in Europe became the province of the actor rather than the playwright.

In Europe and the United States, theatres and touring companies spread out from the old centres of culture. New, and not so new, styles of acting vied with each other for success. The cluttered and overdressed productions of the mid-1800s gave way to a more naturalistic style from Scandinavia and Russia. Henrik IBSEN and later Anton Pavlovitch CHEKHOV wrote plays with powerful social themes. In fact, the rise of realism seems to have given birth to the modern theatre. The tours of the German Meiningen Players after 1874 opened the eyes of actors to the advantages of maintaining permanent ensembles which could then pursue higher production standards. For these new types of theatres plays were written by Maxim GORKY in Russia, Gerhart Johann Robert HAUPTMANN in Germany, George Bernard Shaw (1856–1950), John Millington Synge (1871–1909) and Oscar Wilde (1854–1900) in Britain and Ireland (*see* ABBEY THEATRE).

The 1900s brought in a period of radical experiment in the theatre. German EXPRESSIONISM led to plays of many short scenes, built

around symbolic characters and massed effects. These dramas, by such writers as Ernst Toller (1893–1939), strongly influenced Bertolt BRECHT and his Berliner Ensemble. Brecht rejected formal dialogue in many of his plays, and preferred to present his view of the truth without engaging the emotions of his audience. A French style of EXISTENTIALISM influenced the plays of Jean-Paul Sartre (1905–1980) while several playwrights in France explored the absurdities of the human condition, often described as the 'theatre of the absurd'. Samuel BECKETT and Eugene IONESCO are the main writers in this branch of theatre.

After World War I, American writers made a powerful contribution to drama, none more so than Eugene O'NEILL. He led a group of playwrights who burst the bonds of the earlier fad for superficial realism, producing a new confidence that led to a fresh look at Old World styles.

The 1900s have seen more experiment in drama than any other century. The results have produced a theatre of 'isms: futurism, impressionism, CONSTRUCTIVISM, DADAISM and many others. Some of these avenues may lead to rich new fields, but ultimately great plays will grow only from the minds of great writers inspired to write for a theatre that seizes their imagination.

Above: Peter Brook's London production of Shakespeare's *A Midsummer Night's Dream* caused a stir with its rejection of the play's long tradition of a lavish use of colour in sets and costumes. The monochrome decor of his production, in the eyes of its many admirers, brought a refreshing concentration to the glorious poetry of this favourite of fantasies.

S **Scene dock** is a scenery storeroom with a high ceiling.

Shakespeare, William (1564–1616) was the most profound poet ever to write for the stage. From about 1585, he worked as an actor and playwright in London, where he became a partner at the Globe Theatre, and later in the Blackfriars Theatre. His plays may be divided into 4 periods. The first includes light comedies and some of the history plays, among which are *Henry VI* (1590–91), *Titus Andronicus* (1591), *The Comedy of Errors* (1592) and *The Taming of the Shrew* (1592–93). His lyrical period produced some of the finest comedies and chronicle plays, such as *A Midsummer Night's Dream* (1594), *The Merchant of Venice* (1596), *Julius Caesar* (1599) and *Henry V* (1599). The third period included most of his great tragedies: *Hamlet* (1600–01), *Othello* (1604), *King Lear* (1605), *Macbeth* (1606) and *Antony and Cleopatra* (1607). His final period included *The Winter's Tale* (1611) and *The Tempest* (1612).

Sightlines are drawn on a theatre plan and elevation. They tell the designer where any blind spots might be on stage.

Socialist Realism became compulsory for dramatists in the USSR after it was introduced in the years immediately following the Revolution. It demanded that writers should present reality, be truthful about the progress of the Communist revolution, and educate people in the spirit of socialism.

Stage left is the left side of the stage to the actor when he faces the audience.

Stage right see STAGE LEFT.

Surrealism was a movement in art and literature which grew from DADAISM in the 1920s. It was influenced

Frank Wedekind

by the ideas of Sigmund Freud (1856–1939) and called on the powers of the unconscious mind in artistic creation.

U **Upstage** is the rear part of the stage.

W **Wedekind,** Frank (1864–1918) was a forerunner of the expressionists in the theatre (see EXPRESSIONISM).

**The spread of radio and television has reduced audiences at certain forms of
entertainment, including the circus and the now moribund music hall. But music hall
traditions survive in revue and cabaret.**

Variety

Few entertainers succeed in pleasing an audience with an act that lasts longer than about 20 minutes, and most audiences expect much more than that. They want either a longer show or a more varied one than a lone performer can offer. From early in history, entertainers have joined forces to provide collections of acts in many forms now grouped under the general title of variety.

Circus Spectacular

Travelling circuses, so numerous between the two world wars, are now rare. The survivors maintain traditional acts of wild animal trainers, acrobats, clowns and horsemen. It was the long connection between circus and horse that gave the circus its shape. Antoine Franconi (1738–1836), manager of a Paris circus, so influenced the circus of his day that he established the size of most rings since. His ring of 13 metres diameter offered the best curve for equestrian events. It allowed horses to move briskly enough for good balance, but made it hard for them to gallop.

Horses have been essential to circuses from their beginning. Romans built amphitheatres to accommodate horse and chariot races that were preceded by processions of animals, men and images, rather like parades later circus owners organized for publicity when they entered a town. The Roman circus degenerated into a horrifying spectacle of torture and slaughter of men and beasts in which the savagery of animals could not match the bestiality of man.

Itinerant acrobats and animal trainers probably kept the idea of the circus alive in the Dark Ages. Certainly they flourished in the Middle Ages. Dancing bears, acrobats and rope walkers travelled the roads of Asia and Europe. The Chinese developed a high tradition of acrobatics that culminated in the present state companies. It was in the 1700s that the circus began to

Above: Medieval entertainers, such as this jongleur with dancing bear, pipe and drum, travelled Europe's roads.

Above: Dancing was a popular form of entertainment in Ancient Greece. This dancing girl acrobat uses her toes to pick up objects and place them in a large vase.

Left: The 3-ring circus of Barnum and Bailey in the US begins with a grand procession in which animals and artists look spectacular.

Reference

B **Barnum and Bailey** were 2 of America's greatest showmen and circus owners who formed a brilliantly successful partnership in 1881 when they launched the Barnum and Bailey 'Greatest Show on Earth', a combination of circus, menagerie and museum. James Anthony Bailey (1847–1906) was the organiser who introduced the star attraction, Jumbo the elephant. Phineas Taylor Barnum (1810–1891) had discovered the midget General Tom Thumb who proved to be a goldmine. The circus was a mammoth affair with 200 horses, 500 men and women and a convoy of caravans and wagons.

Burlesque in its earlier form was a play that expressed a satirical point of view of a topical event. One of the first was *The Rehearsal* (1671) by George Villiers, 2nd Duke of Buckingham (1627–87), a parody of John Dryden (1631–1700). This type of burlesque became much broader and cruder in style in the 1800s. In a later form of burlesque, established in the USA, the emphasis was upon the chorus line and tableaux of showgirls. These numbers were interspersed with variety acts, especially comics using broad material and slapstick humour. Finally, burlesque in the USA became synonymous with striptease.

C **Café Concert** in France was the term for all kinds of entertainment found in boulevard cafes and restaurants. *Café concerts* were a rich proving ground for artists who later made their names in variety theatres and musical comedy.

Maurice Chevalier

Chevalier, Maurice (1888–1972), displayed his remarkable talents in variety, revue, musical comedy and films. He began his career in Paris at the age of 12 years. By the time he was 16, he was playing in Paris as a red-nosed comic. His dancing which became known as 'Chevalier style', and his singing established him as a great success in the *Folies Bergère* seasons from 1907–1910. He was soon touring outside France and, as his English improved, he became a favourite in Britain and then in the USA.

assume its modern form. Out-of-work trick riders set up as showmen, and the horse became an indispensable part of the circus. Circus crafts reached a peak in the 50 years before about 1925, but the circus school of Moscow and the centres in Berlin and Budapest keep to admirable standards today.

Music Hall

The typical form of music hall, which dominated popular entertainment in Britain for some 60 years from about 1860, consisted of a series of acts performed under the witty and voluble direction of a master of ceremonies. He introduced the acrobats, magicians, jugglers, comics, singers and other performers while sitting at a table placed to one side of the stage and facing the audience. He frequently invited a member of the audience to join him in this privileged place.

With variations, this type of entertainment succeeded all over Europe and the cities of Australia, New Zealand, South Africa and the

Below: Many variety theatres had stages that were technically good. The auditorium in most of them was horseshoe-shaped in plan. The balconies projected well forward so that the audience was close to the stage. This plan allowed intimate exchanges between stage and audience. In some American theatres, ramps projected deep into the area of the stalls, bringing some of the artists right among the audience. Most acts played against simple, but well-executed, backdrops. The theatres were generally well equipped to accommodate demanding shows, such as illusionists, aerialists and other circus acts, including animal acts.

USA. Americans called their version vaudeville. Its entertainers worked on circuits, touring from one theatre to another, in a way closely similar to that practised in Europe. Entertainment of a cruder kind thrived in the BURLESQUE theatres. Here, emphasis was on the girls of the chorus line – especially on their legs – bawdy comedians and burlesque sketches. Burlesque houses, which by the 1940s staged little but striptease, were banned in New York in 1942.

Before music hall evolved, popular entertainers displayed their talents at *al fresco* gatherings on village greens, at fairs and in taverns, but in the 1700s the rapidly growing populations of towns sought more frequent entertainments. These found three main expressions. Taverns accommodated catch and glee clubs and 'harmonic' meetings where song and drink mixed agreeably. Groups of men formed song-and-supper clubs at which members and guests sang or did 'a turn' for the diversion of their fellows. Club managers sometimes employed circus artists and opera singers for special evenings. At the most dignified end of the scale were the pleasure gardens, such as the one at London's Vauxhall, with their saloon theatres.

These establishments evolved into music halls. Impresarios arranged circuits for their shows, and music halls spread outwards from the large cities. Music-hall songs were the popular music of their day, closely associated with the artists

Cochran, Charles Blake (1872–1951) was a leading British musical and revue producer and impresario-agent for MISTINGUETT and HOUDINI. He had great success with his productions of Nöel COWARD musicals.

Coward, Nöel (1899–1973) was a British actor, dramatist and revue artist of sharp wit and elegant style. His prolific run of success began with *Vortex* written when he was 25. By the following year he had 4 plays and one revue running in London at one time. His songs, for which he wrote both words

and music, and sketches did much to set new standards in intimate revue in Britain.

Crazy Gang was the name for 3 pairs of famous British music hall comedians who

Nöel Coward

were very popular on stage from 1935–1962. They were Bud Flanagan (1896–1968), Chesney Allen (1893–), Jimmy Nervo (James Holloway) (1890–1975), Teddy Knox (c. 1898– c. 1960), Charlie Naughton (1887–1976) and Jimmy Gold (1886–1967).

D **Durante,** Jimmy (1893–1980) American comedian. He was known as 'Schnozzle' because of his large nose. He had a long career in vaudeville and clubs and also appeared in films and on television.

F **Fit-up** is the term used to describe companies who travelled the countryside, setting up their performances in church halls and barns. In the 1800s this 'barn-storming' tradition was well established.

G **Grimaldi,** Joseph 'Joey' (1779–1837) the British clown, was one of the great names in variety who also had a far-reaching effect on pantomime and circus. He was an acrobat, singer, dancer, mime and satirist who appeared regularly at London's Sadlers' Wells.

Guilbert, Yvette (c.1869–1944) was a French comedienne, born in Paris. She won fame for her songs and sketches which were sometimes sentimental, sometimes satirical. She was a product of the Parisian CAFE CONCERTS and sang the songs of the artist Aristide Bruant (1862–1932) who owned a famous nightclub called 'Le Mirliton' in Montmatre.

H **Houdini** (1874–1926) was born in Budapest, and named Erich Weiss. He became the most accom-

By the 1840s the form was highly popular, and had begun to look much further than the world of theatre for its subject matter.

Theatrical traditions in Britain were well prepared to adopt the new form from France. Pantomime and burlesque, entertainments in which events and well-known characters were mocked, had a long history of success with British audiences. James Robinson PLANCHE, musical director of Vauxhall Gardens, one of 200 pleasure gardens opened, created the first revues seen in London. By the 1850s, several revues had succeeded, but it was not until England enjoyed the general lightening of public solemnity encouraged by King Edward VII and the *entente cordiale* that revue found a ready place in the nation's theatrical life. By 1912, revue was the craze of the London stage. American ragtime rhythm, sweeping music halls and variety theatres changed the style of popular music and influenced revue profoundly.

In the USA, revue had developed along lines parallel to its British version, but gradually producers reduced the satirical content in favour of flamboyantly staged song and dance numbers and displays of beautiful showgirls. Florenz ZIEGFELD staged the most lavish revues annually in New York. They were known as *The Follies* (1907- c. 1930). His style won popularity in Berlin, London and Paris, where great names of musical comedy and variety played in the spectacular revues of the capitals.

who sang them on stage. Such songs as 'I'm Burlington Bertie', sung by Vesta TILLEY, a male impersonator, and Harry LAUDER's 'Stop your ticklin' Jock' rang through drawing rooms and dock sides alike.

Strangely, two inventions that contributed to its decline appeared as acts in music hall bills. The moving pictures and phonograph, shown as amazing and freakish oddities, eroded the audience's dependance on music hall as a popular entertainment. Artists who survived the withering circuits began to turn to radio and stage variety shows for a substantial part of their income. The growth of workingmen's clubs and, later, television variety shows improved some artists' chances of a good living, but apart from isolated survivals, music hall was dead by the 1930s.

Review to revue

A revue is a collection of 'numbers'. They may be dances, songs, sketches, choruses or mixtures of those. The essence of revue style is satire. Its writer exposes the follies latent in contemporary events, personalities and manners. The revue, as its name suggests, originated in France about 200 years ago, when theatres associated with the old Paris fairs reviewed theatrical events of the year.

Above: *Beyond the Fringe* reached London in 1961. Its huge success was due to the comedy talents of its main artists, Alan Bennett, Peter Cook, Jonathan Miller and Dudley Moore.
Below: The film *Cabaret* showed typical acts seen in German nightclubs in the 1930s. They were bitter and witty satires against the politics of the Nazis.

plished escapologist the world has ever seen. He began his career at the age of 17 at Huber's 'Dime Museum', New York. Forming a team with his brother Theo, the Houdinis played successfully, using escapes from locked and roped trunks. After Erich's marriage in 1894, his wife replaced his brother in his act, and Theo worked solo under the name Hardeen. Houdini frequently added new escapes to his act. He escaped from a padlocked barrel, from a straight-jacket and from police handcuffs.

In 1901, he threw himself, manacled from the wall of the Paris morgue into the river Seine in a daring

Houdini in chains

escape. Perhaps his most remarkable escape was from a glass tank of water in which he was secured upside down by the ankles, the slide that pinioned his ankles was held by 6 padlocks outside the tank. He died after performing his escape from a tank of water while suffering from appendicitis.

L **Lauder,** Harry (1870–1950), Scottish comic singer and composer was a music hall star who had an immense following both in Britain and abroad.

Lloyd, Marie (1870–1922) was the best known and most popular music hall performer of the Edwardian era in Britain. Her most famous songs include 'The Boy I Love Sits Up In The Gallery'. 'Oh! Mr. Porter' and 'A Little Of What You Fancy Does You Good'.

Lee, Gypsy Rose (1914–1970) was America's most celebrated striptease artist. The secret of her success was probably the impression of grace and 'lady-like' restraint she brought to her act. Her true name was Rose Louise

Hovick. Their mother put Gypsy Rose and her sister June on the vaudeville stage from 1919. They were billed as 'Dainty June and her Newsboys'. After a few lessons from Tessie the Tassle-Twirler, Gypsy Rose began her career in striptease in Kansas in 1929. In 1936, she appeared with success in the *Ziegfeld Follies* (see ZIEGFELD).

M **Mistinguett** (1875–1956) is often described as the Queen of the French music hall. When she was 20 she appeared at the Casino

Above: The spectacular revue reached one of its most celebrated peaks in the shows presented at the *Folies Bergère* in Paris. The programme still consists of songs, dances, comic acts and grand display numbers where the gorgeous costumes of the chorus girls create the theatrical spectacle.

Come to the Cabaret

The large nightclub is now the home of the spectacular revue, to which it is almost wholly confined. Its glittering splendours are seen well expressed in the star-studded casts of Las Vegas, USA and the Crazy Horse Saloon, Paris. Their preoccupation is no longer satire, but female beauty. Producers dress their shows with bizarre extravagance, fantasies of sequins, feathers and undressed showgirls.

In smaller nightclubs, restaurants and coffee houses, a more intimate kind of cabaret, whose 'numbers' are closely related to those of the intimate revue, thrives. The cabarets of Berlin and Paris in the two decades preceding World War II were remarkable for the bitterness and brilliance of their satire. Cabaret artists often attacked the ascendant political ideas and figures of their day, using the techniques of burlesque and revue in songs and sketches. This, especially in pre-war Germany, brought several artists into painful conflict with the authorities. Some of the cafés and nightclubs of Paris's left bank community remain places where singers and poets can entertain their followers in a fashion that is curiously reminiscent of the gentlemen of London's song and supper clubs in the 1800s and the CAFE CONCERTS of Paris at the time. The style of the bitter-sweet French cabaret song, exemplified by Edith PIAF's powerful rendering of '*Je ne regrette rien*', is thought to be the best of cabaret.

After this grand period, the revue declined into tawdry imitations of the spectacular revues of the *Folies bergère*. These continued touring Britain until shortly after World War II, by which time they had degenerated further into nude shows. In the 1930s, the impresario C. B. COCHRAN grasped the opportunity presented by improving conditions for the theatre as Europe climbed out of the Depression. He championed the brilliant young revue artist Noël COWARD, commissioning him to write music, lyrics and sketches for an intimate form of revue. These and many other intimate revues were unlike the spectaculars, much more the expression of a consistent view of life. At first, one or two writers composed an intimate revue, bonding its satire and humour in a more cohesive style than the spectacular with its many different kinds of number.

In the 1960s, a sharp gale fanned the revue to a blaze. A revue called *Beyond the Fringe* produced for the 1960 Edinburgh Festival fringe assembled the talents of the Cambridge University 'Footlights' revue group. With the scantiest of stage accessories, they convulsed audiences with some of the funniest numbers seen for years. In the 1970s, Danny La Rue (1927-), a superb drag artist (female impersonator) starred in *At the Palace*, a revue that looked back to the grandiose days of the spectacular.

de Paris. In 1911 she launched into spectacular revue and began a 10 year working relationship with Maurice CHEVALIER. She spent the 1920s playing a succession of revues built around her talents. In these she frequently sang the song for which she became famous, 'Mon Homme'.

P Piaf, Edith (1915–63) was a French cabaret singer whose powerful voice, in contrast to her frail physique (she was nicknamed 'Little Sparrow'), made her one of the greatest cabaret artists of her time.

Planché, James Robinson (1796–1880) was an English playwright who wrote many dramas, BURLESQUES and extravaganzas as well as the first revues.

R Relph, Harry (1868–1928), a British comedian, was the first variety artist to make a big reputation outside his own country. He was only 4ft 6in (1.3 metres) tall and used the name 'Little Tich' on stage. He starred in Berlin, Paris, Rome and London.

Robey, George (1869–1954) was a British comedian who made a name for himself in musical shows like *The Bing Boys* (1916). His trade marks were a bowler hat, long black frock-coat, hooked stick and thick eyebrows.

S Soubrette is the description given to a minor female role, often a maid. The Soubrette is usually addicted to intrigue, passionately loyal to her mistress, and often saucy. She is a character much met in burlesque and revue of the early European type.

T Tilley, Vesta (1864–1952) was the professional name of Lady de Frèce, *née* Matilda Alice

Vesta Tilley

Powles, who was an English comedienne and male impersonator of great charm, wit and vivacity.

Z Ziegfeld, Florenz (1869–1932) was an American Theatre manager who devised and perfected the American revue spectacle based on the *Folies Bergère*. His *Follies of 1907* was the first of an annual series that continued until 1931. It combined acts with women in lavish but revealing costumes, with comedy sketches, songs and extravagant numbers.

Until it was superseded by television, cinema was the great popular art form of the 1900s. In the 1930s and 1940s, long queues were common sights outside cinemas in all parts of the world.

Cinema

Following the invention of photography, many inventors in the 1800s sought ways of making moving pictures. The problem was a technical one – requiring a camera on which a rapid succession of photographs could be recorded, flexible film and a device to project the film at the same speed at which it was taken.

The principle on which moving pictures are based had been understood for more than 2,000 years. Called the 'persistence of vision', it was exploited in the 1800s in such toys as the Zoetrope. It means that an image persists, or is imprinted, on the retina in the eye for a fraction of a second after it has passed from view. For example, if a cigarette is rotated quickly in the dark, we see a complete circle of light. Thus if a

Below: The Zoetrope, or 'wheel of life', was one of several toys in the 1800s which employed the principle known as persistence of vision, which makes cinema possible. The Zoetrope was devised in 1860 by a Frenchman, Pierre Hubert Devignes. It was a rotating cylinder on the inside of which was a circular strip of cartoonlike drawings. As the drum rotated, the pictures were viewed through slits in the side of the drum, creating the illusion of movement.

series of photographs is projected at a speed of, say, 24 frames per second – the standard speed for sound film – the images merge on the retina to give the illusion of movement.

No one person invented cinema. The work of many pioneers culminated in the late 1800s when the American George Eastman (1854–1932) invented a celluloid film in 1889. William Dickson, a colleague of the inventor Thomas Alva EDISON, built a camera that could take 46 pictures per second on the celluloid film. Edison then built a kinetoscope, a peep show through which short loops of film could be viewed.

Meanwhile, in France, Louis and Auguste LUMIERE invented the *cinematographe*, which was both a camera and a projector. In December 1895 they organized the world's first public film show. One film showed workers leaving the Lumière's photographic factory and another showed a train arriving at a station. It is said that many in the audience were terrified as the train appeared to approach them. Whether true or not, this story illustrates the magic and the showmanship associated with the cinema.

Right: The Kinetoscope was invented by Thomas Alva Edison and patented in 1891. It was a peepshow through which short loops of film could be viewed. The film was made of flexible celluloid which was invented by the American George Eastman. The pictures were taken with a Kinetograph camera, devised by Edison's colleague William Dickson. The first film is said to be of a sneeze, delivered by Fred Ott, a laboratory assistant. The Kinetoscope was first used commercially in New York City in 1894. Early films included scenes of boxing, dancing and variety acts.

Reference

A **Allen,** Woody (1935–), an American actor/writer/director, became known as a comic actor in such films as *What's New Pussycat?* (1965). As a writer, he created for himself an anxiety-ridden, neurotic character, trying to cope with life's complexities. He has also directed several films with distinction, including *Annie Hall* (1977), *Interiors* (1978) and *Manhattan* (1979).

Altman, Robert (1925–), an American director, has employed a wide range of subjects and explored a variety of techniques, including the use of improvisation, in order to involve his actors. His bitter comedy *M*A*S*H* (1970) was a great commercial success. Other notable films include *Thieves Like Us* (1974) and *Nashville* (1975).
Antonioni, Michelangelo (1912–), an Italian director and writer, has made films that are generally more concerned with character and moods induced by environment rather than plot

development. As a result, some praise him for his subtlety while others find his films boring. His films include *L'Avventura* (1960), *La Notte* (1961), *Blow-up* (1966) and *The Passenger* (1975).

B **Bergman,** Ingmar (1915–), a Swedish director in the theatre and cinema, won international recognition with a comedy *Smiles of a Summer Night* (1955), an evocation of the Middle Ages, *The Seventh Seal* (1956) and a study of old age, *Wild Strawberries*

(1957). His later films, such as *Shame* (1967), *Cries and Whispers* (1972) and *From the Life of the Marionettes* (1980), reflect a personalized

Bergman's The Seventh Seal

and rather bleak view of life.
Berkeley, Busby (1895–1976), an American musical director, is best known for his spectacular sequences in films made by other directors, such as *42nd Street* (1933) and *Dames* (1934). These sequences often consisted of changing, kaleidoscopic patterns on the screen formed by a large number of pretty girls with various props. Berkeley also directed many musical films in his own right.
Bertolucci, Bernardo (1940–), an Italian director, became known for his intri-

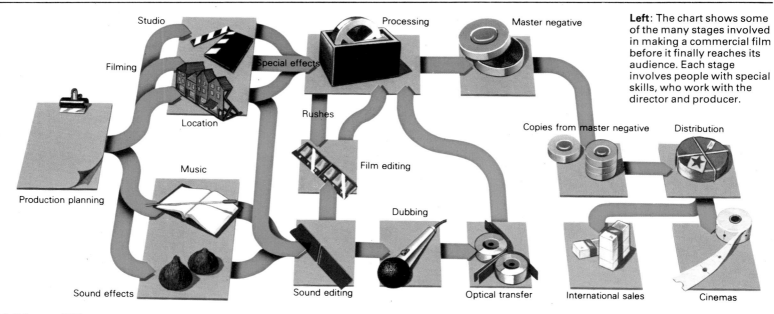

Studio
Filming
Location
Music
Production planning
Sound effects
Special effects
Processing
Rushes
Film editing
Dubbing
Sound editing
Master negative
Copies from master negative
Distribution
Optical transfer
International sales
Cinemas

Left: The chart shows some of the many stages involved in making a commercial film before it finally reaches its audience. Each stage involves people with special skills, who work with the director and producer.

Making a Film

Commercial film-making today is a complex business, requiring contributions from people belonging to one of 250 or more occupations.

Film-making usually starts with a 'property'. This may be the film rights for a novel, play or musical, an original film script or even just an idea. With a suitable property, a producer sets out to raise money. This may come from the studio or company for which the producer works. Independent producers, however, have to raise loans from banks or investments from one or more private sources.

With sufficient finance, the producer prepares a budget, which he or his nominee, an 'associate producer', will try to enforce during the film-making. The producer normally appoints the director and together they find a writer to develop the property. Jobs in the film industry often overlap. For example, some producers are also directors; some directors, such as Woody ALLEN, write their own films; and other directors, such as John HUSTON and Billy WILDER, invariably co-author their films. The producer and director, with the casting director, usually engage the actors and actresses. Suitable star names are often important to convince the financiers that the film is a sound investment.

Before 1909 film companies did not disclose the names of performers in films. However, early audiences showed such intense curiosity about their favourites that producers realized that stars meant profits. Early stars, such as Charles CHAPLIN, were worshipped by the public. From the 1960s the star system declined and today films without stars, such as *Jaws* (1975) and *Star Wars* (1977) can be phenomenal successes. However, a few performers, such as Marlon Brando, Clint Eastwood, Liza Minnelli, Robert Redford and Barbra Streisand, still have star status.

In the early days of cinema, audiences knew the names of stars, but few had ever heard of the directors. Today, however, some directors are as well known as the stars. The role of the director varies. He may be one member of a team of equals or he may dominate the production, imposing on each of his films his own personal stamp. The director is essentially a co-ordinator. He works with writers, photographers, art directors, designers, composers, film editors and so on to achieve exactly what he wants, shot by shot, scene by scene. The extent to which he is involved in any aspect of the film-making depends on his approach. Some directors spend much time supervising the actors, controlling each movement and voice inflexion, leaving the photographers a fairly free hand to use their skills. Other directors give the players considerable freedom and are more concerned with the lighting and composition of each shot.

Various decisions must be made before filming can start. For example, some scenes have to be

Producer
Director
Actors
Hairdresser
Make-up
Wardrobe
Publicity director

Above and right: The diagram shows some of the most important people involved in commercial film-making. It has been estimated that people with about 250 separate occupations are required to make a single film.

cate and exciting films that explored political and personal themes, including *The Spider's Stratagem* (1969), *The Conformist* (1970) and *The Last Tango in Paris* (1972). Recently his socio-historical film *1900* (1976) and *La Luna* (1979), an overwrought study of a mother/son relationship, disappointed many of his admirers.

Bresson, Robert (1907–), a French director, is known for his austere style, his use of non-actors (from 1950) and his belief that human suffering is redeemable only through faith. His films include *Le Journal d'un Curé de Campagne* (1950), *Pickpocket* (1959), *Mouchette* (1967) and *Lancelot du Lac* (1974).

Buñuel, Luis (1900–), a Spanish writer/director, collaborated with the painter Salvador Dali in France in making *Un Chien Andalou* (1928) and *L'Age d'Or* (1930). These films contain surrealist images, anarchic humour and a mocking attitude towards the Church and bourgeois values, features which recur in his later films, including *Los Olvidados*

(1950), *Viridiana* (1961) and *That Obscure Object of Desire* (1978).

Charlie Chaplin in Modern Times

C Chaplin, Charles Spencer (1889–1977) learned his craft as a clown in the English music-hall. From 1913 he made film comedies in the United States, most of which he wrote and directed as well as starring in them mainly as a tramp, who represented the underdog in society. His films include *Easy Street* (1916), *The Gold Rush* (1924), *City Lights* (1931), *Modern Times* (1936) and *Monsieur Verdoux* (1947).

Clair, René (1898–81), a French director, became known for his sparkling comedies, notably *The Italian Straw Hat* (1928), *Sous les Toits de Paris* (1929), *Le Million* (1931) and *A Nous la Liberté* (1931). He worked in Hollywood in World War II but returned home when France was liberated. His post-war films included the fantasy *Les Belles de Nuit* (1952).

Coppola, Francis Ford (1939–), an American writer/director, made *The Godfather* (1972), which was extremely successful commercially, and *The Godfather Part II* (1974) which was probably a better film.

shot on location (in real surroundings), while some films may be shot entirely on sets built in a studio. In the studio, the production manager has the job of organizing the often huge production crew, which contains, to mention only a few, make-up artists, carpenters, scene shifters, painters, electricians, wardrobe designers and dressers. Particular films pose special problems. A film featuring ferocious sharks, dinosaurs or journeys into space will require the talents of a special effects department, while dangerous scenes will often be filmed with stunt men or women, because insurance companies do not permit the actors to take risks, even if the players are so inclined.

The studio and location shots are assembled by the film editor who arranges them into a correct and dramatic sequence. The film editor may work independently, but the director

Left: The American director Joseph Losey is seen here directing Elizabeth Taylor in *Boom* (1968), a film based on a play by Tennessee Williams. Filming in specially built studio sets can be cheaper than filming on location, where the film crew are faced with such problems as poor weather, bad light or inappropriate noises.

Below: Most westerns are made substantially on location, because the subject requires natural scenery. Here wagons prepare to cross a river in *How the West Was Won* (1963). American film-makers are fortunate in having magnificent scenery and plenty of dry, sunny weather in the southeastern United States.

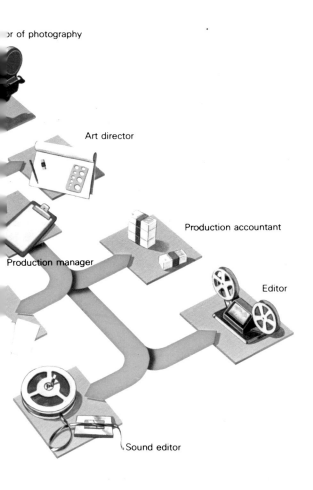

or of photography

Art director

Production accountant

Production manager

Editor

Sound editor

He also made the very costly *Apocalypse Now* (1978) about the Vietnamese war.

Corman, Roger (1926–), an American director/producer, is best known for his horror films, such as *The Raven* (1963) and *The Masque of the Red Death* (1964). As a producer, he gave work to such directors as Peter Bogdanovich, Francis Ford COPPOLA and Martin Scorsese, helping them to learn their craft.

Curtiz, Michael (1888–1962), who was born in Hungary, was a prominent Hollywood studio director.

For example, he made 44 feature films between 1930 and 1939. He worked in most genres, including adventure films like *The Adventures of*

Casablanca director Michael Curtiz

Robin Hood (1938), gangster films like *Angels with Dirty Faces* (1938), romantic films like *Casablanca* (1942), and so on.

D De Mille, Cecil Blount (1881–1959), an American producer/director, was a pioneer of cinema. His *Squaw Man* (1913) was the first film made in Hollywood. His biblical epics, such as 2 versions of *The Ten Commandments* (1923, 1956) and *King of Kings* (1927), were highly successful.

De Sica, Vittorio (1901–74), an Italian actor/director, was

a leader of the Italian neorealist movement of the 1940s and his film *Bicycle Thieves* (1948) was one of the first Italian films to be shown widely around the world. In the 1950s he returned to commercial filmmaking.

Disney, Walt (1901–66), an American animator, introduced his most famous character, Mickey Mouse, in 1928. His full-length cartoons include *Snow White and the Seven Dwarfs* (1937), *Pinnochio* (1939) and *Fantasia* (1940). As a producer, Disney also made live

adventure films documentaries and comedies. Between 1931 and 1969, he was given 35 Academy Awards.

E Edison, Thomas Alva (1847–1931), an American inventor, developed a kinetograph camera which used celluloid film and the kinetoscope, a peep-show through which one person could view a short film. In 1894 Edison opened the Kinetoscope Parlour in New York City.

Eisenstein, Sergei M. (1898–1948), a Russian director, greatly influenced

usually collaborates on the editing as well as on the other stages in the making of a film. Meanwhile, the sound department assembles the sound track. The dialogue may have been recorded when the shots were filmed, but special sound effects and music must be added. In many countries, the film is shot silent and the dialogue, with the other sounds, is added later. Finally the master sound track and the optical film track are matched and prints are made for distribution.

Art and entertainment

The films of the Lumière brothers were no more than brief glimpses of real life. The first film-maker who made films with actors and stories was Georges MELIES, who is now remembered most for his elaborate fantasy films. In the early 1900s, France and Italy were in the forefront of world cinema. One Italian film, *Quo Vadis?* (1913), was extremely significant. It lasted two hours, an unheard-of length at that time. Its success finally dispelled the notion that audi-

ences would be bored by films that ran for more than 15 minutes.

Quo Vadis? was shown in the United States, where it encouraged David Wark GRIFFITH, who had been making short films since 1908, to play a three-hour film, *The Birth of a Nation* (1915). This film, together with another masterpiece, *Intolerance* (1916), demonstrated that film could achieve effects in a quite different way from theatre. Before this time, most films had been static. Directors clamped their camera to a tripod in front of a set where the actors performed, obtaining an effect that was much like a filmed play. But Griffith showed that the camera could move and that individual shots could be composed, like paintings, for dramatic effect. Above all, he demonstrated that a scene can be built up from tiny fragments of film, including close-ups, medium-shots and long-shots. Griffith's films had tremendous influence throughout the world and film-makers realized that a film language had been created.

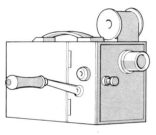

Above: The earliest standard movie cameras took 16 frames per second. They were cranked by hand.

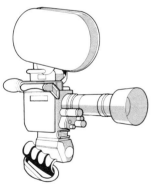

Above: Modern movie cameras take 24 frames per second. These cameras are driven by electric motors.

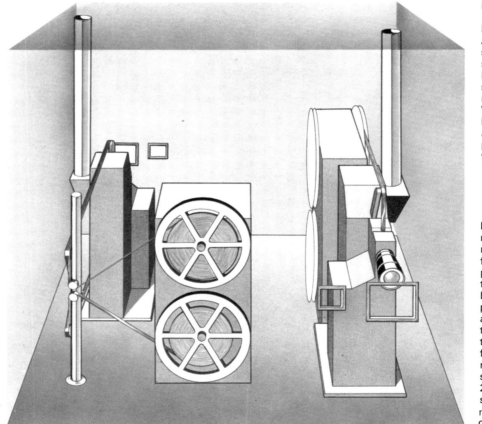

Right: This huge studio set of the Palace of Belshazzar in ancient Babylon was built for David Wark Griffith's *Intolerance* (1916). The towers in the picture were more than 60 metres high. The film cost US$2 millions and, on a relative scale, is probably the most expensive film ever made. It pioneered film technique and many directors, such as Sergei M. Eisenstein, have acknowledged the influence it had on them.

Far right: *Gold Diggers of 1933* was a musical directed by Mervyn LeRoy, a prolific American director. But the spectacular musical sequences were made by Busby Berkeley. This shot shows girls with violins in a number called 'The Shadow Waltz'. Berkeley is best known for the kaleidoscopic and often almost abstract patterns which he created on the screen.

Left: Modern projection rooms are highly mechanized. Huge spools of film are fed into the projector from a separate tower mounting which may be to the side or behind the projector. When the tower is at the side of the projector the film must be twisted through 90° before it can be fed into the projector or returned to the spool. Film spools once held only about 20 minutes of film, but large spools can now provide more than 2.5 hours of continuous performance.

other film-makers through his theoretical books and such films as *Battleship Potemkin* (1925) and *October* (1927). His last work, *Ivan the Terrible* (1942–6), comprised two parts. It brought Eisenstein into disfavour with the Soviet government, which considered it to be a criticism of Joseph Stalin.

F **Fassbinder,** Rainer Werner (1946–), a German director/writer/actor, made many films that commented on various social and political issues. Notable

films include *Fear Eats the Soul* (1973), *Fox* (1975) and *The Marriage of Maria Braun* (1980).

Fellini, Federico (1920–), an Italian director, first made films that showed the influence of neo-realism, such as *I Vitelloni* (1953) and *La Strada* (1954), but his later work is more personal in nature and filled with his fantasies. For example, *Amarcord* (1974) was about childhood, while *City of Women* (1980) revealed of his fantasies about women.

Flaherty, Robert (1884–1951), an American

pioneer of the documentary film, was especially concerned with man's relationship with his environment. His films included *Nanook of*

John Ford's Stagecoach

the North (1920), *Moana* (1926), *Man of Aran* (1934) and *Louisiana Story* (1948).

Ford, John (1895–1973), an Irish-American, directed over 120 films. He is best known for his westerns, which reveal his love of the outdoors and celebrate the myths of the Old West. His westerns include *Stagecoach* (1939), *My Darling Clementine* (1946) and *The Searchers* (1956). Ford made many other kinds of films, such as *Grapes of Wrath* (1940), *They Were Expendable* (1945) and *The Quiet Man* (1952).

G **Griffith,** David Wark (1874–1948), an American film pioneer, originated techniques which influenced film-makers everywhere. In particular his editing, which mixed long-shots and close-ups for dramatic effect, represented a great advance in the development of film as art. His first masterpiece *The Birth of a Nation* (1915) was marred by its prejudice against American blacks. *Intolerance* (1916) was a brilliant epic, combining 4 stories to illustrate the theme expressed in the title. Griffith's Victorian attitudes

high standards of filming and photography.

In 1927 a film called *The Jazz Singer* marked the end of silent cinema. Although it contained only a few lines of spoken dialogue and songs for its star Al Jolson, it was a great success. Film companies switched to sound and a new era began. The style of films changed. For example, new acting techniques were needed because silent acting methods looked exaggerated. However, sound also brought advantages and film-makers soon learned to use it creatively to enhance visual dramatic effects.

In the 1930s and 1940s, people looked forward to new films with great anticipation, fan magazines flourished and long queues were common sights outside cinemas. The most successful commercial film industry was in Hollywood, California, where films were made by large studios, with their own stars, and directors under contract. But despite its popularity, many educated people dismissed cinema as an escapist and often tawdry entertainment.

The 1920s were the heyday of the silent cinema. Major directors in the United States included Cecil B. DE MILLE, Erich VON STROHEIM and King VIDOR, while Charles CHAPLIN and Buster KEATON were great clowns as well as directors. In France there was René CLAIR, in Germany Fritz LANG, F. W. MURNAU and G. W. PABST, in Japan Kenji MIZOGUCHI, and in the USSR Sergei EISENSTEIN and Vsevolod PUDOVKIN. The 1920s were also an era of stars who were household names. like Rudolph Valentino (1895–1926).

Silent cinema was a unique art form. It was a universal medium of communication, which could be understood by anyone anywhere. In fact, when the cinema gained a voice, the distribution of films became restricted. Even today with dubbing, which often looks artificial, and sub-titling, which is not to everyone's taste, the international distribution of films is less widespread than it was in the 1920s.

Of course silent films were never really silent. Most major films had special musical scores composed for them which were played, in the cities at least, by large orchestras. Another misapprehension about silent films is that the photography was poor, a myth created by later generations who saw old and battered prints. But new prints made from the original negatives reveal

made his work less popular in the 1920s. He spent his last 17 years out of films.

Hawks, Howard (1896–1977), an extremely versatile American director, made important contributions to many genres, including his gangster film, *Scarface* (1932), his zany comedy, *Bringing up Baby* (1938), the detective story, *The Big Sleep* (1946), his western, *Red River* (1948), and so on. He began his career as a writer and editor.

Hitchcock, Alfred (1899–1980), a British director, is American director, began his film career as a writer. He has also appeared as an best known for his tense but often tongue-in-cheek thrillers. His films were carefully planned. He shocked audiences by such cinematic techniques as the sudden jump-cut that brings a surprising revelation. His British films include *The Thirty-Nine Steps* (1935) and *The Lady Vanishes* (1938). In the United States he made such fine films as *Strangers on a Train* (1950), *Psycho* (1960) and *The Birds* (1963).

Huston, John (1906–), an actor. The first film he directed was *The Maltese Falcon,* (1941) possibly the best detective film. Many of his films involve tough heroes at odds with life such as *Treasure of the Sierra Madre* (1947). He has tackled many other themes, including 2 fine studies of urban America, *Fat City* (1972) and *Wise Blood* (1979).

Keaton, Buster (1895–1966), a brilliant American comedian, starred in and directed a series of great silent comedies, including *Our Hospitality* (1923), *The* *Navigator* (1924), *The General* (1926) and *Steamboat Bill Junior* (1928). He played a serious, unsmiling character who finally triumphed against great odds, which often involved Keaton in dangerous stunts. His career declined after the 1920s.

Kubrick, Stanley (1928–), an American director, made several films which were clearly intended to shock his audiences, such as *Dr Strangelove* (1963) and *A Clockwork Orange* (1971). One of his most successful films commercially was the sometimes obscure but beautiful *2001: A Space Odyssey* (1969).

Kurosawa, Akira (1910–), a Japanese director, made 2 films, *Rashomon* (1950) and

Buster Keaton in The Navigator

Above: *Citizen Kane* (1941) was directed by Orson Welles who played the main role of a newspaper tycoon. The film is often hailed as the greatest ever made. It shows dazzling virtuosity in technique, including its elaborate construction based on overlapping flashbacks, the dramatic lighting, camera angles and deep-focus photography.

Above right: The *Seven Samurai* (1954) is a superb Japanese adventure film directed by Akira Kurosawa. Kurosawa has acknowledged his debt to the American director John Ford, who is known for his westerns. It is, therefore, interesting to note that the *Seven Samurai* was remade as *The Magnificent Seven*.

Developments in countries other than the United States challenged this view. For example, in post-war Italy, a group of directors, including Vittorio DE SICA, Roberto ROSSELLINI and Luchino VISCONTI, made films that were called neo-realist. Escaping from the studios and filming in real locations, these film-makers often used non-actors and their films had a documentary feel. Neo-realism was praised by many as the opposite of Hollywood escapism, but we now see that this view was an over-simplification, because some of the most influential neo-realist films are as carefully plotted and as sentimental as many Hollywood films.

Another important post-war trend was the emergence of some directors as independents. For example, Orson WELLES soon found that he was unable to work within the studio system and began a long, though erratic career as an independent, free to make the films that he wanted.

Together with new trends in cinema, there were also new attitudes among audiences. From the 1940s the number of film societies increased rapidly and national film theatres and archives were established around the world. People were given the opportunity to explore the cinema of the past and discover the works of overseas film-makers never seen before in their country. However, as serious interest in the cinema increased, audiences declined because of competition from television.

One of the film industry's responses to television was to produce fewer but increasingly lavish films which television could not rival. But there was room for low-budget films made by young and talented directors. Such films often found outlets in small 'art' cinemas which were steadily increasing in numbers, especially in the 1960s and 1970s. One movement which benefited from this development was the French New Wave which was launched by such films as François TRUFFAUT's *Les Quatre Cents Coup* (1959).

With a serious, albeit small audience concerned with enjoying cinema both as entertainment and art, new critical approaches were formulated. On of the most influential was the *auteur*, or authorship, theory. This suggests that some directors are as much authors of their films as are novelists, despite the fact that film-making is a collaborative process. This theory was advanced by French critics who applied it mainly to American films, many of which had once been dismissed as escapist. They said that the authorship of a director, such as Alfred HITCHCOCK or

---

The Seven Samurai (1954), which were very popular in western countries. They paved the way for the world distribution of many other Japanese films. Other Kurosawa films include *Throne of Blood* (1957), *Red Beard* (1965) and *Kagemusha* (*Shadow Warrior*, 1980).

Lang, Fritz (1890–1976), a German, directed several distinguished films in Germany, including *Metropolis* (1926) and *M* (1931), before going to the United States. His American films often displayed his interest in crime and human psychology. They include *You Only Live Once, Scarlet Street* (1945) and *The Big Heat* (1953).

Metropolis director Fritz Lang

Lucas, George (1945–), a remarkably successful American director, won attention with his low-budget *American Graffiti* (1973), which dealt with 1950s pop culture. However, *Star Wars* (1977) proved one of the greatest of all money-spinners. The sequel to *Star Wars*, which he wrote and produced, appeared in 1979.

Lumière, Louis (1864–1948), with his brother Auguste (1862–1954), were French pioneers of film-making. They perfected the *cinématographe*, a device combining a camera, a film printer and a projector. They organized the world's first public film show in Paris in 1895. It included 10 films and lasted 20 minutes.

Méliès, Georges (1861–1938), an early French film-maker, pioneered trick photography. He was an ex-conjurer and his best-known films, such as *Voyage to the Moon* (1902), were fantasies.

Minnelli, Vincente (1910–), an American director (and father of Liza Minnelli), became known for his stylish films, particularly such musicals as *Meet Me in St Louis* (1944) and *An American in Paris* (1951).

Mizoguchi, Kenji (1898–1956), a great Japanese film-maker, began to direct in 1923, although much of his early work has been lost. He became known internationally through such period films as *Ugetsu Monogatari* (1952), but the bulk of his films have contemporary settings.

Murnau, Friedrich Wilhelm (1889–1931), a German director, made several influential silent films, including *Nosferatu* (1922),

Vincente MINNELLI, is evident in such features as recurrent themes or in style (the way they are made and look).

Narrative Films and Genres

Over the years most films, especially those made in the United States, have tended to fall into one of a series of broad categories, or 'genres'. Film genres include westerns, comedies, musicals, romances, epics, horror films, and so on. The origin of some genres, such as westerns and comedies, dates back to the early years of cinema history. Other genres, such as musicals, developed later. Genres came into being because film-makers and their financial backers tended to favour those kinds of films which were already proven box office successes. This still happens today, as evidenced by the spate of 'disaster' films in the 1970s, including Steven SPIELBERG's *Jaws* (1975).

One of the most popular of all genres is the western. The first important western was Edwin S. Porter's 11-minute-long *The Great Train Robbery* (1903). Over the years the western became a particularly versatile genre, because it could be used in so many ways. It could incorporate comedy, romance, adventure, suspense or even social and political allegory, as in Fred ZINNEMANN's *High Noon* (1952). Westerns, of course, are a particularly American genre, although this has not prevented Italians and others from making contributions to it.

In understanding cinema, genres are important because they employ conventions or signs, which audiences recognize because they have come across them before in films in the same genre. For example, if we see a brief extract from a western showing a lone figure walking slowly down an empty street, we feel a sense of menace. Even though we have not seen the rest of the film, we still expect the lone figure to be attacked at any moment by hidden gunmen. Clothes in westerns, and often also in other genres, are signs, because they give us information about the people wearing them. For instance, we can readily distinguish between a gambler, say, and a cattle rancher or between a saloon girl and a more respectable matron simply by the way in which they are dressed.

Conventions are widely used because they are a form of short-hand, enabling film-makers more easily to pack an often highly complicated story into the brief span of a two or three hour film. Audiences find pleasure in recognizing signs and signs can add to our enjoyment providing that they are not always used in the same way. The skilled film-maker is always looking for ways of using conventions to gain fresh insights. Sometimes film-makers react against the conventions and reverse them so as to achieve the opposite effect to that which is expected.

Conventions have always been important in comedy. For example, early slapstick films contained shots of banana skins and open manholes. Both signalled disaster for an approaching character, but the convention was often turned

Below: *The Magnificent Seven* (1961) was directed by John Sturges. This popular film was based on the Japanese *Seven Samurai*. It observes all the conventions associated with the western genre.

around so that the character (unwittingly) missed the obvious danger but ran into another, which the audience had not been expecting.

Over a period of time, genres develop, change and sometimes even decline. For example, the end of the American studio system led to a decline in the musical. The American musical traced a dazzling path from the 1930s, with the spectacular Busby BERKELEY films and the stylish Fred Astaire and Ginger Rogers collaborations, to the 1950s, with such joyous films as *Singin' in the Rain* (1952). However, musicals are extremely expensive to make and after the fall of the studios, far fewer of them were made and most of those were adaptations of proven theatrical successes. Such films often seemed static by comparison with their vigorous predecessors. Public attitudes also change. In the 1960s and 1970s, changing attitudes towards sex and the status of women in society undermined the traditional romantic film genre. But even then there was a reaction to the mass of violent and sexually explicit films being made and the romantic genre reasserted itself with the successful *Love Story* (1970).

Other genres, such as horror films, continue unabated. Dracula and Frankenstein stories are as popular as ever. Dracula began his screen career in F. W. MURNAU's *Nosferatu* (1922), while

Above: *The Empire Strikes Back* (1979), produced by George Lucas, is a sequel to his incredibly successful *Star Wars* (1977). These films were expensive to make but they blended the right ingredients – technical skill, excitement and fantasy – to attract audiences.

Left: These picture boards show camera set-ups for a sequence in Alfred Hitchcock's *The Birds* (1963), in which birds attack a group of children, and their teacher. Hitchcock meticulously planned his films in advance in order to achieve the maximum effect on his audience. Before shooting began, he compiled a shot-by-shot, detailed breakdown of the film. As a result, he filmed only what was required, making editing simple.

American films about the creation of monsters date back to before World War I. Science fiction has survived although the Space Age has made much science fiction literature outdated. Such films as Stanley KUBRICK's *2001: A Space Odyssey (1969)* and Steven SPIELBERG's *Close Encounters of the Third Kind* (1979) prove the continuing appeal of the genre. Thrillers also do well at the box office, as evidenced by Francis Ford COPPOLA's two films of *The Godfather* (1972, 1974), Roman POLANSKI's *Chinatown* (1974) and many films made by Donald SIEGEL.

Animated Films

Animated film-making is a time-consuming business and one film is generally put together by a sizeable team. Animated films are made by photographing drawings (or models) one frame after another. One second of film time represents 24 frames or drawings and so a five-minute cartoon contains 72,000 separate drawings.

son of the painter Auguste Renoir. Two of his films, *La Grande Illusion* (1937) and *La Règle du Jeu* (1939), constantly recur on critics' lists of the best films of all time. Renoir made several films in the USA during World War II, notably *The Southerner* (1944) and *Diary of a Chambermaid* (1945).

Resnais, Alain (1922–), a French director, is noted for complex films in which flashback memories are blended into the narrative, and actuality and imagination are interwoven, such as *Hiroshima Mon Amour*

(1959) and *Last Year in Marienbad* (1961). Other films include *Stavisky* (1974), *Providence* (1977) and *Mon Oncle d'Amérique* (1980).

Riefenstahl, Leni (1902–), a German actress and director, is best known for her extraordinary documentaries *Triumph of the Will* (1934), which glorified a Nazi rally, and *Olympic Games 1936,* a film of great beauty. Her post-war career was damaged by her former association with Hitler.

Rossellini, Roberto (1906–1977) was an Italian dir-

ector, known for his neorealist films, *Rome – Open City* (1945) and *Paisa* (1946), but he made a variety of other films, including comedies, historical films and documentaries. Much of his later work was made for television.

Siegel, Donald (1912–), an American director, is best known for tense thrillers, such as *Coogan's Bluff* (1958), *Dirty Harry* (1972) and *Escape from Alcatraz* (1979). He has also made a fine science fiction film *Invasion of the*

Body Snatchers (1956), a stylish historical melodrama *The Beguiled* (1971) and films in various other genres.

Spielberg's Close Encounters

Spielberg, Steven (1946–), an American director, is best known for his extraordinary box-office successes: *Jaws* (1975) and *Close Encounters of the Third Kind* (1977). However, some prefer his earlier films: *Duel* (1971) and *The Sugarland Express* (1973). *1941* his comedy about World War II, was greeted with rather less enthusiasm in 1979.

Tati Jacques (1908–), a French actor, wrote, directed and starred in a series of comedies, including *Jour de Fête* (1949),

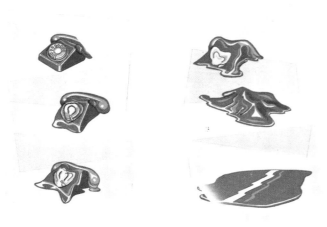

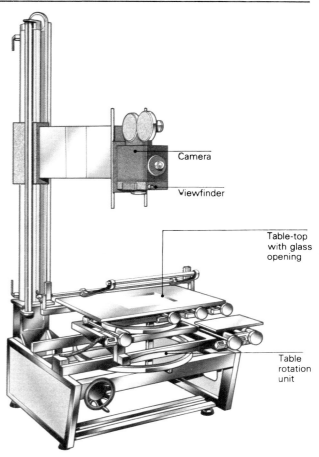

Left: This group of drawings showing a telephone melting comes from a sequence used in an animated film. The drawings are photographed one frame after another, although in slow movements the same drawing may be repeated on 2 or 3 frames.
Right: This animation stand is widely used for photographing animated films or for superimposing titles, subtitles or credits on previously shot film. It is also used when animation and live action are combined.
Below: The American director Robert Flaherty is seated on top of a station wagon during the filming of the documentary *Louisiana Story* (1948). His films contain superb visual images and are generally concerned with the interaction between people and their environments. *Louisiana Story* tells of the idyllic, almost dream-like existence of a boy and his pet raccoon in a Louisiana swamp area. An oil company arrive and the mysteries of oil-prospecting are seen through the boy's eyes.

Camera

Viewfinder

Table-top with glass opening

Table rotation unit

The most famous animator was certainly Walt DISNEY, whose first film appeared in 1923. However, his international popularity began with a film called *Plane Crazy* (1928) which introduced, for the first time, his most outstanding character, Micky Mouse. In addition to short cartoons, Disney also made a series of remarkable feature-length cartoons from 1937.

In the 1950s, animators generally reacted against Disney's lavish style and cartoons became more spare in form. Recently, many of the best cartoons have come out of Eastern Europe, notably Czechoslovakia and Yugoslavia.

Documentary Films

The documentary has played an important part in film history, especially because of its influence on other films. One important early documentary-maker was the Russian Dziga Vertov (1896–1954) who sought to educate people about the 1917 Revolution. By contrast, Robert FLAHERTY made lyrical films showing life in places such as the Arctic, the South Seas and Scotland.

In Britain such documentary films as *Drifters* (1929) and *Night Mail* (1936) influenced later narrative films which aimed at realism. During World War II, many documentary film-makers made films to aid the war effort. In fact propaganda has been the aim of many documentary film-makers. Perhaps the most brilliant and notorious film-maker of this kind was the German Leni RIEFENSTAHL, who glorified Hitler and the Nazi party in her *Triumph of the Will* (1934). In recent years television has provided the main outlet for documentary film-makers.

Monsieur Hulot's Holiday (1952), *Mon Oncle* (1958), *Playtime* (1968) and *Traffic* (1971). The comedy arises from the character played by Tati who inadvertently creates chaos around him.
Truffaut, François (1932–) was perhaps the most interesting of the French New Wave directors. his *Les Quatre Cent Coups* (1959) and *Jules et Jim* (1961) established his reputation internationally. Some of his films contain autobiographical elements, which seems appropriate in that, as a critic, Truffaut had

formulated the *auteur* theory. Other films include *Stolen Kisses* (1968), *Day For Night* (1973) and *La Chambre Verte* (1978).

V Vidor, King (1894–), an American, began his career as a director in 1918. His concern about various social issues was expressed in such early films as *The Big Parade* (1925), *The Crowd* (1928) and *Our Daily Bread* (1934). He also made fine commercial films, such as *War and Peace* (1956).
Visconti, Luchino (1906–76), an Italian director,

was noted for his bravura, near operatic style. His first films, *Ossessione* (1942) and *La Terra Trema* (1948) were neo-realist. But later he made elegant period films, such as *Senso* (1953), *The Leopard* (1963) and *Death in Venice* (1970).
Von Stroheim, Erich (1885–1957) was one of the great pioneers of cinema. He directed *Greed* (1923) which, although it was cut from an original 9 hours to 2, remains a masterpiece. He lost his job as a director because of his extravagance with money.

W Wajda Andrzej (1926–), a Polish director, won international fame with the World War II trilogy: *A Generation* (1954), *Kanal* (1955) and *Ashes and Diamonds* (1958) Wajda, like like Roman POLANSKI, learned craft in a film school.
Welles, Orson (1915–), an American, began his career by directing *Citizen Kane* (1941). This tour de force is still rated among the 10 best films by most critics. But Welles, unable to adapt to the studio system, went to Europe and became an independent. He often raised

money by acting in the films of others. His work as a director is uneven, but he made some fine films in Europe, including *Chimes at Midnight* (1966).
Wilder, Billy (1906–), an Austrian-born American director, is best known for taut melodramas, like *Double Indemnity* (1944) and *Sunset Boulevard* (1950), and bitter-sweet comedies, often bordering on the outrageous, like *Some Like it Hot* (1959) and *Kiss Me Stupid* (1961). He is a director who works, successfully, within the system.

Radio and television provide inexpensive entertainment in the home. Both media employ techniques borrowed from the other arts, but they are also creating their own unique forms of art and entertainment.

Broadcasting

Radio and television are the two most modern forms of art and entertainment. In a way that even printing cannot, radio and television bring the outside world into the home. The first radio signal through the air was made in 1895, but it was not until the 1920s that regular broadcasting became established in several countries. Television broadcasting began in 1936 in Britain and the United States, but had to be suspended during World War II. Effectively, television really got under way in 1946 after the war was over. From the start broadcasting has generally aimed at informing and entertaining, often doing both at the same time.

Above: A typical radio set of the 1930s. Made by Philips in 1933, it had highly efficient tuning coils.

Borrowing Art Forms

Much of the material broadcast, especially on television, has been borrowed from other forms of art and entertainment. The two principal borrowings have been from the theatre and from cinema (which itself owes a debt to the theatre). In many countries television has very largely taken over the rôle of the cinema as a source of entertainment. Not only does it screen numerous old films, but frequently programmes made specially for television are almost indistinguishable in character and technique from cinema films.

Radio has made some of its biggest borrowings from the concert hall. Some countries, particularly Britain and the United States, have one radio CHANNEL devoted largely to broadcasting serious music and other channels devoted almost entirely to pop music. Television is less successful in presenting straight music, but does well where there is spectacle involved, as in opera and ballet. Other forms of stage shows also translate well into the medium of broadcasting, such as variety and music hall. With most forms of sport, television succeeds in giving the viewer a seat at the event, as it were – and in some, such as racing, the viewer at home sees more than the spectators

at the racecourse. With news and its background, broadcasting has borrowed the techniques of newspapers and translated them into either purely sound or sound and visual terms.

Pictures in Sound

Radio has created art forms as well as borrowing them. This is particularly true of radio drama, where the effect is similar to that produced by reading a novel. The listener, like the reader, builds up a mental image of what is happening. Radio drama must do this entirely by the dialogue, with a few SOUND EFFECTS to help set the scene and complete the illusion.

Two outstanding radio broadcasts show how vivid a mental picture can be created. In October

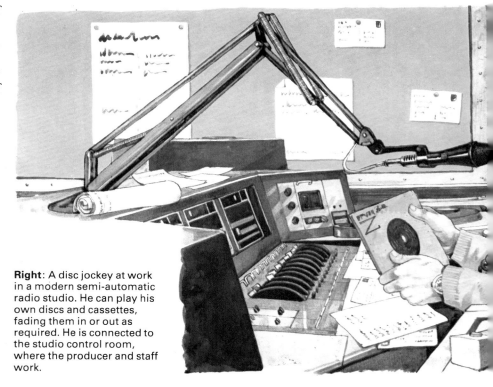

Right: A disc jockey at work in a modern semi-automatic radio studio. He can play his own discs and cassettes, fading them in or out as required. He is connected to the studio control room, where the producer and staff work.

Reference

B Baird, John Logie (1888–1946), a Scottish engineer, was one of the pioneers of television. In 1926 he gave the first public demonstration of it. His mechanical system was replaced by an electronic system for general use.

C Cameras for television have lenses like ordinary cameras, but instead of film they have a mirror system which splits the light into the 3 primary colours. Each col-

John Logie Baird

our is directed through its own cathode ray tube (as in the tube of a colour tele-vision set) which turns light signals into electronic pulses.

Catch-phrase is a popular saying. Many such phrases are picked up from radio and television shows, especially comedy.

Channel is a wavelength or group of wavelengths allotted to a particular radio or television station.

Commentator is a broadcaster who describes an event for the benefit of listeners or television viewers.

D Disc-jockey is a person who announces and

plays records, generally of pop music, on radio.

Documentary is a factual account of some topic of general interest. Programmes of this kind range from travel and natural history to political investigations.

E Echo occurs when sound is reflected in a large, resonant building, such as a church. Echo can be added to broadcast sound by playing the material recorded in the studio through a loudspeaker into a resonating chamber and picking up the result with

the aid of a microphone.

I Inlay is an electronic device whereby a figure, such as a newsreader, is televised against a plain background colour which can be 'lost'; the figure can then be superimposed on a different background, such as an outdoor shot, seen by a second camera.

J Jingle is a catchy tune with words used in a television or radio commercial (advertisement). Many jingles have given rise to CATCH-PHRASES.

Above: Children's programmes are a special category aimed at a particular market in the fields of education and leisure.

1938, the actor-producer Orson Welles (1915–) produced a radio drama entitled *The War of the Worlds*. It contained apparent on-the-spot reports of an invasion of New Jersey by men from Mars. Despite preliminary announcements that the programme was fiction, people believed that it was true and widespread panic ensued. The other broadcast was Dylan THOMAS's *Under Milk Wood*, first heard in January 1954. Thomas called it 'a play for voices', and in it he produced a word-picture of an imaginary Welsh town from midnight to midnight.

The ability of radio to leap through space and time gives it an advantage over theatre, cinema and television. It can also create impossible situations, which comedy writers have been quick to take advantage of. This was particularly so in the case of the *Goon Show*, a popular British radio series of the 1950s, in which such unlikely events as a race between two pipe organs across the Sahara were made to seem quite credible, and very funny.

Great Occasions

Radio, and even more so television, excel in bringing great occasions to life. To do this radio, which was first in the field, created the COMMEN-TATOR, who could describe to listeners the scene he was watching. Television, by actually showing the event, has an even bigger impact, though commentators are still employed to explain what the viewer is seeing. Such OUTSIDE BROADCASTS form some of the most exciting aspects of radio and television. The advent of VIDEOTAPE in the

1950s has made it possible to record daytime events so that people can see them in the evening or the next day or whenever the broadcasting authorities decide to screen it. It has also made possible the REPLAY, a great help in clarifying what really happened. One of the most sensational 'great occasion' broadcasts of all time was the landing of men on the Moon in July 1969.

Great occasions, and indeed all forms of PRO-GRAMMES, have been enhanced by the many technological improvements in broadcasting. Much radio output is now broadcast in STEREO and some even in QUADRAPHONY. Colour, first demonstrated in 1928 by John Logie BAIRD, started coming into general use for television broadcasts in the 1950s. Although television normally requires very bright lighting, modern CAMERAS have been devised that can 'see' in the dullest light.

Special Programmes

Broadcasting has given rise to numerous special kinds of programmes. On the entertainment side, the best-known is the serialized drama, often called a 'soap opera' because in the early days of such dramas on radio many had a soap company as their SPONSOR. Halfway between entertainment and information is the 'chat show', in which well-known people take part in informal and often unscripted discussions. In quiz programmes professional teams and members of the public are invited to answer questions.

The DOCUMENTARY, a style of programme adapted from the cinema, has proved one of the main-stays of serious television. Programmes of this kind, bringing unfamiliar material to the screen, have helped viewers to understand how other people live and work; they are educational without appearing to be so. Purely educational programmes have been a feature of broadcasting for many years. Radio has been used to help children in scattered communities for whom conventional schooling is impossible, for example in Australia and the Soviet Union. Germany was one of the earliest countries to set up an adult education broadcasting programme. This concept has been taken to the ultimate in Britain with the OPEN UNIVERSITY, in which special radio and television broadcasts form an essential part of the students' study programme.

M **Marconi,** Guglielmo (1874–1937) was an Italian physicist who developed radio. By 1897 he had managed to send signals over a distance of 19km and by 1901 succeeded in transmitting across the Atlantic Ocean.

O **Open University** was founded in Britain in 1969. It provides courses of study by a mixture of correspondence material, television and radio broadcasts, and tutorials, and awards degrees. Its system and teaching materials have been used in other countries.

Guglielmo Marconi

Outside broadcasts, also called remote broadcasts, are television or radio programmes produced on location away from the studio. Conferences, sports events and similar occurrences are broadcast in this way.

P **Personalities** are entertainers of various kinds who have made a name for themselves on radio or television, but do not necessarily fall into a category such as actor, musician or sportsman.
Programmes are the individual items in a day's

broadcasting, ranging from news bulletins to plays and films, but not including advertisements.

Q **Quadraphony** is a form of 4-channel STEREO, in which sounds coming from the sides and rear of a concert hall or drama studio are reproduced to give a feeling of depth. The listener needs 4 loudspeakers in the 4 corners of the room to appreciate quadraphony.

R **Replay,** in television, is an instant recording and

playback device which enables viewers to see an action for a 2nd (or 3rd) time almost as soon as it has taken place. It is particularly useful in sports telecasts. The replay can be in slow motion.

S **Signature tunes** are immediately recognizable pieces of music that are used to introduce regular programmes. Some are specially written; others are adapted from music already composed.
Sound effects are the various noises, such as doors

Religious broadcasting has enabled housebound people to join in acts of worship. The Communist-dominated countries are among the few in which there is no religious broadcasting, but in Communist-ruled Poland a series of strikes in the summer of 1980 won regular broadcasting of Mass as one of several concessions.

One special category of audience that has received careful attention is children. Apart from educational programmes, broadcasts aimed exclusively at children are put out in most countries. Teenagers and young adults are catered for by the pop music shows, which have produced a new style of broadcaster, the DISC-JOCKEY.

Almost as popular as the actual programmes are the commercials, the advertisements which are broadcast by commercial radio and television stations to pay for the service. Advertising JINGLES, with their catchy tunes, have passed into the lore and language of children, and many famous PERSONALITIES are willing to take part in them. Commercials provide many of the CATCHPHRASES which broadcasting has helped to put into everyday speech. A form of musical catchphrases are the SIGNATURE TUNES which introduce the majority of regular programmes.

Tricks of the Trade

Radio and television employ tricks of the trade to make their programmes more enjoyable and realistic. For example, a broadcast from a small STUDIO may sound as if it is coming from a church or other large building because ECHO has been introduced. A television performer can appear against a background apparently far from the studio. Originally this was done by back-projection – throwing film of the background on to a transparent screen behind the performer – but this effect can now be produced electronically by a process known as INLAY. A simpler device is superimposition, in which an image from one camera – such as a title or other wording – appears on top of the image from another.

In a sense, the majority of television pictures are special effects, because the action takes place on a set in which scenery is used to create an apparently real situation. But as in the theatre, the audience is really looking at a room with one wall missing. For some particularly lavish effects the television cameras are taken 'on location'; for example, a drama set in a medieval castle may well be filmed in an actual castle.

Above: A television 'chat show' looks very cosy and intimate when you see it on the screen, but the reality is very different. Besides an audience, the studio is crawling with cameramen and other technicians, while in the control box the director and his assistants select every shot the viewers see.

Right: Seeing is not always believing: a special effects man adjusts lights behind a group of candles.

opening, motor-cars starting up and bird-song, which are added to braodcasts to create a realistic effect. Today many effects are pre-recorded on disc or tape, but in the earlier days of broadcasting many sounds were clever imitations: for example, the sound of an execution by guillotine in the French Revolution was made up by drawing a sword along the metal frame of a piece of furniture, while a hard cabbage was chopped in two with a cleaver. Add a horrified gasp and the effect was complete.

Sponsor is an advertiser who pays most or all of the cost of a radio or television programme, with which the advertiser's name becomes closely associated. Sponsorship is practised mainly in the United States.

Stereo is 2-dimensional sound. The sound is picked up by twin microphones and fed through a pair of amplifiers to 2 loudspeakers, to give a spatial effect.

Studio is the room from which radio or television programmes are broadcast. It is in 2 parts: one is the main area where the perfor-

Dylan Thomas

mers are, the other a sound-proofed cubicle which looks on to the main area through a large window. In the cubicle are the programme director and technical staff.

T **Thomas, Dylan** (1914–1953), was an English-speaking Welsh poet who gave many radio readings of his works in Britain and the United States. His passionate style was matched by his stormy life and heavy drinking.

V **Videotape** is a magnetic tape on which pic-tures as well as sound can be recorded. It first came into use about 1955. Today most programmes are recorded on tape, which means they can be broadcast at times when it might not be convenient to do a live broadcast. Videotapes can be edited, so errors can be corrected easily.

Index

Acknowledgements

Contributing artists
Marion Appleton, Peter Dennis. Edwina Keen, Kevin Maddison,
Jim Marks, Nigel Osborne, Jenny Thorne, Gerald Whitcombe, David Worth

The Publishers also wish to thank the following:
Adespoton 33T; 38TR
Albertina Graphische Sammlung, Vienna 4t
Alte Pinakothek, Munich/Kuns⁻ Dias Blauel 12TL; 17C
American Museum In Britain/Derek Balmer 47TL
Heather Angel 23B
Architectural Association 35CL; 41C
BBC Hulton Picture Library 89E; 101B; 111B; 113B; 114B; 116B; 126B; 127B; 128B
John Bethell 43C; 44TR; 51CL
Bettmann Archive 76T; 113C
Bildarchiv Preussischer Kulturbesitz 72T
Bridgeman Art Library/Glasgow Art Gallery 59TL
Bridgeman Art Library 68C
Brecht Einzig 98C
Brecht Einzig/Architectural Press 98T
Castle Museum, York/Woodmansterne 47CR
City of Manchester Art Galleries 57T
Colorpix 25B
Corpus Christi, Cambridge 109B
Courtauld Institute Galleries 5TC
Daily Telegraph Colour Library/Judith Aronson 102T; 103T, C
Daily Telegraph Colour Library/Michael Hardy 112C
Mike Davis Studios/Jesse Davs 77CL & cover C; 87T; 93C; 95C
Douglas Dickins F.R.P.S. 19TR; 94T; 105C
Zoe Dominic 88T
Mary Evans Picture Library 61⁻; 62B; 64B; 68B; 73B; 74B; 77B; 88B; 90B; 93B; 100TL & cover TL; 102B; 106B; 107B; 108B; 112B
Mary Evans/Mrs Barbara Edwards 58CR
Mary Evans/Hodder & Stoughton 56TR
Mary Evans/Harry Price Library, University of London 115B
Sally Fear/Courtesy Rowntree Mackintosh 128C
Werner Forman Archive 32CL
Werner Forman Archive/British Museum 106T
Werner Forman Archive/John Friede Collection, New York 9TR
Werner Forman Archive/Phillip Goldman Collection, London 29TR
Werner Forman Archive/Metropolitan Museum, New York 49TR
Werner Forman Archive/Peking Palace Museum 74T
Werner Forman Archive/Pullan Collection, London 22TR
Fotomas Index 5B; 19B; 31B
Giraudon 39T
Glasgow Art Gallery 59TL
Guy Gravett/Picture Index 85C; 87C
Sonia Halliday 6T, CL; 8T; 10T; 20; 34B; 37C; 38B; 39B; 63C
Sonia Halliday/Jane Taylor 45CL
Hamburger Kunsthalle 27B
Robert Harding Associates 26. 29CL
Robert Harding Associates-Bodleian Library 56TL & cover CL
Robert Harding Associates/British Museum 62TL; 67T; 85TR; 109CR
Robert Harding Associates/Museum of Fine Arts, Boston 60C
Robert harding Associates/Stedelijk Museum, Amsterdam/S.P.A.D.E.M. 18TR & cover BR
Robert Harding Associates/Victoria & Albert Museum 52CL; 81T
Robert Harding Associates/Walter Hampden Memorial Library, Players Theatre, New York 111T
Michael Holford 5CR; 30B; 37B; 48TL; 50B
Michael Holford/British Museum 52TL
Michael Holford/Science Museum 55CL
Michael Holford/Victoria & Albert Museum 56B
Alan Hutchison Library 75T
Alan Hutchison Library/ Bernard Gerard 91T
Edward James Foundation/A.C.A.G.P. 31
A.F. Kersting 37T; 42C
Kobal Collection 59B; 117B; 118B; 119T, B, C
121B, C; 122TR, B; 123CR, B
Kunsthistorisches Museum, Vienna 23C; 53T
Kunsthistorisches Museum, Vienna/photo Meyer 92CL
London Features International 80C
Lucasfilm UK Ltd 124T
Macdonald & Co Ltd. 58TL, B; 68TL & cover CR; 72B
Macdonald & Co Ltd./David Cripps 48C & cover BL
Macdonald & Co Ltd./Shaun Skelly 41T; 127T
Macdonald & Co Ltd./Victoria & Albert Museum 100CR
Macquitty Collection 14T
Mander & Mitchenson 86T, C 98B; 105B; 115T
Mansell Collection 3B; 11B; 13B; 18B; 21B; 26B; 42B; 44B; 52B; 61B; 63T, B; 67B; 91B; 94B; 95B; 97B; 110B
Mas/Prado, Madrid 30T
Mayor Gallery/©Andy Warhol 3C
Metropolitan Museum of Art, New York, H. O. Havemeyer Collection 13C
Tony Morrison 20B
Museum Boymans-Van Beuningen, Rotterdam 13TL
National Film Archive 59TR; 96C; 115C; 120B; 121T; 122TL; 123TL; 124CL; 125CR
National Gallery, London 3T; 6B; 7B; 18CL; 20CR; 21TL; 70TL
National Gallery, Washington 27TR

National Portrait Gallery London 15CR; 57B; 60B
National Theatre/Brecht Einzig 98T
National Trust/A. Bartel 55T
National Trust/John Bethell 53CR; 54T
Chris Niedenthal 67C
Norlin Music UK. Ltd. 78T
John Ogle 16B
Philadelphia Museum of Art: The Louise & Walter Arensberg Collection A.D.A.G.P. 15TL
Photri 42TL
Picture Post 32TR
Polydor/Neumeister 78B
David Redfern 71B
Rex Features/Cinello/Spa 116T
Rijksmuseum/Theatermuseum, Nederlands Theater Institut 109T
Scala 4B; 11TL, TR
Scala/Museo Archeologico Nazionale, Cagliari 17TL
Scala/Naples Museum 107TR
Scala/Pitti Palace, 27TL
Scala/Uffizi Gallery, Florence 28T
Science Museum 7T; 117C; 126T
Ronald Sheridan 23TR; 35T; 44CL; 62TR
Snark International 79B; 99B; 103B; 104B
Snark International/Louvre 26TL
Snark International/Musee des Arts Decoratifs 70B
Snark International/Musee de versailles 93TL
Snark International/Metropolitan Museum of Art, New York 110
Sotheby's Belgravia 14B
S.P.A.D.E.M.
Spink & Son Ltd. 50TL, CR;
Tate Gallery, London 10B; 14C; 24B; 31C
Tate Gallery, London/S.P.A.D.E.M. 25C; 30C
Teatro la Scala, Milan 82TL
Theatermuseum Munich/photo Klaus Broszat 70C
Titus/Picturepoint 12CR
Trinity College Dublin/Green Studio 10C
Victoria & Albert Museum/Crown Copyright 8C, B; 9TL, B; 12B; 15B; 17B; 19CL; 22TL; 24T, C; 28B; 29B; 32B; 43B; 45B; 46B; 47B; 48B; 51TR, B; 53B; 54B; 55B; 90T; 104C; 108T
Walker Art Gallery, Liverpool 25T
Elizabeth Whiting Associates 45CR
Reg Wilson 80B; 82B; 83B; 84C, B; 85B; 86B; 92B; 111C; 112T
Yale University Art Gallery/A.D.A.G.P. 21BR
Zefa 35CR; 36TL & cover TR
Zefa/Anatol 72C
Zefa/P. Keetman 40T